JAGS

TO

RICHES

THE
CINDERELLA
SEASON
OF
THE
JACKSONVILLE
JAGUARS

JAGS
TO
RICHES

JOHN OEHSER
AND PETE PRISCO

ST. MARTIN'S PRESS
NEW YORK

To my wife, Cheri, and my son, Jacob,
for the time, and the belief
—J. O.

To my mom, Joann, your dream has come true and
I know you're smiling from above; and to my dad,
Angelo, thanks for everything you've done—
I couldn't have done it without either one of you
—P. P.

Design by Stanley S. Drate/Folio Graphics Co. Inc.

Library of Congress Cataloging-in-Publication Data

Oehser, John.
    Jags to riches: the Cinderella season of the Jacksonville
Jaguars / John Oehser and Pete Prisco.
        p.   cm.
    ISBN 0-312-17123-4
    1. Jacksonville Jaguars (Football team)—History.   I. Prisco,
Pete. II. Title.
GV956.J33035   1997
796.332'09759'12—dc21   97-16520

First edition: September 1997

10   9   8   7   6   5   4   3   2   1

Foreword

Let's tell you this before we begin—we never thought we'd be writing this book. Not yet. Not so soon. Just as you never thought you'd be reading it.

Jags to Riches?

The Cinderella season of the Jacksonville Jaguars?

Not yet. No way. Not so soon. Any success story involving the Jaguars wasn't supposed to be written during the 1996 off-season, but in the future, maybe after the '97 or '98 season. That was when the team planned to have success, and in keeping with that plan, any books about this team figured to be written around then.

More on that soon. First, we'll tell you about ourselves, the authors. That's what this foreword is for—to give you, the reader, an idea about the people who wrote what you're about to read, and why their story means something to them. We're a couple of guys who love football, who have written about sports for more than two decades between us and have seen pretty much everything that's ever happened to the Jaguars.

Pete Prisco, who has worked for the *Florida Times-Union* since 1987, has covered professional football in Jacksonville since the 1980s—a span that covers events ranging from the strange to the dramatic to the important, all of which are covered in these pages. Pete was there when the idea of the NFL in Jacksonville was a dream, of men named Rick Catlett, Tom Petway, and

Chick Sherrer. John Oehser, who joined the *Times-Union* in 1988, didn't start covering the NFL or the Jaguars until after the team was established—in 1995, six months before the Jaguars' first game.

Tom Coughlin, the Jaguars' coach, lives football. His players live it to a lesser extent. You, the reader, love football, or you wouldn't be reading this book.

We share the passion.

We don't share the love most people reading this book have for the Jaguars. That's not our job. Our job—as we explain endlessly to fans, players, and coaches who call us negative and cynics, and can't understand that we don't root, root, root for the home team—is to report, and at times to analyze, the news. We strive to be objective, and that means praising when it's warranted, and criticizing when it's warranted. That means we fight with players sometimes. Sometimes it means we don't write what fans want to read—that their team is the greatest, each and every week. We are accused of being negative, unfair, and cynical, and many couldn't imagine us writing 80,000-plus words on the Jaguars with the overriding theme being a positive one.

Those people are wrong, and here's why—

We may be cynical, but it doesn't mean we don't appreciate a great story. We do.

Sportswriters live for a great story. They're why you write about sports. It's just that great stories don't happen often, but if you know anything about the 1996 Jacksonville Jaguars, know this—

They were a great, great story. It's why you're holding this book, which, incidentally, has been a dream of both of ours for some time.

During the first year or so we covered the Jaguars, we talked often of possibly doing a book on the team. It was something that interested each of us. Anyone in our business, we would think, cherishes the idea of publishing something solid and permanent, rather than writing something that usually gets thrown away with the day's trash and dinner. So that was a distant dream, an idea we kicked around occasionally, but to be honest, it seemed far away early in the Jaguars' history.

The first year? The 4–12 season?

The Camp Coughlin days?

That team certainly didn't seem bookworthy. Not yet.

Early in 1996, it didn't either. The Jaguars were struggling, and eventually fell to 3–6, then 4–7. A .500 season seemed impossible, and you don't often write books about sub-.500 teams. Then, however, magic happened at the facility that was then Jacksonville Municipal Stadium. The Jaguars, who had found ways to lose for a season and a half, suddenly found ways to win. They won four consecutive games and surged into the playoff hunt, and even a couple of cynical sportswriters often accused of being down on the team couldn't deny we were watching something special.

Finally, late on the afternoon of December 22, there we were—

In the end zone of JMS.

We had walked from the press box to watch the Atlanta Falcons' final drive against the Jaguars that day. The Falcons, 3–12 entering the game, were supposed to be an easy opponent for the Jaguars, who needed a win to cap a miracle run and make the playoffs at 9–7 in only their second season.

Most people reading this book know the Falcons game was hardly easy for the Jaguars. Late in the game, the Jaguars led 19–17, but the Falcons drove easily, and with eight seconds remaining, they set up for a 30-yard field goal by Falcons kicker Morten Andersen.

We stood in the end zone, under the uprights, each

thinking what everyone in the crowd was, too—it was over. Nice run. Nice season. Time to enjoy Christmas. Our emotions, we admit, were mixed. Covering big events such as the NFL playoffs is why you write about and report sports. Still, after training camp, four preseason games, and a 16-game regular season, staying home for the holidays had appeal.

Andersen slipped. The ball sailed wide. Merry Christmas.

We each stood in the end zone. Under the uprights.

Pete, interestingly, can be seen on highlights of the play retrieving the ball.

"Unbelievable," he said.

Which was the theme of most of our conversations about this team much of the season. What went on in 1996 was unbelievable, even to objective onlookers.

As the 1996 season continued, the Jaguars made it increasingly hard to be negative. The team improved, they became legitimate, and by the end of the season, they were worthy of their tag as one of the most talented young teams in the NFL. That team became the team that shocked the sports world in December 1996 and January 1997.

Then again, why should anyone have been surprised? Since well before there was a team named the Jaguars, this had been a story with dramatic, unexpected twists and turns.

Pete, as we mentioned, covered the expansion process throughout, and we'll take this opportunity to say—for the record and for posterity—that he was one of the few people aside from the main players who believed from early on the city had a chance to land the team.

If you don't believe it, look it up. Or just ask him.

Enough self-adulation. We mention this because the foreword is about memories, and about giving the reader

an idea what this book will be. It's about the unbelievable, and from the beginning, covering this team was
about covering unbelievable, amazing stories.

None were more amazing than that which occurred
November 30, 1993, when the franchise was awarded.
Pete was in Rosemont, Illinois, site of the NFL owners
meetings. The 30th expansion franchise was to be an-
nounced. Whispers began circulating around the Hyatt
Regency O'Hare.

"It's Jacksonville. It's Jacksonville."

As Pete waited by the stage where the announcement
was to be made, owner Wayne Weaver walked through a
door, and winked. That was when he knew.

John, then covering the University of Florida, was in
Gainesville. He called the office, learned of the news, and
called his wife, Cheri, a supervisor at Prudential Insurance. He told her, and when she relayed the news, a mur-
mur went through her unit, and a cheer. It was that sort
of day.

That was the end of the expansion process, a process
in which Jacksonville was such a long shot that Pete was
an odd man out among even media covering the process.
Always, it was the other cities mentioned first, with Jacksonville the other team.

Charlotte, Memphis, Baltimore, St. Louis . . .

And Jacksonville.

It got so bad Pete even wrote a column on the matter.

And you can look that up, too.

The real Jaguars story began in February of 1994,
when Weaver hired a largely unknown coach from Boston College, Coughlin, to be the Jaguars' first coach.
Much of this book is about the massive change Coughlin
underwent from those early days. Much of the book also
chronicles the sometimes difficult relationship between
Coughlin and the local media, and particularly the news-

paper. That's unavoidable. It's our book, seen through our eyes, and it's part of the story.

This was not always an easy team to cover. Coughlin was paranoid, and the team was, too. In the early days, a typical Coughlin press conference began with him walking in and looking at Pete, and shaking his head because of a story.

"You, you, you," he would say.

Most of that first season was about memories like that. The team was undertalented, and while it played hard much of the season, there were few memorable moments. The most vivid?

Standing on the sidelines in Cleveland as journeyman running back Vaughn Dunbar milked the clock in a 23–15 upset victory. On those sidelines, veteran defensive end Jeff Lageman led his teammates pumping their fists and urging the team to an unlikely victory.

That was the highlight, but the reality is they weren't very good. We, of course, wrote this, too, and many other negative stories in the first year—and the second. With each was a conflict.

"You can't help yourself," Coughlin would say.

Well, no, we can't help ourselves. We're reporters, and our job is to cover the team, and report the news—good and bad, and in good times and bad.

That's what you'll read about in this book—the good times and bad.

The Jaguars began the 1996 season convinced they were better than the year before. We thought so, too, and that made the 3–6 and 4–7 start something of a mystery. We can remember talking to second-year offensive tackle Tony Boselli after losses, and Boselli being so upset he was almost unable to express himself.

"We should be winning. We are better than this."

Boselli is a prodigy, and supremely confident, but

there was something in what he was saying. Finally, in Baltimore they got a break. Ravens quarterback Vinny Testaverde fumbled late with the Ravens sitting on a lead. The Jaguars forced overtime, and won it with a field goal.

With that, the bad breaks and sometimes unbelievable way fate worked against this team seemed to turn 180 degrees. They won that game, then beat Cincinnati at home, and we started talking about how this suddenly looked like a real team. They went on the road to Houston, and won. That night, Pete wondered aloud—

"Can this really happen?"

John: "No way."

But by then, there was a way. The Jaguars beat Seattle, and then when Andersen missed that field goal, they were in. The next Saturday, on a cab ride through snowy Orchard Park, New York, Pete said, "You know, they might actually win this game today."

John: "No way."

The scene continued in the press box that day, showing vividly two things: 1) our cynical nature and 2) our complete lack of prognostication skills. The Bills took a 7–0 lead. The Rich Stadium crowd was intimidating the Jaguars.

Pete: "It's over."

John (nodding): "It's over."

Our friend, columnist Mike Bianchi, always one to keep our cynicism from overcoming us, shook his head—

"It's not over."

We laughed at his naïveté. The Jaguars rallied to tie it 7–7, but the Bills took a 14–7 lead.

Pete: "It's over."

John: "It's over."

Bianchi again disagreed, shaking his head and coining a phrase he'd use again and again during January—

"You can't count the little Jaggies out."

And you couldn't. The Jaguars rallied, won 30–27. Afterward, Lageman spotted Pete in the tunnel. "You didn't pick us, did you?"

Pete shook his head. Lageman playfully, and forcefully, pushed his helmet into Pete's chest. The Jaguars moved on, and Pete had chest pains for a week. The next week, in Denver, same scene. The Broncos, the team with the best record in the AFC, took a 12–0 lead.

Pete: "It's over."

John: "It's over."

Bianchi: "You can't count the little Jaggies out."

And he was right again. The final—

The Jaguars lost the next week in New England, 20–6. Their dream season ended, and the most memorable thing either of us ever had seen in sports did, too.

We may be cynical, but like we said, we know a good story when we see it.

As we write this in May 1997, it's natural to wonder about the Jaguars' future. Perhaps they'll soon win a Super Bowl, or perhaps the 1996 season will be the best of their early years, a bright memory and a moment so magical that it's impossible to match. Either way, they'll have 1996, and we'll be able to say we wrote the book on it. It's special to us, and we hope it will be special to you, too.

We just didn't figure it would be so soon.

Then again, no one else did, either.

JOHN OEHSER and PETE PRISCO
Jacksonville, Florida
May 1997

Acknowledgments

The week before the Jaguars played the New England Patriots in the AFC Championship Game, we received a telephone call from a literary agent, Stuart Gottesman, asking if we had considered doing a book on the season. We had thought about it, but wondered if there would be a market for us, even if they were to lose the coming Sunday, which they did.

Stuart assured us there was a market, so we decided to go ahead with the project.

Four months later, in May 1997, *Jags to Riches* is a reality.

So, to begin these acknowledgments, we thank Stuart, without whose vision—and early advice and editing—it's hard to imagine this book existing.

When we received that early phone call from Stuart, we imagined the work that might be involved in writing a book in what—because of our April 15 copy deadline—was essentially a three-month turnaround. We were right, and it was worth it, and as might be expected in such a project with high production and a short time frame, it couldn't have happened without the help of those close to us.

So thank you, Cheri Oehser, who allowed Pete in the house daily for a month, and thank you Jacob Oehser, who barely saw Dad for several weeks during this process.

And thanks to Pete Wolverton at St. Martin's Press, who believed in the idea enough to allow it to happen.

And thanks to Paul Prisco, Pete's brother, for making sure all his bills got paid in February and March.

And finally, but not leastly, thanks to the following, without whom *Jags to Riches* would hardly have been possible: Dan Edwards, Dave Auchter, Rick Korch, Rick Wilson, Alissa Abbott, Vahati Van Pelt, Tom Coughlin, Michael Huyghue, Wayne Weaver, Mike Richey, Mary Kress, Richard Allport, Carl Cannon, Jim Nasalla, Bob McClellan, Mike Bianchi, Gene Frenette, Tony Boselli, Ben Coleman, Kevin Hardy, Jeff Lageman, Kevin Gilbride, John Jurkovic, Ron Hill, Rick Reiprish, David Seldin, Tom Petway, Rick Catlett, Chick Sherrer, Hugh Culverhouse Jr., Roger Goodell, Dana Hall, the Jaguars organization, the *Florida Times-Union*, Tom McManus, Natrone Means, and Jimmy Smith.

JOHN OEHSER and PETE PRISCO
Jacksonville, Florida
May 1997

1
DOUGHNUTS
AND A CRISIS

*"There are certain things about which
there are no compromises."*

—TOM COUGHLIN
February 1997

Early on Saturday morning, October 12, 1996, eleven football players sat on a cluster of sofas and soft, low chairs in the locker room at Jacksonville Municipal Stadium. The players laughed. They talked.

They ate doughnuts. Everywhere, there were smiles.

This was a special time, a friendly time. Saturday morning, doughnuts time. The players ripped, ribbed, and ridiculed one another, and when a guy said something, he got it right back. Fast. And then some.

Televisions blared in the background. This was loose. This was fun. No coaches here. The players talked over the TV. They joked. They teased. Eleven professional football players. Eleven members of the Jacksonville Jaguars.

1

Boxes of doughnuts lay open on two long, thin tables amid the sofas and chairs. The players continued laughing. On the sides of the room, players sat by their lockers, listening to the banter, preparing for a light walk-through later that morning. This was their routine. Doughnuts time was the players' time, a time for bonding. A time away from the media, away from team meetings, away from fans. A time to relax.

Early on the morning of October 12, the day before a home game against the winless New York Jets, the Jacksonville Jaguars—in their second NFL season—needed such a time. This was a team struggling for identity—a team as noted for inexcusable losses and inconsistency as it was for a stable of young stars. Those players—Tony Boselli, Mark Brunell, Kevin Hardy, and Tony Brackens, to name a few—might have been the answer for the future, but in the present, there were questions.

Why was Brunell—considered a potential second coming of San Francisco 49ers quarterback Steve Young—not yet comparable to the four-time NFL passing champion? Why was the running game ineffective? Why wasn't their star free-agent signee, wide receiver Andre Rison, getting the ball more?

Why did the defense play well one week, then poorly the next?

Why did the offense do the same?

Most of all, fans in Jacksonville, who had waited patiently and desperately for 15 years for an NFL team, wanted to know this: Why weren't the Jaguars good yet?

Or at least, why weren't they better than 2–4, a game better than their record after six games the previous season? One and five was OK in 1995, as was a 4–12 season-ending record. That year, the Jaguars were a ragtag team of free agents and "youth with potential." Fans expected little. Even when the other 1995 expansion team—the

Carolina Panthers from the hated city of Charlotte, North Carolina—went 7–9 and set an NFL record for expansion victories, Jacksonville fans didn't mind much. They had a team, after all, and team officials promised a bright future—sooner rather than later.

Now, six games into 1996, things weren't OK. After a season-opening victory over the AFC's defending champions, the Pittsburgh Steelers, the Jaguars lost consecutive games to the Houston Oilers, Oakland Raiders, and New England Patriots. They followed that streak with a dramatic victory over the Panthers, but lost to the then winless Saints in New Orleans on October 6. To some, the losses diminished any positives—even the Panthers victory. Carolina, despite the loss, was 4–1, leading the NFC West. Given a choice—Panthers or Jaguars—many in Jacksonville no doubt would have preferred the Panthers' gaudy record and first-place status.

That their only loss came to the Jaguars was no consolation—particularly with the Panthers garnering positive press nationwide as the NFL's feel-good story of 1996.

What was wrong? Fans weren't the only ones asking.

Players and coaches were, too, so the Jaguars needed Saturday morning doughnuts. They were a way for players to escape the pressure of the NFL, and escape the pressure of losing. Most of all, they were a way of escaping the often overwhelming pressure of playing for the Jaguars' head coach, Tom Coughlin.

Coughlin had built the Jaguars in his image. His total control extended into his players' lives. Doughnuts were relaxation. Coughlin was stress.

Early on the morning of October 12, some players wondered if that stress was too much. The Jaguars spent big money in the 1996 free-agent market, and had high hopes for the season. A 6–16 overall record in nearly a season and a half meant something was missing, something was wrong. Some players believed that something was Coughlin. This talk of Coughlin being too unreasonable, and out of control, was spoken in whispers. That's the only way anyone talked about Coughlin around the Jaguars—a whisper. Anything else meant risking your job.

Coughlin was more than the Jaguars' coach. He was coach, general manager, and personnel director in one militaristic package. He, in many ways, *was* the team; his power, absolute. He hired players, and fired them—and in the first year, he was so intimidating that players avoided looking at him when passing in the halls, walking with their heads down to avoid eye contact.

Once, Coughlin told a player to cut his Mohawk, then released him that afternoon—after he cut his hair.

Coughlin was distant and controlling, and some wondered if he didn't push his ways too far—and if his image was right for a young franchise. He was more infamous than famous, and his old-fashioned image made him an easy target for media and cynics.

One Coughlin quirk made him an easy stereotype: a laundry list of rules (assistant coaches could not wear sunglasses on the field, and players' phones were turned off in their hotel rooms at 11 P.M. the night before games) that ranged from nitpicky to comical.

National media picked up on the rules, painting a picture of a red-faced, silver-haired maniac.

He didn't mind a bit.

He embraced his image. The rules, the tough approach—to listen to him, it was part of the Jaguars' building plan. "There has to be a period of orientation," Coughlin said after the 1996 season, explaining his philosophy in the early days. "There just has to be. There has to be a period where people have to understand that this is the way it's going to be. There are certain things about which there are no compromises."

The style, planned to the detail, alienated players in an era of "players' coaches" who offer hugs on the sidelines. "It's a dictatorship," Jaguars defensive tackle Kelvin Pritchett said late in the 1995 season.

Coughlin, until October 12, 1996, didn't seem to care. A coach's role, in his mind, was to coach. A player played, and if a player didn't like the coach . . .

Well, there always were 29 other NFL teams.

So, doughnuts time was important to the players, but early on the morning of October 12, it turned strange. Doughnuts time had started the previous season. A few veterans told a few rookies to bring doughnuts on Saturday morning. It became tradition, and that morning, the players laughed and joked and drank coffee as usual. Then, for the first time, Coughlin walked into the locker room, and to everyone's surprise, sat in the middle of the group.

Stunned silence followed.

"They were probably shocked that it happened," Tom McManus, a second-year linebacker who played for Coughlin at Boston College, said.

The players sat still for a moment, and when Coughlin spoke, a few players replied, breaking the awkward, stony silence. Was this an olive branch, or an invasion? Or an attempt to show his players there was more to the man than the myth? Who knew? Coughlin tried to loosen the mood, joking with a few players, some of whom stared at one another in disbelief. Others looked away, or at the floor.

Those not in the circle watched, amazed at what came next: One by one, those seated around Coughlin stood and walked away, leaving him alone with the doughnuts.

"Anytime the boss comes into the employees' locker

room it becomes an uncomfortable situation," defensive tackle John Jurkovic said. "We were struggling at the time, and we weren't playing well. That adds a little stress. Guys' nerves are edgy and raw anyway, so when the boss comes down to the locker room, it's a stressful situation."

The first two seasons were full of difficult times, but as Coughlin sat alone that morning, the gravity of his situation became more real. His team was struggling, and he had made a conscious decision to change—"It was part of the plan," he said later—but his players, bewildered, rejected the effort. After two years of distance, Coughlin trying to be a buddy didn't register.

Coughlin, players said later, never mentioned the incident, and at first, little changed. The next day, the Jaguars needed a rally to beat the Jets, 21–17. They then lost two games to fall to 3–6. Coughlin knew he needed to change, but changing—and convincing his players the change was real—wouldn't be easy.

And then there was a question, one Coughlin may have contemplated as he sat alone with the doughnuts, early on the morning of October 12: Even if the change was real, had it come soon enough?

2
THE LEGEND OF WATERLOO

"You cursed him . . . like your parents. You get angry at the time they're doing those things to you, but you know they're doing it for your benefit. It was the same with him."

—PETE MITCHELL
August 1995

"Nobody outworked the guy."
—GLENN FOLEY
August 1995

The scene was tiny Lafayette Field in Waterloo, New York, a town in the north of the state. This was a Saturday afternoon, late fall, 1963. More than 4,000 people packed into Lafayette Field to watch Waterloo High School play a football game against Mynderse High from nearby Seneca Falls.

The boys from Waterloo played that day for town pride. Mynderse—bigger, mightier, stronger Mynderse—had beaten Waterloo 11 consecutive years.

"The rivalry with Seneca Falls was so bitter people in Waterloo didn't even want their kids born in Seneca's hospital," said Mike Ornato, then coach at Waterloo High.

Waterloo, this year, was unbeaten—thanks to a core of seniors who grew up together playing sports and bringing pride to a small town. They were childhood friends, and the star was a gritty running back—Tom Coughlin, the oldest of the seven children of Waterloo natives Lou and Betty Coughlin. Young Tom personified the team and the town. Already, he was a legend. "A dynamic focal point for all our success," the quarterback on the '63 Waterloo team, Bob Baldwin, called him years later.

"He was a leader from Day One," Waterloo's baseball and basketball coach, Bill Carey, said.

Coughlin was that, and more.

Native son. Driven. Clean-cut. Disciplined. Well behaved.

A model early-1960s kid.

"The all-American boy if there ever was one," said then Waterloo resident Paul Whitaker, who later became Young Tom's father-in-law.

These kids, these seniors, Coughlin would later say, "were good, and we knew we were good." They had won Little League baseball and basketball championships, and won a section title in basketball and a league title in baseball as seniors, but football was never big in Waterloo. Nearby Syracuse University and its coach, the legendary Ben Schwartzwalder, made football popular in the area with its great teams of the late 1950s and a national championship in 1959. Waterloo, however, was small and its football teams were just OK. Never had an athlete from Waterloo received a Division I football scholarship, much less one to Syracuse.

This year was different. Coughlin was talented, and the offensive line cleared his way all season. Early against Mynderse, the game went well for Waterloo. The line overpowered Mynderse, and Waterloo led 7–0. Later, when Coughlin returned a punt 60 yards for a touchdown, Waterloo led 14–0, and the town had a memory to last forever.

"I'm sitting at the top of the railing when that happened, and I forgot where I was," Coughlin's younger brother, John, told the *Florida Times-Union* years later. "I went over the back of the stands and this girl broke my fall. They took her to the hospital, but I was fine."

The final: Waterloo 27, Mynderse 0.

The run secured the only perfect season in Waterloo history, and the next summer, Lou and Betty Coughlin drove their oldest child 40 miles up the New York Thruway to Syracuse, where he was to play football on scholarship. "When Lou and I left the driveway the first time to take him to college," Betty recalled years later, "there was a kid at every downstairs window. They all cried the day he left for college."

So did the people of Waterloo.

Their legend was leaving home.

Thomas Richard Coughlin was born August 31, 1946. His was the story of a small-town hero—a driven, disciplined kid destined for success. Succeed he did. Always. And always, the backbone was discipline. For Coughlin, discipline was the only way, a way first shown him by his father, Lou.

Lou Coughlin, a warehouse operator for 38 years at the Seneca Army Depot, served in the army in World War II, and applied a military, ordered touch to rearing his children. Lou was a sports fan who played soccer and basketball at Waterloo High, but he never pushed young

Tom to play sports. Education and discipline were more important to Lou, which was one reason Coughlin said his childhood was diverse.

He was an altar boy, an honor student, a junior Rotarian, and the treasurer of the Varsity Club. When he graduated Waterloo High, he had an 88.4 grade point average.

His favorite sport was basketball, and he averaged 11.9 points a game as a senior point guard before hitting .425 as a senior catcher on the baseball team, but it was football in which he most excelled. Wearing number 44—same as his idol, former Syracuse great Ernie Davis—he rushed for 1,852 yards in 1962 and 1963, scoring 36 touchdowns. His 20 touchdowns as a senior was still a Waterloo record in 1997. "He had a great work ethic, was very intense, and made the most of what he had," Ornato said of Coughlin, nicknamed "Ernie" in high school, after Davis.

Rarely did Coughlin deviate from a path to success—so rarely that such stories take on a legendary tone. Once, he and his best high school friend, Terry Manfredi, bought a six-pack of beer. This was a lazy, hazy, crazy day of summer—or as close as Young Tom got to such things. They drove to nearby Junius Ponds, but before they opened the first beer, Terry's mom, Laura, found them. "Tom almost jumped out of the car," Laura recalled in a 1997 interview with the *Finger Lakes Times* in Geneva, New York. "No, he did jump out of the car. I said, 'You two better get home in a hurry because Bill Carey called, and he knows what you're up to.'

"They said, 'Oh, no.' They came right home and didn't dare do it again."

Winning brought out what rebel there was in Young Tom. Once, a day after winning a baseball sectional, he and some friends skipped school to go swimming at Junius Ponds. Another time—hours after winning a sectional basketball championship—he and friends drove around in a friend's 1959 Chevrolet. Coughlin and his friends dared the driver, Kenny Sitterly, to cut across a yard to get to another street. Sitterly did.

The car stuck in the snow. Police freed the car, by which time "his friends" had abandoned Sitterly.

"Being the buddies they were, they all took off and ran on me," Sitterly later recalled, laughing at the memory.

"Normal kid stuff," Coughlin called it.

So, Young Tom wasn't perfect. He was just very close—and always, he was a leader. "Tom was always a good speaker," Carey said. "When people weren't doing too good, they looked up to him. He knows how to pick people up and get them going."

Despite his football success, Coughlin wasn't highly recruited. The University of Buffalo—with future NFL coach Buddy Ryan then an assistant—and Syracuse showed the most interest. Syracuse, the school of his idol, Davis, was the easy choice, and he signed there, but there was nothing easy in those days about playing for the Orangemen.

Schwartzwalder built a power as most coaches did in his era—casting a broad, militaristic shadow over his program. No one used the term "players' coach" in those days, and if they did, they didn't use it referring to Schwartzwalder. "He used the old military tactics to run his football team," former Syracuse all-American Gary Bugenhagen later said. "I'm sure a lot of that wore off on Tom."

Coughlin agreed, saying, "The leadership has to be strong, and the coach has to stand for something. Otherwise, you don't know where you're going."

Coughlin started three years at Syracuse, playing alongside Floyd Little and Larry Csonka. In three seasons, he carried 65 times for 336 yards, caught 34 passes for 367 yards, and returned punts and kicks. Once after fumbling a punt, Coughlin returned to the sideline. Schwartzwalder met him there.

"Fumble again, kid, and you'll never play again," the coach yelled.

"That happened a lot," Coughlin said, remembering the story.

"I'm sure he picked up a lot of Ben's discipline and toughness and the type of football it takes to win," said Jim Shreve, who recruited Coughlin to Syracuse.

Little and Csonka played in the NFL. Coughlin graduated with a degree in history, and the next fall, returned to Syracuse working on a master's degree and serving as a graduate football assistant for the freshman team. Coaching became his career choice.

After a season at Syracuse, he became head coach at the Rochester Institute of Technology for four years, where he took the school from a club program to Division III. Coughlin treated it as big-time football, compiling a 16–15–2 record. A season finale demonstrates how much Coughlin had come to love his profession.

A blizzard covered Rochester with a foot of snow. The finale against New York Tech, it appeared, would be canceled. Coughlin, however, felt RIT should win, and having shoveled widows' snow for years in Waterloo, he saw no reason snow should ruin a chance at a victory. He and his assistants shoveled the field clean, and the game was played.

"We won," Coughlin recalled years later, smiling.

Another story from RIT goes as follows:

Before a September game against Albany State, Coughlin and his assistants were pounding in stakes that would hold the rope surrounding the field during the game. The Albany State bus arrived. The Albany coaches wore suits; Coughlin and his assistants stood, sweating in the sun in shorts and sweaty T-shirts, swinging sledge-hammers.

"They thought we were crazy," Coughlin recalled.

RIT won that game, too.

He returned to Syracuse in 1974, staying seven seasons as an assistant. He then spent three seasons as offensive coordinator at Boston College, where he coached Heisman Trophy–winning quarterback Doug Flutie. In 1984, Philadelphia Eagles coach Marion Campbell hired him into the NFL as receivers coach. "He didn't know shit about the pro game," then Eagles wide receiver Kenny Jackson said, "but he learned. He became a good coach by learning. He was so technical we always called him 'Technical Tom.' He always seemed to have everything in order."

He learned under Campbell two years, then with Green Bay another two before being hired to coach receivers by New York Giants coach Bill Parcells in 1988. In New York, his receivers called him "Maniac Coach."

"Was he intense," then Giants receiver Stephen Baker said. "We always worried he'd become a head coach, because we thought if he did, he just might have a heart attack."

Coughlin didn't endear himself to all his receivers. "There are ways to discipline people, and the way he went about it turned a lot of people off," then Giants receiver Mark Ingram said. "All the wide receivers had run-ins with him. He didn't let you chew gum, wear a hat, or bring food into a meeting. A lot of guys rebelled."

Coughlin, all the while, angled for a head coaching job—college or pro. Late in the 1990 season, Boston College hired the 44-year-old Coughlin to replace Jack Bicknell, his former boss and the coach at BC for 10 seasons.

He spent his final months in New York helping the Giants to Super Bowl XXV and hiring assistants and recruiting at BC. From the locker room, while celebrating the Giants' 20–19 Super Bowl victory in Tampa, Florida, Coughlin called several BC recruits. Most signed with BC, convinced this driven, disciplined coach could turn the Eagles around.

They were right.

But few knew how driven and disciplined Coughlin could be.

Coughlin started at BC a day after the Super Bowl victory. A believer in discipline and hard work, he found at BC a program desperately needing both.

He had stored away the lessons learned first from his father, then from Schwartzwalder, Campbell, and Parcells. In time, they had evolved into a philosophy. The series of lessons was now a belief system. When he was an assistant, the coaches for whom he worked bridled the system. At BC, he was decidedly unbridled.

A program in disarray; lazy, out-of-shape players; players who considered attending class optional—that was what he found at BC. So began his winter workouts—or, as players referred to them, "throw-up-fests."

"Guys puked all over the place," Tom McManus, a Jaguars linebacker who played for Coughlin at BC, said.

"The most hellish thing I've ever been through," said Gordon Laro, who played for Coughlin at BC and spent the 1995 training camp with the Jaguars. "He got rid of a lot of people who didn't want to play."

Players missing class received Coughlin's most brutal punishments. He was ruthless on such players, figuring they had three choices—obey, not play, or leave school. "It's not that you feared him physically," said former BC quarterback Glenn Foley, who played with the New York Jets in 1995 and 1996. "It's just that you did what he said or you were gone."

Missing class meant running at 6 A.M. The player did that, the rule went, or rolled 300 yards on a wet, muddy field, or did 300 yards of a drill known as up-downs, in which a player ran the length of the field—dropping to the ground and up again every five yards. "At those times, you hated him," Laro said, "but you learned it was good for you."

Punishment wasn't just for habitual hooky. It was as fierce for first-time offenders. Tight end Pete Mitchell, a key player for Coughlin's first two Jaguars teams, was late for a meeting once. He ran every day at 6 A.M. for five weeks. "You cursed him . . . like your parents," Mitchell said. "You get angry at the time they're doing those things to you, but you know they're doing it for your benefit. It was the same with him."

Victories came hard. The Eagles went 4–7 that first season as Coughlin weeded out players, implementing his way. Losing heightened his desire, and he worked later and later each evening. Coughlin started with a 5 A.M.-to-midnight, seven-day-a-week schedule. As the losses mounted, he worked later, began to weaken, and grew sick. The sickness became viral pneumonia. At first, he ignored the symptoms, knowing there was something wrong.

"My head was affected to a point where I was a little slow on the draw," Coughlin said later. "From the top of my shoulders up, it was a constant ache."

When his fever reached 104 degrees, he agreed to stay home—but only after doctors told him he was contagious. Still, he barely rested. His staff brought practice tapes nightly, and he called assistants at the office from home. Assistants brought game plans for that week's opponent, Georgia Tech, to his house. Saturday, he was on the sidelines, although he gave up play calling midway through the game because his senses weren't sharp. BC won, and Coughlin earned the respect of his team.

"I was the head coach," he said of the story, shrugging.

That was the side his players saw, all anyone at BC saw at first. Then, something happened showing a different side. Jay McGillis, a defensive back in Coughlin's image—self-made, tireless—was diagnosed with leukemia.

Coughlin loved McGillis as a son. One day, in the first off-season program, "Jay leans over on the track, pukes, and then keeps right on running," Coughlin recalled five years later. "He was that kinda kid."

McGillis started 10 games that first year before developing what was thought to be mononucleosis. Blood tests revealed the leukemia. Coughlin visited McGillis almost daily for eight months. He watched sickness overcome Jay, and watched Jay throw up from chemotherapy. The two grew closer. McGillis called Coughlin the day a bone marrow transplant he hoped could save him failed. On July 3, 1992, Jay died at home.

"Talk about dying with dignity," Coughlin said. "Never once did Jay say to me, 'Why me? Why me?' Never once. He never complained. He never lost hope."

For months after his death, Coughlin wore McGillis's windbreaker. He hung McGillis's number 31 jersey in his old BC locker, and during his first two years with the Jaguars, he kept mementos of Jay in his office in his Ponte Vedra Beach, Florida, home. As of 1996, Coughlin called Jay's parents on his birthday each year and held a golf tournament each spring in his honor to benefit leukemia research.

The summer Jay died, Coughlin worked on, determined not to repeat the losing season. Once that summer, after a night out, Laro looked out his dorm window, and saw a light in Coughlin's office window.

It was 3:30 A.M.

"Nobody outworked the guy," Foley said. "When he first came in, everything was his way or the highway. He wanted to instill fear, but as time progressed, he gave the leadership role to the seniors."

That year, BC went 8–2–1 and played in the Hall of Fame Bowl. In 1993, his third season, they went 9–3, beating Virginia in the Carquest Bowl. The 1993 season included his signature victory at BC, a 41–39 victory over No. 1–ranked Notre Dame, an event as unlikely as one occurring several weeks later—the city of Jacksonville being awarded an NFL team.

The timing of BC's victory over Notre Dame thrust his name to the top of NFL coaching candidates as Jaguars owner J. Wayne Weaver began searching for a coach. Weaver, however, focused first on football's biggest names. Some, such as former Bears coach Mike Ditka, were out of football, looking for jobs. Lou Holtz of Notre Dame and Bill Walsh of Stanford were candidates, too, but Walsh—who had coached the 49ers to three Super Bowl victories—didn't want to rejoin the NFL, and the Jaguars weren't sold on Holtz. Also considered was Tony Dungy, defensive coordinator with the Minnesota Vikings. Weaver liked Dungy, but wondered if he was aggressive enough with players. Weaver passed, and in 1996, Dungy became coach at Tampa Bay.

The Jaguars' most wanted: Jimmy Johnson.

Weaver wanted to give Johnson total control of football operations. Johnson, the plan went, would build from nothing—much as he had done with the Dallas Cowboys. There was one problem: Johnson was under contract with Dallas. Still, Johnson was unhappy with Cowboys owner Jerry Jones, and a few weeks after Johnson coached the Cowboys to a second Super Bowl victory in two years, Weaver and Jaguars officials met with John-son on a South Florida boat.

The meeting was a violation of the NFL tampering policy, so the Jaguars and Johnson kept it quiet. Word leaked to NFL officials, who warned the team to back off Johnson. Two months later, Johnson left the Cowboys, but before then, Weaver turned to a coach whose name he heard often during his search—a college coach capa-ble, perhaps, of doing what Johnson did in Dallas after leaving the University of Miami. Coughlin was that coach.

"His name continued to move to the top of the list," Weaver said.

Coughlin fit the Jaguars' profile. The Jaguars, Weaver decided, would be a young, forward-thinking franchise. Coughlin, then 47, was young, and as a college head coach, not inclined to be swayed by NFL status-quo thinking and theory.

Coughlin wanted into the NFL, but on his terms. He longed for total control, which prompted him to turn down offers from the Atlanta Falcons and the Giants, two teams with powerful general managers.

"That's something that absolutely attracted me to the position—the responsibility," Coughlin said.

At first, even offered control, Coughlin balked. The Jaguars called in the first week of February, and Coughlin at first wanted to decline. He was happy at BC, unsure about taking over an expansion team. At first.

"It kept growing—the interest, the real challenge of the opportunity," Coughlin said. "Whenever I would try to put it out of my mind, it just wouldn't stop."

Weaver offered him the job Saturday, February 19, 1994. Coughlin slept restlessly, and the next day, ac-cepted the job. On February 21, at a press conference in Jacksonville, Weaver announced Coughlin as the Jaguars' first coach, signing him to a five-year, $4 million contract that made him the highest-paid rookie coach in NFL history. Coughlin would have total control of personnel, power few NFL coaches had at the time.

Coughlin, a Division I coach for three seasons, never even had been an NFL coordinator—a stepping-stone assistants used for a head job. The lack of experience prompted questions of Tom Who? Who was this college coach who would lead the city's franchise through its first seasons? One of his former Giants receivers knew.

"They couldn't have picked a better guy to start up a team," Baker said. "He'll work his butt off to make that team a success. That's the way he is. Work, work, work. Give him a few years, and he'll have that team a winner."

Tom Who? The people of Jacksonville, hungry for the NFL, would find out over the next few months. His BC reputation preceded him. Workaholic. Tyrant. Control freak. Many wondered, Was this the right choice? This was a college coach, not an NFL coach, and besides, it wasn't even a college coach named Bowden or Spurrier, two names of legendary status in the state.

Anyone doubting the hire need have looked no further than a tiny town in northern New York that still remembered this man as Young Tom Coughlin, a disciplined, driven legend destined for success.

The Legend of Waterloo had made it. He was in the NFL with total control, and if he failed . . . well, if he failed, it wouldn't be because anyone outworked him. Anyone in Waterloo could tell you that.

3
THE QUEST FOR
A FRANCHISE

"We got it."
—J. WAYNE WEAVER
November 30, 1993

On August 16, 1979, more than 50,000 people stuffed the Gator Bowl in downtown Jacksonville, Florida, on the banks of the St. Johns River. The field they looked upon long had been a site for college and minor-league professional football games, but fans gathered this night for another reason.

They gathered for a hope, and a dream.

They gathered for civic pride.

They gathered for the National Football League.

As the 50,000 cheered, skydivers fell from the darkening summer sky, landing on a freshly painted "Jacksonville Colts" emblem at midfield.

That was the dream in the summer of '79—that the Baltimore Colts, one of the most tradition-rich of the NFL's 28 teams, might move to a little-known, football-crazy town in northeast Florida. It was a dream, fore-

most, of then mayor Jake Godbold, who thought professional sports the best way to catapult Jacksonville to
national-city status. Jacksonville was a football town—
having supported teams from Florida State University
and the University of Florida, as well as the World Football League in 1974 and 1975. Godbold thought the NFL,
while an unlikely dream, was the best professional sports
option.

That summer, Colts owner Robert Irsay was unhappy
with his lease at Baltimore Memorial Stadium. He
wanted a new city with a better stadium deal. A Jacksonville funeral director, Doug Peeples, sent a letter to Irsay,
asking him to consider Jacksonville. Irsay flew to Jacksonville on August 16. That afternoon, he and Godbold
discussed the Colts moving to Jacksonville.

At 8:46 P.M., a helicopter fluttered over the Gator Bowl
turf. Fans chanted, "We want the Colts. We want the
Colts." The helicopter landed. Irsay emerged. Fans, wearing "Jacksonville Colts" and "Colts Fever" T-shirts, continued to chant, "We want the Colts. We want the Colts,"
as Godbold spoke to the crowd. "Jacksonville is on the
threshold of becoming a great, national city," he said.
"We know it, and Mr. Irsay knows it."

Irsay then said, "It's too early to say what will or what
can happen. I'm very impressed with officials and the
people who came out here to welcome not only me, but
the Baltimore Colts."

They were grand words—optimistic words, giving the
city brief hope—but they were empty.

In the next 15 years, Jacksonville would hear them
often.

Irsay declined Jacksonville's offer within a month. Three
years later, he moved to Indianapolis, the first of many

disappointments Jacksonville would face in what became a decade-and-a-half quest to join the NFL.

"I thank Mr. Irsay for this opportunity," Godbold said at the time of the Colts courtship. "I think we just may have gotten more use out of him than he did out of us. We had everything to win, and nothing to lose. This is not the end of the road."

Far from it.

Godbold's words, however, proved prophetic in several ways. Who was using whom became a debate over the next 15 years as team after team talked with city officials only to move elsewhere, or return to their city. Disgruntled owners used Jacksonville's enthusiasm as the ultimate bargaining power with their cities. Jacksonville became a target of national jokes. "Want to sweeten the deal in your city? Give Jacksonville a call. Those folks will darn sure help," became the credo. The city's citizens, and some public officials, grew tired of rejection, and questioned the effort, but the city's mayors—first Godbold, then Tommy Hazouri and Ed Austin—continued the quest in the face of national ridicule.

From 1980 to 1987, four teams—the Cardinals, Saints, Oilers, and Falcons—flirted, only to leave the city jilted.

Five years after Irsay, Godbold received a phone call informing him the New Orleans Saints were for sale, and could be moved. The call led to negotiations between then-Saints owner John Mecom and several Jacksonville businessmen in Amelia Island, Florida, a resort city near Jacksonville. The sides agreed to a deal. "They were coming to Jacksonville," Dr. Roy Baker, one of the executives negotiating for Jacksonville, said later. "At one point we had a handshake deal."

Mecom instead sold the team to Tom Benson, who kept the team in New Orleans. "Out of all the negotiations I was involved with, this is the one I thought was for real," Godbold said later. It also would be his last.

In 1987, with Hazouri mayor, Houston Oilers owner K. S. "Bud" Adams—upset with his Astrodome lease—threatened to move to Jacksonville. The city made an offer of $128.5 million, which led to an October visit from Adams. The deal impressed Adams, but he continued to play Jacksonville against Houston. For a few days, it appeared the Oilers were moving to Jacksonville, but on October 26, Adams signed a letter of intent to stay in Houston, which offered less money than Jacksonville. "I said all along this would come down to love or money," Hazouri said. "He chose love, and I respect Mr. Adams for that."

That offer was enough to interest two more teams within a month. St. Louis football Cardinals owner Bill Bidwill—disenchanted with that city's failure to build a new stadium—included Jacksonville with Baltimore and Phoenix as sites for possible relocation. Bidwell moved the team to Phoenix.

In 1988, Falcons owner Rankin Smith, who grew up in Jacksonville, spoke with city officials about a possible move, a continuation of discussions that began the previous year. Smith was upset with delays in Atlanta's plans to build the Georgia Dome. Many believed Smith's ties to the city made the Falcons a possibility for Jacksonville.

The Georgia Dome became reality, and Jacksonville's NFL dreams did not. By now, the NFL had announced plans to expand in the early 1990s. Jacksonville, its business leaders determined, wouldn't be left out again.

After five rejections, Jacksonville citizens increasingly felt the NFL was an unattainable love. Many tired of the same story—hope, then disappointment.

Thomas Petway and Rick Catlett weren't among these people.

In August of 1989, four months after a group of Jacksonville businessmen formed Jacksonville/North Florida Leaders to draw an expansion team, Petway formed another group, Touchdown Jacksonville! The groups merged, with Petway chairman and Catlett—a former mayor's aide who knew many NFL owners—executive vice president. Petway and Catlett began building an ownership group that compared favorably with its competitors in an 11-city expansion race that included Charlotte, Oakland, Baltimore, St. Louis, and Memphis.

The group spent two years planning. The NFL didn't set an expansion date until May of 1991. The league then announced a two-team expansion for 1994, a date later delayed until 1995. In October of 1991, on the eve of the ownership applications due date, TD Jax!—as it was now known—announced a nine-man ownership group. Net worth: $500 million. Included were Petway; Jeb Bush, son of President George Bush; and a then relatively unknown shoe executive/multimillionaire from Connecticut named J. Wayne Weaver.

In March of 1992, after a shoddy presentation at a league meeting, NFL owners nearly dropped the city from the expansion list. By May, it was one of five finalists including Charlotte, Memphis, Baltimore, and St. Louis. Also in the early 1990s, the city had a final flirtation with an existing team. In 1990, New England Patriots owner Victor Kiam spoke with Barnett Banks chairman Charles Rice about selling to a Rice-led group, with that group moving to Jacksonville. The NFL warned Jacksonville to stay away. Kiam sold to Robert Kraft.

Expansion, then, was the city's hope, and in March of 1993—six months before the NFL planned to announce the new teams—it was a distant hope. The city lacked the reputation of its competitors. Charlotte had the NBA. St. Louis and Baltimore not only had professional sports teams, but had been in the NFL only to have teams move. Another factor against Jacksonville: ownership.

TD Jax! had money, but owners questioned if it had the right kind of money—a so-called money man with deep pockets and a free-flowing checkbook. In March of 1993, Weaver filled the void.

TD Jax! restructured its ownership group. Petway became a limited partner. Weaver became majority owner. Now, owners saw Jacksonville as having a potential owner like themselves—rich and powerful, with business savvy, and ready to join their exclusive fraternity. Weaver had a net worth estimated at $250 million—well within the range NFL owners considered worthy of membership.

"Having one guy who has that kind of money is a big plus," said Hugh Culverhouse Jr., son of then Tampa Bay Buccaneers owner Hugh Culverhouse Sr., and a member of the NFL's finance committee.

"We have found a way to profoundly enhance the Jacksonville case," Petway said at the time. "Solid, deep-pocket ownership is a critical factor in the expansion race."

The pockets of Jerry Wayne Weaver, born January 1, 1935, in Columbus, Georgia, weren't always deep. He excelled at football and wrestling in high school, but after transferring before his senior year, he was ineligible for sports. It was then he became what he called "a bad boy."

"I never was arrested or anything like that," Weaver said, "but I took out my frustrations of not being able to play in the wrong way. I was a terrible student," he added, laughing, "but I can read the balance sheet with the best of them."

Few imagined the bad-boy senior as a future millionaire. "I'm not so sure anybody thought he would even get out of high school—much less accomplish what he has," his wife, Delores, said. "Certainly, he wouldn't have won any awards for the most likely to succeed. Wayne had quite a temper. He thought he could solve all of his problems by reacting instead of acting on the situation. He had a lot of growing up to do."

With no money for college, he went to work selling shoes. Soon thereafter, he and Delores married. He was 20. She was 18. "I can remember worrying about paying the rent," he said. "Or hoping we had three dollars on Saturday night to go to a movie."

Weaver worked his way into management at Brown Group, a St. Louis Missouri–based shoe company, then to executive, before being hired to run Fisher Camuto. That company became Nine West, a leading retailer of women's shoes. Nine West provided Weaver not only wealth, but a reputation as business leader—from high school troublemaker to millionaire 250 times over.

"He is the American Dream," Petway said.

In 1993, he resigned from Nine West to concentrate on a new venture, Shoe Carnival, and to devote more time to Jacksonville's NFL venture, but until late in life, the NFL was far from Weaver's plan. He had season tickets to the St. Louis football Cardinals while living there, but his dreams didn't include sports ownership, and he only joined the Jacksonville effort at the urging of his brother, Ron Weaver, also a limited partner.

"It was a process that kind of evolved over time," Weaver said, "My first reaction was, 'Are you kidding? Jacksonville?' I think along the way, there was some subtle arm-twisting, but when I got involved, I never had any idea of stepping up as the lead guy. It was an evolution over a long period of time."

The NFL challenge was hardly the first Weaver attempted in the face of doubters. In 1989, he climbed Mount Kilimanjaro in Tanzania, training for the climb by running the 11 flights of stairs in his Connecticut office an hour and a half each day. In 1991, he ran the Boston Marathon, a 26.2-mile race, although until three months before, he had never run more than five miles in a day.

"I've never done anything I don't do well," Weaver said. "I've never taken on something I didn't complete, never accepted a challenge I didn't master. You just have to want it."

The NFL, it was apparent in the spring of 1993, would be the toughest challenge yet.

Weaver's presence as majority owner made Jacksonville a player in expansion, but it hardly made the city a favorite. Seven months remained before the October announcement. They would be the most turbulent, dramatic months in the city's sports history.

Jacksonville still trailed St. Louis, Baltimore, and Charlotte in the eyes of most, and some believed it even lingered behind Memphis. In July of 1993, that changed. The city was no longer behind.

It was no longer in the race at all.

The city, in the spring of 1993, had only the Gator Bowl as a possible home field. The Gator Bowl's dilapidated state long concerned those pursuing the franchise. It compared poorly to average NFL stadiums, and was far behind modern facilities such as Joe Robbie Stadium in Miami. In the spring of 1993, it became more than a concern. It became a controversial and potentially dream-breaking flash point in the bid.

NFL officials visited the Gator Bowl April 12. The city planned a $49 million renovation, a figure close to the

$60 million TD Jax! said would be needed. NFL officials told TD Jax! the stadium was further below league standards than originally thought, and when TD Jax! calculated the costs of the changes, the tag was $112 million with cost overruns. So began a citywide debate: fund the stadium, or risk losing even the chance of a team.

The changes needed meant rebuilding the stadium. Many city leaders wondered why this was needed when a stadium that was the site for numerous Gator Bowls and Florida-Georgia football games was there. And if a new stadium was needed, those leaders said, why not let the team pay for it? TD Jax! officials wanted the city to finance the stadium—reason being they were paying the $160 million—200 million expansion fee. The debate went public, turning nasty in early June.

"The NFL's not going to put a team in a ghetto," TD Jax! president David Seldin said.

The quote from Seldin—who had alienated some civic leaders with his aggressive style—symbolized the rift between the city and TD Jax! The Gator Bowl was in a rundown downtown area, and was far from beautiful to the eye. Seldin later said he was trying to say the NFL needed modern facilities, and the comment didn't refer to the area. Still, it angered many.

Negotiations continued. TD Jax! and Austin agreed on July 1 to a renovation plan with a $112 million ceiling, with the lone obstacle being city council approval. On July 21, the city planned a ceremony at the Jacksonville Landing—a high-profile, riverfront, central location—to celebrate the lease signing.

The city council, however, voted to delay approval.

TD Jax! officials, who wanted solid backing from the city, perceived the delay as a no vote. Weaver, angry and unwilling to bear the entire risk of constructing a stadium, announced the end of TD Jax!'s bid.

"We're out of business," Seldin said. "We don't care what people say about us anymore. It's over.

Around the NFL, reaction was disappointment. "It's hard to believe all that work . . ." Falcons president Taylor Smith said. "To come this far and see it go to waste . . . what a shame. I know that community, and it would support football. That makes it an even bigger shame. I hope it's not the end of the road. I hope something can be done. But if it is, it's a sad day for Jacksonville."

Weaver stayed quiet for several days. On July 27, however, Weaver met with NFL officials about resurrecting the effort. NFL commissioner Paul Tagliabue, upon learning that Austin and *Florida Times-Union* publisher Carl Cannon were traveling to London on vacation, invited their group to an NFL exhibition game there August 8. Austin declined, thinking it only a social invitation, but Weaver also was invited—Tagliabue having the idea that getting them together might resurrect the bid.

That meeting didn't happen, but city council president Don Davis heard of Tagliabue's intentions. That led to a call to NFL director of planning Don Weiss, a one-time golfing partner. "I wanted to know if the NFL was really interested in Jacksonville," Davis said. "He said, 'Don, I can't speak for the commissioner, but I think the answer is yes.'"

Soon thereafter, Weaver and Davis spoke.

"Wayne," Davis told him, "I can't let this thing die if the NFL really wants Jacksonville."

Two days later, Davis went to Cannon's office and told him the situation. When Davis left, Cannon called Austin, who rushed to the *Times-Union* for a meeting. Cannon asked Austin if he would talk to Weaver if the lease was solved. Austin said yes.

Cannon and Davis relayed that news to Weaver. The

next day, Cannon met with Seldin. Afterward, Cannon called Weaver. "Do you want to get back into the football business?" Cannon asked.

"No, not really," Weaver said.

"Give me a number. What would it take to get you interested again?" Cannon said.

That changed Weaver's mind, secret negotiations began, and a plan emerged: the city would put up $121 million, rather than $112 million, and TD Jax! would be responsible for construction and cost overruns. On August 23, the city council agreed to lease the stadium for 30 years to TD Jax! On August 24, Weaver and Austin flew to Washington to meet with Tagliabue, who welcomed them back in the race.

The city was in, but the rift had set it behind in a league test for the expansion cities—selling premium seats. The NFL asked each expansion group to sell club seats and luxury suites before September 3 as a measure of fan passion. When TD Jax! left the race, it refunded $2 million from such sales, a relatively small number. Now, 10 days remained before that deadline, and Weaver said if 9,000 club seats weren't sold he would not finance the team.

Cannon formed NFL Now!, comprising civic leaders and businesses, to spearhead a drive that was more of a success than anyone imagined. On September 3, NFL Now! announced 9,737 club seats had been sold.

"I'm very excited about the pride in the community," Weaver said. "Now, it's up to Touchdown Jacksonville! to go out and get a football team."

"This is about Jacksonville," Cannon said. "We've shown the community that we can pull together on a common issue."

Would the NFL see that passion? And would it bring a team to Jacksonville? Those were questions for the next four months, and it was hardly a given in August that the answer would be yes. At the time of club-seat sales, St. Louis and Baltimore seemed the favorites. Charlotte, with strong ownership, was a likely choice if a leader faltered, or if the NFL decided not to expand to two former league cities. Word soon leaked that Tagliabue was against Baltimore because he didn't want a team so close to Washington, the Redskins' market. That left St. Louis and Charlotte as the leaders.

In October 1993, the NFL owners gathered in Rosemont, Illinois, to announce the two franchises. Jacksonville, many thought, had a chance because St. Louis was struggling to put together an adequate stadium proposal.

Instead, Tagliabue announced Charlotte as the 29th NFL team, but did not announce a 30th, delaying a decision until November 30. The delay, he said, was because there was no clear choice among other cities. Speculation, however, was heavy that the delay was to allow time to analyze a new St. Louis ownership group.

Weaver, like most in Jacksonville, was furious. Feeling TD Jax! had a more-than-adequate proposal, he demanded a meeting with Tagliabue. If the league was only delaying a decision to ensure St. Louis a franchise, Weaver told him, he wanted to know so he could stop wasting time and money. Tagliabue told him no— Jacksonville was a strong candidate.

Few other than Weaver and TD Jax! officials believed that.

Yet, throughout November, NFL officials privately indicated that the league was serious about Jacksonville. Weaver, officials said, was a strong owner candidate, and owners wanted him in the club. Also, the Jacksonville ticket drive impressed owners, who were tired of lagging ticket sales league-wide. A city so passionate about football, they figured, might be a solid site for a franchise—

even in a small market. Mostly, the league had tired of the St. Louis situation. The expansion was four years old, and St. Louis had yet to provide a clear financial package, and had no lease for a new stadium.

"It's still a wide-open race," Denver Broncos owner Pat Bowlen said after initial delay. "I know I haven't made up my mind yet. And I don't think a lot of others have either."

Jacksonville media, speculating that the delay was only to help St. Louis, criticized the NFL, prompting one NFL official to say, "What are they doing? Jacksonville's the favorite."

Still, as the day approached, it was hard to imagine Jacksonville—so often jilted by the NFL—a favorite.

On November 30, 1993, Weaver spent the morning and midafternoon in a 27th-floor suite in the Hyatt Regency O'Hare hotel in Rosemont, Illinois. "I've never been so damn nervous in all my life," Weaver told *Times-Union* columnist Gene Frenette as he paced the room.

Downstairs, the NFL owners meetings—in which the final expansion vote was to be taken—were to conclude at 3:15 P.M., and in Weaver's suite sat many who had spent the last six months trying to secure an NFL team, including Petway and Seldin, among others. Former Kansas City Chiefs safety Deron Cherry, now a limited partner in the effort, was there, too. "It was just like being in a locker room waiting to come out before kickoff," Cherry said. "My hands were sweaty and I just wanted to go out there and tear somebody's head off."

Until then, the days immediately before the announcement were full of uncharacteristically good news. People in Jacksonville were starting to believe . . . .

Maybe . . .

Late Monday, the night before the announcement,

word had leaked that a lease agreement that would enhance St. Louis's bid had failed to develop. "I was optimistic last time [when Charlotte got its team]," Weaver said that day, "but I didn't have the total gut feeling I do now. I just can't see the league going to St. Louis. If that happens, it'd be pretty Machiavellian after encouraging me so much the last couple of weeks. If they pick St. Louis, they're going to have an enormous public relations problem. They'd be sending the wrong message to the other NFL cities."

Two hours before the announcement, two owners told people close to the Jacksonville effort that it looked good, and rumors filtered into Weaver's room—2706. Around this time, an NFL source told Cherry that Jacksonville was approved by the expansion and finance committees. The league told all pursuing groups if they received the team they would be escorted to the meeting; if they didn't receive a team, they would be told in their suite.

"There had been so many rumors going around and no matter how good they sounded, we had been down that road before," Seldin said.

At 2:30 P.M., Warren Welsh—NFL director of security—approached Weaver outside the suite. "Mr. Weaver, do you have a couple of compatriots you want to bring down with you?"

Weaver turned to Petway. "We got it," Weaver said.

Downstairs, Tagliabue told the world at 3:13 P.M. CST that Jacksonville was the NFL's 30th franchise. "You can't describe how I feel," Weaver said.

If Weaver felt happy, it was a feeling shared by Jacksonvillians. When he learned of the decision in Rosemont, Austin spun like a ballerina, dancing and laughing. In Jacksonville, fans did the same, drinking until the next morning at the Landing—unrehearsed reveling; joy and pride. That afternoon, before the party downtown, a former mayor was watching television in his downtown law office. Fourteen years before, Godbold had stood at midfield of the Gator Bowl near a "Jacksonville Colts" logo, waiting to shake the hand of Robert Irsay while 50,000 fellow citizens watched, cheering. Around 4:15 EST on November 30, 1993, a special report bulletin flashed on his television.

"I've been through this so many times," he said. "I want it to be real, but I'm not going to believe it until the commissioner comes out and says it's official."

Minutes later, the report aired. It was official. Godbold, who had waved Irsay good-bye that night never really knowing if the NFL would ever fly back to Jacksonville for good, dropped his face in his hands.

And he cried.

"I've lived this dream for 15 years," Godbold said. "To see it finally come true, how lucky can a person be? . . . This will bring pride and enthusiasm and a feeling of community we've never experienced before. There's not a doubt in my mind: This is the best thing that's ever happened to Jacksonville.

"I don't think Jacksonville will ever be the same again."

4
THE BUILDING
OF THE JAGUARS

"He [Tom Coughlin] wanted everyone to know who was in charge, that he was the boss. If you don't come in and put forth 100 percent like you're supposed to, like you're paid to do, then you're going to be up and out of here."

—JIMMY SMITH
November 1996

The 1994 college football season began in late August. A week later, the NFL season began. Making both dates difficult for Tom Coughlin was being involved in neither.

Coughlin was hired 19 months before the Jaguars' first game, which meant that for the first time since 1968 he wouldn't spend fall weekends on the sidelines. "It's the fish-out-of-water syndrome," Coughlin said that August. "It's withdrawal. As coaches, we live by the calendar, and this time of the year, usually it means it's time for training camp. It's only natural you feel something's missing."

Coughlin was a college coach. He had 19 months to

learn the professional game, and now, he had what he never wanted—a season away from football. He filled the void the only way he knew: work, work, and more work.

Coughlin spent his first month in Jacksonville planning the next 18, and when he was done, the Jaguars' schedule through opening day 1995 was set—at least tentatively.

At first, Coughlin didn't even have an office. No one on the Jaguars did. Coughlin and the staff worked out of several trailers outside the Gator Bowl for a year while the new stadium was constructed.

"That required a second gulp of air," Coughlin said, "but when they offered me the job, and I thought about not taking it, I kept asking myself, 'Don't you want the challenge?' What was here was the opportunity to do something historical. We would build this from nothing."

Wayne Weaver had heard stories of Coughlin's work ethic. Up close, it was more fanatical, and more impressive.

"I've been around some motivated people in my career," Weaver said, "but I can honestly say I don't think I've met anybody as motivated or as driven as Tom Coughlin, or as detail-oriented. He knows what he wants to do, and he doesn't waver in his decision to get something done."

What Coughlin wanted in 1994 was to learn the league. Total control over personnel meant he was responsible for decisions regarding players about whom he knew comparatively little. Coughlin brought five assistants—Pete Carmichael, Randy Edsall, Mike Maser, Steve Szabo, and Jerald Ingram—from BC for 1994, and assembled a scouting staff, too. He toured training camps, he and his coaches attended games, and his scouts scouted colleges.

This time proved invaluable. While scouting Green

Bay that year, he first noticed a young, mobile quarterback named Mark Brunell, whom he soon acquired in a trade and who became the team's starter by the end of the first season. So thorough was his scouting that it extended beyond quarterbacks, and even starters. Most NFL coaches are hard-pressed to name even every player on their team. Midway through the Jaguars' first season, Coughlin's knowledge of opposing personnel was so deep that when describing the Houston Oilers' linebackers, he mentioned that although Al Smith was injured, a then obscure reserve, Barron Wortham, would replace him. He gave a detailed report on Wortham as if he were one of his players—a scene Coughlin repeated for other players throughout that first year.

That was Coughlin's 1994 fall: Scout. Study. Sweat. And hope, somehow, he could get it all done in time. "There's so much to do," Coughlin said. "Next year is just around the corner."

The Jaguars signed their first players on December 15, 1994. It was only the beginning.

A month later, Coughlin hired two coordinators—Kevin Gilbride on offense and Dick Jauron on defense. Gilbride had been a coordinator in Houston, where he ran the controversial run-and-shoot, and had a sideline fight with then Oilers defensive coordinator Buddy Ryan, but he was a familiar name, and a proven coach. Jauron coached defensive backs in Green Bay, and most in the NFL believed he deserved a coordinator's position.

The Jaguars were signing players, too—bigger names than any expansion team before. The 1995 expansion process was different from any in NFL history. The league, wary of saddling franchises into losing histories such as the 1976 Tampa Bay Buccaneers', determined Carolina and Jacksonville would receive a chance to compete quickly for their $201 million expansion fees. That meant the most talent-rich player pool ever available to expansion teams. Each received two selections in each round of the 1995 rookie draft, and had the same access to the free-agent market as established teams. With a full salary cap, experts predicted unprecedented success.

That made the 1995 off-season an exciting, expensive time. First came the expansion draft, when they drafted a known quarterback, Steve Beuerlein, and a wide receiver who won the Heisman Trophy at the University of Michigan, Desmond Howard. Defensive end Jeff Lageman, center Dave Widell, cornerbacks Mickey Washington and Vinnie Clark, defensive tackles Kelvin Pritchett and Don Davey, and guard Shawn Bouwens—all signed big-money free-agent contracts.

The Jaguars had been an idea. Now, they had names and faces.

Later came the rookie draft. The Jaguars selected Tony Boselli, an offensive tackle from the University of Southern California, and James Stewart, a running back from Tennessee, with their first two draft selections, and by the time April ended, the first season's roster was all but set.

Coughlin was preparing for the first season with a maniacal approach anyone who knew him expected. Some liked it, some didn't. No one ignored it.

One of the assistants hired after the 1995 season was Larry Pasquale, a respected special-teams coach. That summer, Jaguars coaches spent several weeks reviewing techniques. It was part of Coughlin's master plan—to have all assistants know the Jaguars Way, no matter the position. Coughlin devoted a week to special teams, having Pasquale teach him the techniques and theories in that area. "In my career, no coach had ever done that before," Pasquale said.

A passionate attention to detail was only part of Coughlin's growing reputation. As at BC, he believed there was but one way. His way. "I'm demanding because I know human nature well," Coughlin said. "If given the opportunity, the individual will take the easy way out. I'm trying to force people to be all they can, and not accept rationalization, crutches, and lame excuses that go along with failing to achieve."

Beginning in March 1995, his players learned how serious he was when he implemented his off-season conditioning program. Off-season conditioning in the NFL was different from college and far different from Coughlin's BC program. Most NFL teams have off-season programs. They are voluntary, and many players work out at hometowns, following workouts suggested by the teams.

Coughlin's was voluntary—volunteer or risk being released.

Attendance at the program, held in Jacksonville, was nearly 100 percent, and although it wasn't punishment-oriented, the intensity and demand for on-field participation and practices not only surprised players, it stretched league rules. The NFL and most players saw the off-season as a time for relaxing; Coughlin saw it as a time to familiarize himself with new players—and this season, as a way to get players accustomed to his ways. At one of the first team meetings, Coughlin noticed a player slouching, one leg crossed over another. He yelled at the player, telling him to sit up straight and put his feet on the floor. "That got some guys' attention right away," then wide receiver Shannon Baker said. "That told you how it would be."

Coughlin's approach, coupled with the unusual expectations for the workout program, caused immediate grumbling. "He's not a hard-ass simply to be a hard-ass," then tight-ends coach Nick Nicolau said. "He does things for a reason. It's like if your doctor told you to go on a diet for health reasons. He's not telling you that to be a hard-ass. He's telling you that for a reason. That's what Tom does."

Players, however, protested to the NFL Players Association, which led to stricter rules governing off-season workouts the following season. Some called them the Coughlin Rules.

Coughlin was more than rules. Already, he preached psychological tactics picked up throughout his career, but mostly from Giants coach Bill Parcells. Coughlin studied such techniques, and in Jacksonville, they became a trademark. Each week during a season, Coughlin presented a motivational theme, usually accompanied by a saying. In the team's first training camp in Stevens Point, Wisconsin, players got a glimpse when Coughlin installed a "Concentration Line" sign at the gate entering the practice field. A player was to think of nothing but football once across the line.

The sign became a fixture over the door leading out of the team's facility to the practice field.

On the third day of the Jaguars' first minicamp, a promising defensive tackle named Ferric Collons fought with offensive guard Tom Myslinski. The fight ended when Collons threw Myslinski's helmet half the length of the field. Coughlin told Collons to retrieve the helmet. Collons refused. Coughlin, furious, told Collons he was cut, and afterward, Coughlin fumed about the incident. Collons, a run-stuffing player whom the Jaguars could have used in the first two seasons, started for the Patriots in 1996. Another time before that first season, Coughlin told a player with a Mohawk haircut, Andrew Moore, to cut it.

Moore did. That afternoon, Coughlin released him.

After that, most players lived by a rule: Don't cross Coughlin.

Coughlin's style set the tone in that first season. Setting the structure were the infamous "Coughlin Rules."

Coughlin's rules were many, and nitpicky, but he considered them important. As he saw it, none were difficult—so long as that player was as serious about football as Coughlin.

"I hate loose ends," Coughlin said of his style. "I don't like things that are not absolutely spelled out. I don't like things that aren't organized. Discipline goes along with a good organization. I'm demanding, but I'm only demanding if I've spelled things out. If I did that, you're not talking about discipline anymore. You're talking about accountability."

The structure extended to Coughlin's life. He was in bed at 10:10 P.M. nightly—not before, or after. And only after a bowl of ice cream. Every night. Same time. When his four children were at home, he handed each a list of chores to do every Saturday. His football rules were as strict. Once, he saw his teenage daughter, Katie, sitting at practice. He ordered her to stand. Among his team rules:

—No sunglasses. (This applied to coaches and players.)

—Collared shirts when out of room in hotels on road trips.

—No feet off the floor in team meetings.

—No spatting. (This is common NFL practice in which players tape over their shoes.)

—Movies and phones turned off in team hotel at 11 P.M.

—No apparel from other NFL teams worn at team facility.

—No kneeling or sitting in practice.

—No sitting on helmets during practice.

"He came in and really set the tone for the inaugural season," wide receiver Jimmy Smith said. "He wanted everyone to know who was in charge, that he was the boss. If you don't come and put forth 100 percent like you're supposed to, like you're paid to do, then you're going to be out of here."

The rules were an easy story, and became a symbol for the Jaguars. When a writer arrived in Jacksonville for the Coughlin Story invariably it was a Rules or Dictator story the writer sought.

Many players resented the rules. They were making millions and supporting families, and yet were treated as if they were showing up for their first day of high school football practice. "It reminds me of a college team," safety Monty Grow said.

The first season was full of such comments, but included highlights. The team lost its first four games; then, on October 1, in the Houston Astrodome, Brunell passed 15 yards to Howard with 1:03 remaining for a 17–16 victory. Two weeks later, they stunned the Pittsburgh Steelers 20–16, the first time an expansion team beat an eventual Super Bowl participant. A week later, they won on the road again, 23–15 over the Browns in one of the league's most tradition-rich venues, Cleveland Stadium.

So began premature playoff talk. Inexperience, injuries, and a lack of depth caused a decline after the victory in Cleveland, and while Carolina surged toward .500, the Jaguars lost seven consecutive games before finishing on a high note—a 24–21 victory over the Browns. That made them 4–4 against the AFC Central, the first time an expansion team had a .500 division record. Brunell, who took over for Beuerlein as the starter after Houston, ran for a tying touchdown in the fourth quarter, and drove the team for a last-second game-winning field goal. Afterward, talk was of a future that suddenly seemed very bright indeed. "It's something we can carry into next year," Vinnie Clark said.

"There were three other games we could have won," Coughlin said. "We don't talk about that, but that's the truth. All the crap that was said—all the negatives—we worked through it."

Coughlin's reputation was established after the first season. What was not established was the Jaguars' roster. The Jaguars, from Weaver to Coughlin, had Year Three as a target date for the playoffs, but in Coughlin's mind, they were far from ready to do what he wanted in Year Two—go at least .500, and with a break or two, compete for a playoff spot.

The goal was to get younger, and late in the 1995 season, the team released two veterans—wide receiver Ernest Givins and linebacker James Williams. First-season fill-ins, it was clear, wouldn't be safe in the 1996 offseason.

The Jaguars established a core in the first season—Brunell, Boselli, and middle linebacker Bryan Schwartz, a second-round draft choice the year before. Also in the core were a few veterans who could contribute several more seasons, players such as Lageman. But with free agency providing an attractive market for talent, few Jaguars' jobs were safe in February of 1996.

"Last year, we got our ass kicked," Lageman said after the 1996 season. "When you looked around the locker room, you saw a bunch of guys without any experience."

As free agency began, the Jaguars had $10 million–$11 million to spend. They spent freely, and immediately. "You don't get things done by screwing around," Jaguars senior vice president of football operations Michael Huyghue, the team's point in contract negotiations, said.

Would free agents, with the choice of 29 other teams,

volunteer for Camp Coughlin? The answer was a resounding yes. On the first day of free agency, the Jaguars signed Alonzo Spellman, a 26-year-old defensive end with the Chicago Bears, to an offer sheet worth $12 million over four years. Spellman was the first '96 free agent to sign with another team, but because he was a transition free agent, the Bears had a week to match the offer and keep him. "I think [Spellman signing] sends a huge message," Huyghue said at the time. "People want to play here. They see this as an opportunity to build a championship football team."

The next day, they signed Leon Searcy, an offensive tackle from the Pittsburgh Steelers, to a five-year, $17 million contract, which then made him the highest-paid offensive lineman in NFL history.

A term Coughlin used often before free agency was "playmaker." The Jaguars lacked such players, and in Coughlin's mind, playmakers weren't just players who scored, intercepted passes, and sacked quarterbacks. A playmaker was any player who dominated—for instance, a run-blocking offensive tackle from a team that made the Super Bowl largely because of its running game. Searcy, a 26-year-old, four-year veteran, gave Coughlin his first new, young playmaker. Searcy, in Coughlin's plan, would play right tackle, clearing holes for Stewart, and protecting the blind side of the left-handed Brunell. Brian DeMarco, a 1995 second-round draft choice who played right tackle as a rookie, would move to right guard, next to Searcy. Boselli, outstanding as a rookie, would stay at left tackle.

"Leon Searcy is the finest offensive lineman in free agency," Coughlin said. "We have our bookends [Searcy and Boselli]."

The Jaguars had one impact player signed, and were waiting on another. This was their status when they signed another transition free agent, Quentin Coryatt of the Indianapolis Colts. The Jaguars the previous year produced a league-low 17 sacks. Spellman was one way to remedy that. A blitzing linebacker such as Coryatt was another.

The Jaguars' free-agency scorecard looked like this:

—One player signed and secure.
—Two players signed and waiting.

Another important number to consider was $47 million. That was the price for the three players if neither the Colts nor the Bears matched the Jaguars' offers. In the high-spending mood of the early years of free agency in the 1990s, such spending was common, but coming so quickly from an expansion team, it attracted the attention of front-office types league-wide. Many disliked what they saw.

When the expansion rules were announced in the 1995 season, many in the NFL protested. Green Bay general manager Ron Wolf, who helped build the 1976 Buccaneers, was particularly vocal, believing the new teams received "too much," too many advantages with the extra draft selections and equal access to free agents. The Jaguars' '96 off-season signings loudened the cries.

The free-agent status of two of the Jaguars' targets heightened those feelings. The NFL established the transition tag to allow teams to keep those players by matching the offer of the pursuing team, but many felt that in the Jaguars' case, "transition" had a different meaning.

The Jaguars, officials from other teams felt, had so much room under the salary cap that they could offer a transition player more than market value. That meant the teams either lost the player, or paid him so much to stay that they altered their salary structure. The Jaguars, then, cost existing teams not only players, but money—

hardly a recipe for popularity. "We don't break the rules," Huyghue said.

Superagent Leigh Steinberg agreed.

"Those folks have their act together," said Steinberg, who represented Spellman. "They have a huge number of very talented salespeople. When they get focused, there's an energy that administration gives off. That can be a tremendous force. They seem to know what they want, and they go after it. It's a very impressive group from the owner on down."

The euphoria from such praise soon waned. The Bears matched the offer to Spellman, and a few days later, the Colts did the same for Coryatt, but free agency was far from over, and word spread: What the Jaguars wanted, they went after. Reputation be damned.

Losing Spellman and Coryatt disappointed team officials, but left money to make moves elsewhere. The first move was to pursue a cornerback.

Enter Aeneas Williams, an unrestricted free agent from the Arizona Cardinals. Williams was the best available cornerback, and one of the best overall. The Jaguars negotiated with Williams for four days, offering between $3.2 million and $3.5 million a season. Williams re-signed with the Cardinals for similar money.

The pursuit of Williams set off even more ill will league-wide toward the Jaguars—and this time, it stemmed from a suspicion that the Jaguars may have tampered with Williams.

NFL rules prohibit team officials from speaking to potential free agents before the signing period. It was a rule often followed with a wink, but many in the league believed Huyghue stepped well over the vague line. Huyghue flew to the Pro Bowl in Hawaii in late January. There, many NFL officials believed, he spoke to potential free agents—in particular, Williams. ESPN reported some NFL personnel were angry over the actions, but the NFL never reported any evidence of tampering. At the next Pro Bowl, the league tightened rules to prevent team officials from talking to free agents, a move many believed was aimed at Huyghue.

After losing Williams, the Jaguars stayed active. A second tier of players was now signing league-wide, and the Jaguars were again head of the league.

First, they signed Houston Oilers linebacker Eddie Robinson, who many believed equal to Coryatt. Robinson, who signed for $10.5 million over four years, was a late bloomer, having signed with Alabama State on an academic scholarship. He developed into a second-round draft selection, and by the time he signed with the Jaguars—choosing them over the Falcons—he was 26 and, many believed, one of the NFL's better pass-covering outside linebackers.

The next day, the Jaguars signed Keenan McCardell from the Browns, now known as the Ravens. McCardell, a former 12th-round draft selection, had emerged the previous season, catching a career-high 56 passes, including seven in the season finale against the Jaguars.

A few days after the McCardell signing, the Jaguars—again trying to fill a need for a corner—signed Todd Lyght, a transition free agent from the Rams, to an offer sheet. That deal was done, but a technical error by the Jaguars in the structuring of the contract allowed the Rams to match. The first wave of free agency was finished. Finally. Addressed were offensive tackle, linebacker, and receiver. Still needed were cornerback and defensive line.

The next addition, surprisingly, was neither.

In early March, the Jaguars claimed running back Natrone Means, a 1994 Pro Bowl player with the San Diego

Chargers, off the waiver wire. Means led the AFC in rushing after nine games the previous season, but sustained a groin injury, and the Chargers waived him in late February for salary-cap reasons. The Jaguars were the only team to claim him. It seemed a departure from Coughlin's plan, but it made sense. The Jaguars were building for Year Three, and the target age for free agents in the 1996 off-season was 26—the age of Searcy, McCardell, and Robinson.

Means was 23 when he was claimed off waivers.

The Jaguars signed two more free agents before the April draft—defensive tackle John Jurkovic from the Green Bay Packers and safety Dana Hall from the Ravens. Coughlin felt a team needed intelligent veterans to win. Jurkovic and Hall were such players.

In late April, the Jaguars drafted a second time. They considered running back Lawrence Phillips, a troubled player from the University of Nebraska whom Coughlin compared to Jim Brown. The Jaguars, however, had Means. And Stewart. Phillips's trouble and the team's depth prompted a defensive draft. They chose Kevin Hardy, an outside linebacker from the University of Illinois, with the second overall selection, and with the third selection of the second round chose University of Texas defensive end Tony Brackens.

"We feel like we got two first-round selections," Coughlin said.

Later in the second round, they selected Georgia Tech center Michael Cheever, then went defense again with a third-round selection, West Virginia cornerback Aaron Beasley.

The draft was finished. Free agency was, too. The Jaguars were younger, faster, and on paper, better. The second training camp was two and a half months away.

5
GETTING READY

"Tom's changed a lot. He has learned a lot about what an NFL camp is all about."

—JEFF LAGEMAN
August 1996

That the 1996 Jaguars season would be different was obvious from the beginning. The first change was in scenery. No longer would they train a country away, as in the first off-season, when training camp was in Stevens Point, Wisconsin. This season, training camp would be at home.

Team owner Wayne Weaver, from the inception of the franchise, wanted camp in Jacksonville, but before the first season, construction at Jacksonville Municipal Stadium prevented it. By 1996, the JMS facility in downtown Jacksonville was ready for in-town camp.

Coughlin liked the privacy of training away from Jacksonville; Weaver loved the idea of camp as an annual way for fans to get to know their team. Weaver easily won.

Weaver pictured a camp with parents and children watching their team, talking excitedly of a new season— the sort of goodwill Weaver felt could make the Jaguars a long-term community presence. On July 17, the day before training camp, a bizarre presence entered this serene setting.

Jaguars fans knew Andre Rison well. A four-time Pro Bowl wide receiver, he had a bad-boy reputation, which he enhanced the year before during a one-year career with the Cleveland Browns. Midway through that season, when the Jaguars visited Cleveland Stadium, the Browns were struggling and Rison was being criticized for production less than his five-year, $17 million salary warranted. Rison, hoping to jump-start a failing team and a damaged reputation, guaranteed a victory over the Jaguars. The Jaguars won, 23–15.

Feuding with quarterback Vinny Testaverde, Rison caught a career-low 47 passes for 701 yards and three touchdowns. The Browns moved to Baltimore after the season, and upon arriving, faced salary-cap problems. The Ravens released Rison in early July. On Tuesday, July 16, he met with Coughlin and Weaver in Jacksonville. He signed the following day.

Rison, at 29, didn't fit the team's build-with-youth philosophy, but the biggest negative was his reputation. The Jaguars would be his fourth team, and his list of enemies in Indianapolis, Atlanta, and Cleveland was long.

Rison and Coughlin? In the same locker room? In the same state?

Coughlin brushed aside those questions. He needed playmakers, and while he thought Keenan McCardell and Jimmy Smith had potential, Rison *was* a big-time receiver—at least, he had been until the previous season.

Factoring, too, was Coughlin's ego. A player with a bad work ethic, or reputation, to Coughlin's thinking, was a player in the wrong system—a system other than Coughlin's. Coughlin believed, given time with a player, he could make any player a dedicated team player. He didn't see why Rison should be different.

"We talked about each phase of his career, and he did not blink an eye when discussing any off-the-field or on-field incidents that had cast him in a bad light," Coughlin said upon signing Rison.

"I think it would be great if we could go to church and get guys who were all former altar boys," Huyghue said, "but that's not the way it is. However, Andre has not done anything to demonstrate that he's a drug guy who has major character flaws. He's matured as a player, and we're catching him at that cycle."

"You could say I had a lot of ups and downs," Rison said. "Now, I'm on the upbeat. I'm more focused than at any time in my career."

As training camp opened, many wondered how true those words were.

Changes were obvious as camp opened. Free agency had added players such as Searcy, McCardell, Hall, Jurkovic, Robinson and now, Rison. Means was new, too, as was a trio of rookies—Hardy, Brackens, and Beasley.

The new meant old faces, some fan favorites, were gone.

Howard had signed as a free agent with Green Bay; Beuerlein, with Carolina. Gone, too, was offensive tackle Bruce Wilkerson, who had also signed with Green Bay. Eugene Chung, an offensive guard, had signed with the 49ers. Also released was Cedric Tillman, a wide receiver. Keith Goganious, a linebacker who started the first season, had signed as a free agent with the Buccaneers after not being asked back by the Jaguars. The safety position had undergone the most turnover. Harry Colon, Mike

Dumas, and Darren Carrington, all first-year starters, were no longer with the team. Only Carrington remained in the NFL, signing with the Raiders.

Those changes were ongoing and expected. Unexpected was a change in Coughlin, who wasn't quite the dictatorial presence of a year ago. Kind and gentle?

Perhaps not, but gone were some of the problems of a year before. There were no "voluntary" days at the beginning of training camp, for example, and rules were less strict.

Players in early practices kneeled and removed their helmets. Gone, too, was Coughlin's habit of postpractice wind sprints after each session of two-a-days, common the year before. "Tom's changed a lot," Lageman said after one of the early sessions. "He has learned a lot about what an NFL camp is all about."

Coughlin denied any changes. "It's just that the players now know what to expect from our practices," he said.

On August 2, the Jaguars played their first preseason game of 1996 in JMS against the New York Giants. The Jaguars took an early lead on a 34-yard field goal by second-year kicker Mike Hollis, then trailed 14–3 at halftime after a 2-yard run by Giants running back Keith Elias and a 5-yard scramble by quarterback Dave Brown.

Rison's 24-yard touchdown reception on a broken play from Brunell made it 14–10 Giants in the third quarter, and after a 2-yard touchdown by Means with 3:19 remaining in the third quarter, the game was tied 17–17. Elias's 3-yard run with 5:09 remaining gave the Giants a 24–17 victory.

The game had high points for the Jaguars. Rison, in his debut, caught two passes for 66 yards, and Stewart— pushed by Means—carried eight times for 45 yards. This was a sign, Stewart believed, that the off-season changes to the offensive line were working. "They opened up some great holes, and they seem like they're going to be a great group of guys to run behind," Stewart said.

"We meshed real well as an offensive unit," DeMarco said after his first game at right guard. "We turned it on. We came to play, and I think we showed we can put the ball in the end zone."

Rison reveled in his performance. His leaping, stretching touchdown reception was the night's highlight, and he relished being in the spotlight again. "He showed the ability to stretch out for the ball, and the ball stuck in his hands," Coughlin said.

"He's quite a receiver," Brunell said. "A big-play guy."

Rison returned the compliments, telling whoever would listen that not only was his new quarterback the best in the NFL, but that he and his new teammates were destined for greatness. "I see a lot of potential with this team," he said. "The faster we come together and gain the camaraderie, I think it will show on the field."

Happy, too, were the defensive linemen and linebackers. Under pressure to create a better pass rush, the team's front seven showed improvement early, sacking Brown once and pressuring him throughout the first half. "Our pressure will be a lot better than it was last year," Kelvin Pritchett said.

The one major concern was Brunell. He completed the two passes for 66 yards to Rison, but apart from those, was just one of eight for 12 yards. Five were dropped, but 30 percent in the first live action from the starting quarterback raised concerns. "We should have thrown the ball better," Brunell said. "Obviously, we've got some work to do."

That work continued the next week in the Trans World Dome in St. Louis, and although the result was the same—a loss to the Rams, 17–10—again there were high and low points. Stewart ran well, carrying eight times for 37 yards, but Means—after rushing eight times for 18 yards in the preseason opener—carried four times for minus-1-yard. The Jaguars sacked Rams quarterbacks twice for 14 yards, again boosting optimism about the rush, but a persistent problem of covering premier receivers was revealed again as Rams receiver Isaac Bruce caught four passes for 88 yards.

This was why the Jaguars had pursued Lyght, Williams, and even former Dolphins corner Troy Vincent in the off-season, and the area—anchored by Washington and Clark again—apparently was not improved.

Brunell improved from the first game, completing 11 of 17 passes for 119 yards. His backup, Rob Johnson, also was impressive for a second consecutive week, completing eight of 10 passes for 70 yards.

Brunell gave the Jaguars a 7–0 lead with a 37-yard run, and after a 46-yard field goal by Chip Lohmiller and a 3-yard run by rookie running back Lawrence Phillips, the Jaguars needed a 59-yard field goal by Hollis to tie it 10–10 on the final play of the first half. With 2:28 remaining in the game, Rams reserve running back Brent Moss scored on a 6-yard run, and neither team scored again.

Coughlin didn't care much about victories and losses, but he didn't like what he was seeing. "What bothers me is we do one thing well one week, and then do something else well the following week," he said. "Part of getting continuous improvement is consistency."

Brunell, meanwhile, was frustrated—not with himself, but with the Jacksonville media. The Jaguars, two games into preseason, were still in training camp, which was headquartered at the Radisson in downtown Jacksonville. On a typical day, the players practiced in the morning, returned to the Radisson for lunch, then returned to the stadium for an afternoon practice, then back to the Radisson for meetings and sleep. Interview time was around lunch, and after being criticized for his performance against the Giants, Brunell ducked most of the media until after the St. Louis game. A few days afterward, when asked about the improvement from one week to the next, he bristled. "It was an interesting week, you know? You guys are all saying that I can't pass the football. Of course, you fail to report there were three dropped footballs. That got me a little frustrated.

"I felt good Week One. I felt good Week Two. As far as the whole passing game, we got better. It comes down to the consistency thing again."

The next Sunday night was a nationally televised TNT game against the San Francisco 49ers. It was the Jaguars' first game—regular or preseason—against either of the NFL's two dominant teams of the 1990s, the 49ers and Cowboys, and the Jaguars treated 67,858 fans at JMS to the biggest margin of victory in franchise history, 38–10. The bulk of the victory was against the 49ers' second team, a fact the fans who cheered into the night didn't seem to mind.

Rison again played to the home crowd, catching his second touchdown of the preseason, a 3-yarder from Brunell for a 7–3 Jaguars lead with 5:58 remaining in the second quarter. The Jaguars pushed the lead to 10–3 on a 22-yard field goal by Hollis, but with 55 seconds remaining in the first half, San Francisco quarterback Steve Young scored on a 4-yard run to tie it, 10–10.

The second half was a Jaguars celebration. First, Means scored on a 2-yard run to make it 17–10 with 7:26 remaining in the third quarter, and with 1:14 remaining in that quarter, Johnson—subbing for Brunell—scored on a 7-yard run to make it 24–10. With 10:24 remaining in the fourth quarter, reserve running back Randy Jordan's 12-yard run made it 31–10, and finally, with 4:57

remaining, the Jaguars scored a final touchdown—a 4-yard run by reserve running back Roger Graham.

The 38 points was the most for the Jaguars in any game, but the defensive effort—in particular, that of Brackens—was equal cause for optimism. The Jaguars sacked 49ers quarterbacks six times. Brackens had two of those sacks, including one in the first half chasing down Young—one of the league's most mobile quarterbacks. The play showed everything that was impressive about Brackens—quickness, strength, and raw speed.

"That's what he can do—he can run like a deer," Lageman said.

The game also featured the first matchup of Brunell and the quarterback to whom he was most often compared, Young. They had the same number, 8; each was lefthanded; and most striking, each was particularly dangerous running in the open field. Young completed 17 of 27 passes for 144 yards; Brunell completed eight of 15 for 95 yards and a touchdown and an interception. They staged a running battle, too. Young ran four times for 29 yards and a touchdown; Brunell, six times for 36 yards.

"I always appreciate a quarterback who can make plays out of the pocket," Young said afterward. "He makes the first guy miss, which I think every good quarterback has to do to set up in the pocket and throw the ball. And when he gets outside, he seems to be smart with his body. He doesn't do anything crazy, but he moves the ball."

Those were the niceties of the victory. Of concern was an offensive line that looked impressive in three preseason games, but suddenly was injured.

After the third play of the 49ers game, Boselli limped from the field with an injured ankle. Jeff Novak replaced Boselli, and on the next possession, he sprained an ankle.

"We lost two left tackles in the blink of an eye," Coughlin said. "It defies normalcy."

With one game remaining in the preseason, the Jaguars suddenly seemed in danger. Novak likely would miss up to four weeks. Boselli, a team source told the *Florida Times-Union* the next day, had a medial sprain of the right ankle perhaps severe enough to force him from the opener 12 days away. Boselli and Coughlin denied the injury was so severe.

"I'll be there," Boselli said.

"We have all intentions that he'll be ready," Coughlin said.

Would the Jaguars be as ready? They had a little over a week to learn.

The day after the 49ers victory was difficult for another reason. This was the first major cut day of the season, and Coughlin trimmed the roster from 78 to 60 players That meant difficult decisions, and saying good-bye to more familiar names.

One significant cut: Chris Doering, a rookie receiver from the University of Florida. Doering was popular among Gators fans in Jacksonville, having set a Florida record for touchdown receptions playing for coach Steve Spurrier's Fun-and-Gun offense. When the Jaguars selected him in the sixth round in the draft, they needed receivers. The signing of Rison, however, pushed Doering down one notch, and the decision to release him wasn't hard for the coaching staff.

"At first, I thought maybe this was the perfect situation for me," Doering said. "Maybe it was too perfect."

The day also was the last for two players who played significant roles in the first season—defensive tackle Ray Hall and linebacker Mark Williams. Hall played 12 games the first season; Williams started the first 10 before a season-ending shoulder injury. The addition of Jurkovic upgraded the tackle position, so Hall was no longer needed. The presence of Robinson and Hardy meant Williams no longer had a spot. "It was a tough day for everybody," Coughlin said. "You're talking about guys who had been with us."

The Jaguars had more cuts to make in a week, but first, there was a final preseason game—in Denver against the Broncos. And while in Denver, the Jaguars made their final major move of a turbulent off-season, signing the pass rusher they had sought for so long.

On the Monday after the 49ers game, the Arizona Cardinals released Clyde Simmons, an 11-year veteran defensive end with 93.5 career sacks. Friday morning, Simmons arrived at the Jaguars' hotel in Denver, signing a three-year deal. Some Jaguars were irked that day by a related incident, although they felt no ill will toward Simmons. The entire team made the trip to Denver, but when Simmons signed, a player had to be released—Corey Mayfield, a defensive tackle who was with the team throughout 1995. He was told of his release in the team hotel, and sent back to Jacksonville that morning on a plane, alone. Several players later said they thought this was an unfair way to treat Mayfield.

The Simmons signing seemed a gift from nowhere. Yet, Huyghue and Coughlin each said there was a plan. The Jaguars didn't know Simmons would be available, but in a changing free-agent market, Jaguars officials did expect teams facing salary-cap problems to release prominent players as the season neared. Simmons was scheduled to make $2 million with Arizona in 1996, but when the Cardinals signed holdout defensive tackle Eric Swann to a new contract, they released Simmons to fit Swann's salary under the cap. The Jaguars, Huyghue said, kept money available for just such a situation.

"You have to put yourself in a position to do that," Huyghue said. "We were in a position to acquire marquee players with little risk. We did that with Clyde and Natrone. Those were very worthwhile risks. They were calculated risks. They gave us the opportunity to try to add a couple of pieces to the puzzles and see if they fit in. If they did, then great, and if they didn't, we knew we'd go in another direction. We weren't afraid to experiment."

This experiment significantly boosted the pass rush. "You're not going to win in the National Football League without a consistent defense, consistent pressure on the passer," Coughlin said. "This gives us a chance to enhance that pressure."

Simmons played for the Jaguars that night. If he was sluggish, he needn't have worried. His new teammates were, too.

The Broncos dominated the first quarter. Broncos quarterback John Elway ran 4 yards for one touchdown, passed 6 yards to tight end Shannon Sharpe for another, and including a 43-yard field goal by Jason Elam, Denver led 17–0 after a quarter. The quarter featured more bad news for the Jaguars. Means tore a ligament in his thumb. He missed the rest of the game, and his status for the opener was uncertain.

Brunell passed 20 yards to Smith to make it 17–7 at halftime, and in the second half, Johnson—improving with each preseason game—passed for three touchdowns: 5 yards to tight end Pete Mitchell, 9 yards to Smith, and 9 yards to Derek Brown. The Jaguars won, 31–24. Coughlin talked afterward about the significance of such a come-from-behind victory, but the image players took from Denver came at halftime.

Furious, Coughlin screamed at his players in the locker room, berating them for a lack of effort, poor execution, and anything else he could imagine. "I was concerned that our football team had decided the preseason was over," Coughlin said later. "It wasn't over. It wasn't going to be over for another 30 minutes, and I wanted everyone to understand that."

Soon into the tirade, they understood. Coughlin, in his rage, slapped over a tray of Gatorade. "It was great," Lageman said. "He had every right to be upset. They came out and smoked our asses."

The tray spilled over, soaking several players, most of all DeMarco.

"Was that really necessary?" DeMarco asked Coughlin.

To Coughlin it was. Preseason was all but over and the opener against the defending AFC champion Pittsburgh Steelers at JMS was nine days away. Not much time, and no one, particularly Coughlin, knew if it was enough.

6
A NOTEWORTHY BEGINNING

"I know we shocked the world. Nobody thinks about Jacksonville except for us. We have our own family. We're going to show the whole world we can win in any kind of fashion."

—ANDRE RISON
September 1, 1996

Birthdays, typically, meant little to Tom Coughlin. He began coaching in 1969, and for 26 years, rarely celebrated his birthday. Falling on August 31, before and often during football season, there was never time.

His 27th birthday in coaching—his 50th in life—was no different, because this time it fell on the day before the opening of the Jaguars' second season.

The opponent was the Pittsburgh Steelers, which meant it was more than just the regular-season opener in Jacksonville Municipal Stadium. The Steelers were the defending AFC champions, having won the AFC Central the year before. They had played the Dallas Cowboys tough before losing Super Bowl XXX in Phoenix, Arizona, 27–17.

"We're ready for Pittsburgh," Leon Searcy said of his former team. "Why wouldn't we be? We have some things to work on, but the bottom line is when it comes time for the dance, we will be ready to tango."

Besides Searcy versus his former team, there were other story lines. Tony Boselli, injured against San Francisco, missed the Denver game, but it appeared he would play against the Steelers. Jeff Novak, however, would miss the game, meaning the Jaguars had five linemen— the five starters—with significant NFL experience. Still, other questions remained unanswered—most notably, was Mark Brunell ready to be a franchise-level quarterback?

Brunell resented the preseason criticism, but the media weren't the only group around the Jaguars suspecting he wasn't ready. Teammates privately worried that although Brunell had potential, this could be a long season while he matured into a leader.

There was even talk, albeit not serious, of a quarterback controversy. Brunell completed 31 of 61 passes for 441 yards and three touchdowns in the preseason, and was intercepted twice. The performance of his backup, Johnson—a 1995 fourth-round selection from Southern California—made the numbers look worse. "I think he'd be the most honest and up-front of all. . . . He's not totally pleased with his performance," Coughlin said.

Johnson, who played in only one regular-season game as a rookie, completed 30 of 43 passes for 336 yards and three touchdowns to the preseason. His preseason rating was 116, which would lead the NFL in any season. "That's ridiculous," Johnson said of the so-called controversy. "I played well in the preseason, but that's preseason."

Nationally, few were aware of the problem, which was why many selected the Jaguars as a contender in the AFC Central. Those prognostications were not only a tribute to the Jaguars' free-agency additions; they were also a not-so-glowing commentary on the division. The Jaguars were picked by many to finish between 7–9 and 9–7, which meant contending for the playoffs. The division title, too, seemed possible because of losses sustained by the Steelers—the division champion in 1994 and 1995. Besides losing Searcy, they had lost quarterback Neil O'Donnell to the New York Jets in free agency. Few considered O'Donnell worth the $25 million over five years the Jets paid him, but fewer expected the Steelers to be as good without him. None of the three quarterbacks remaining—Jim Miller, Kordell Stewart, or veteran Mike Tomczak—seemed an adequate replacement. Free agency had also robbed the Steelers of linebacker/pass rusher Kevin Greene, who had signed with Carolina. If free agency had helped any team, it was the Jaguars; if it had hurt any team, it was the Steelers.

The rest of the division was hardly invincible. Houston and Cincinnati had finished 7–9 the previous season and, along with the Jaguars, were favored to battle for second. All three were improving, young teams. Houston had drafted Heisman Trophy winner Eddie George at running back. The Bengals had one of the NFL's best young quarterback-receiver combinations—Jeff Blake and Carl Pickens. The division's other team, the Baltimore Ravens, had undergone a tumultuous off-season, moving from Cleveland, and were picked by most to finish last.

Coughlin scoffed at the notion any team except the Steelers might be favored—even with their losses. "I don't buy any of that stuff," he said. "Everybody has their problems. They are the gauge for the American Football

Conference. They are the team that has to be beaten before anybody can be the champion of our division."

Of more serious concern to Coughlin was his team. The preseason had had high moments, but the first team had struggled in all four first halves, which left him with significant doubts. He did feel good about one thing that week. A look at the Jaguars' roster, for the first time, revealed players capable of winning in the NFL.

The Jaguars were younger and more talented than in 1995, particularly on offense. Means would miss the opener with the torn thumb ligaments, but Stewart had had a big training camp and preseason, winning the starting job before Means's injury. Keenan McCardell and Andre Rison were starting at receiver, with Jimmy Smith No. 3 and Willie Jackson No. 4. The offensive line also looked new, and had questions. Boselli and Searcy were the bookends Coughlin envisioned, but the interior—guards Ben Coleman and Brian DeMarco and center Dave Widell—struggled to run-block at times. Tight end was a concern, with Derek Brown the starter, and Pete Mitchell playing a receiver/tight-end role.

The defense was new and improved, notably on the front seven. No longer would four starting linemen play 80 or 90 percent of the plays. Ends Jeff Lageman and Joel Smeenge would start, with veteran Clyde Simmons and rookie Tony Brackens playing extensively in passing situations. John Jurkovic and Kelvin Pritchett would start at tackle, with Don Davey in reserve.

At linebacker, Bryan Schwartz—who had improved late in his rookie season—would start in the middle, with Kevin Hardy starting as a rookie and Eddie Robinson on the other side. The secondary seemed the weakest area. Vinnie Clark and Mickey Washington, 16-game starters the previous season, would again start, with two second-year players, Chris Hudson and Travis Davis, at safety.

Aaron Beasley, who had shown promise in the preseason, injured his shoulder against St. Louis, and wasn't scheduled to return for a month. Dana Hall would back up both safeties. Mike Hollis and Bryan Barker would kick and punt, respectively, for a second consecutive season.

"There was no question we were more talented [than in 1995]," Coughlin said after the season. "I thought we were talented, but I didn't get a great feeling [in preseason] we were playing together as a team. I felt we were capable of good things, and that's what I pointed out to the team at the half in Denver. I felt opening day would be good, but in the back of my mind, I didn't have a clue about our team."

Players were more confident, believing they could, and should, win.

Perhaps no player felt that urgency more than Lageman, who felt he was paid for one reason, even on an expansion team. That was to win. He had promised himself when he signed the previous season that he would help turn the team into a winner. As the Steelers game approached, Lageman saw no reason the time to start delivering on that promise shouldn't be now.

Jeffrey David Lageman was born July 18, 1967, in Fairfax, Virginia, and starred in baseball and football at Parkview High School in Sterling, Virginia. His best sports memory before 1996: leading Parkview's baseball team to a state title as a senior—that, and helping the University of Virginia rebuild its football program under George Welsh in the mid-1980s.

Lageman's brother was on the first Virginia team ever to play in a bowl. That was in 1984. Three years later, Lageman was on the second.

That's the sort of thing Lageman said he likes: Building. Being remembered. Being a part of something new.

"I enjoyed that feeling," Lageman said.

Getting that feeling in the NFL took a while. Lageman, a three-year starter at inside linebacker at Virginia, was a first-round draft choice of the New York Jets in 1989. The choice was hardly popular among fans at the Jets' draft headquarters.

"The Jets select Jeff Lageman," came the announcement.

"Jeff who?" came the heckling cries.

Lageman quickly answered the question, successfully moving to defensive end and endearing himself to Jets fans with a combination of toughness, craziness, and most importantly, production. Once, early in his career, Lageman arrived at a training camp aboard a Harley-Davidson, ponytail flapping in the wind. And tough? Lageman missed all but two games in 1992 with a knee injury, but apart from that, never missed a game in six seasons with the Jets. In 1993, he played the season with a herniated disk, once seeking outside advice on whether to retire. In his last season with the Jets, 1994, he injured a shoulder in the preseason so severely doctors told him he needed surgery. Instead, he took a painkilling injection with a nine-inch needle before each game. He started all 16, finishing with six and a half sacks.

"The worst pain I ever had to play through," he said. "It was to the point where some games I really had to do a lot of suffering out there. I'd do a certain thing where my shoulder would have a sharp pain, my arm would go dead, then a dull pain. It was a week-in, week-out thing."

Yet, Lageman shrugged at the tough-guy persona. "You get paid to play," he said. "That's always been my philosophy."

By the end of 1994, Lageman wanted to take that philosophy elsewhere. Six seasons with the Jets produced one playoff appearance, and he realized no matter how tough he was, at 27, he was closer to the end of his career than to the beginning. At the same time, Coughlin was building the Jaguars.

The Jaguars would be young, with players from different NFL teams and some with no NFL experience. Needed, Coughlin felt, was an experienced leader who could communicate with players of all ages, backgrounds, and styles. Lageman, he felt, fit those criteria.

Lageman, in January and February, listened to offers from several teams. By early March, his choices were two—the San Francisco 49ers, the defending Super Bowl champions, or the Jaguars.

Best, or newest?

Building. Being remembered. Being a part of something new.

"I enjoyed that feeling," Lageman said.

On March 14, 1994, he signed with the Jaguars, saying, "It's great to be part of something where everything is so new. In New York, I reached a point in my career where everything was stale. I wasn't getting excited for the beginning of the season anymore. I wasn't getting excited for anything."

Coughlin, in Year One, kept a distance from most players, but used Lageman—the team's representative with the NFL Players Association—as a buffer between himself and the team. Coughlin was the drill sergeant; Lageman was the veteran who understood Coughlin's madness, and who could relay the reasons to others. In the first year, intimidated players referred to their coach as "Coach Coughlin" almost exclusively. Lageman called him "Tom."

No player was too close to Coughlin, though, and the relationship between Lageman and Coughlin wasn't always smooth. Lageman was one of the few players to openly question Coughlin. Early in the 1995 off-season workout program, Lageman—as the player rep—called the NFLPA, notifying officials Coughlin's "voluntary" workouts pushed the rules' limits. This led to rules being more strictly enforced the next year. Also, when Coughlin set dates for the first training camp in Stevens Point, he included four "voluntary" days at the beginning. Lageman was among three players—Smeenge and Pritchett were the others—who opted not to "volunteer," as was their right under league rules.

Yet, Lageman remained a leader in Coughlin's eyes. Coughlin valued performance and work—Lageman's strengths. "His general hate of losing comes through in his style of play," Jaguars defensive tackle Paul Frase, a longtime Jets teammate, said. "If somebody is going half-speed, he gets to them when he comes out and says, 'Don't let that crap happen again.'"

That attitude made Lageman a locker-room leader, and one of the more popular players among teammates and fans. His Monday night television show was well watched, and he never was shy about answering questions candidly. There was more to Lageman than the tough-guy persona. He had a perspective. Football was important, but he also knew it was *just* a job, and *just* a game. The toughest time of his career occurred with the Jets when one of his best friends, defensive tackle Dennis Byrd, sustained a neck injury in 1992. The injury ended Byrd's career, nearly rendering him a quadriplegic. When Lageman saw Byrd in his hospital bed, he broke down, and considered retiring. As of 1996, Byrd could walk, and he and Lageman hunted frequently. In the summer of 1996, they formed a football camp for children on the Navajo Indian reservation in the Southwest United States.

Such experiences gave Lageman perspective few other Jaguars players shared. He was one of the few Jaguars players in the first season who knew when to be serious, when to be loose. He knew when to laugh, and when a spokesman was necessary. Often, that was his role. Early on, his relationship with the media was comfortable enough that one of his daily routines was to walk through the locker room and playfully give the finger to one of his favorite reporters—a routine that continued into the second season.

The first year frustrated Lageman, who thought the Jaguars should win more. Already frustrated, his season came to an early end. In Game 11, a loss at Tampa Bay, he sustained a foot injury that doctors thought would force him out a few weeks. He tried to rehabilitate, but reinjured it. He eyed a comeback for the final regular-season game against the Browns, but late that week, doctors said he couldn't play.

His season was over, and he wasn't sure how many he had left.

That made 1996 important, and he liked what he saw. He had hoped the Jaguars could win in 1995; by 1996, he felt they should win consistently—partially because of massive improvement on the defensive line. The previous season the Jaguars had sacked the quarterback just 17 times, the league low. Lageman felt this shortcoming had been caused by a lack of depth. He had played more than 80 percent of the plays in 1995 when healthy, difficult for any lineman, but particularly for one who played at 265 pounds.

The signing of Simmons and Jurkovic, and the drafting of Brackens, Lageman thought, would change that number drastically—and contribute to more victories.

Lageman wasn't alone. As September 1 approached, a player not confident, ready, and willing was hard to find. "This game will show us where we are right now," McCardell said. "We get a quick test to see exactly where we're at as a team. We have big expectations. They've been on top the last couple of years, and that's where you want to be. You have to go through them to get there."

They had gone through the Steelers before, winning 20–16 at JMS. Searcy, now with the Jaguars, said the Steelers were embarrassed after the game. They were determined not to lose to an expansion team again. The Jaguars were determined to prove it was no fluke—and to prove they were worthy of being considered a rival for their AFC Central opponent.

"As far as we look at it, we've developed a rivalry," Brunell said. "I don't know how much they think we have a rivalry, but it's a little extra going against the Steelers. We did beat them last year, and got them pretty fired up. Something developed there. We're not going to take anything from them."

On September 1, a day after Coughlin's 50th birthday, 70,210 packed into JMS, ready to see if the off-season acquisitions would mean an improved team. The expansion season was past. This, they hoped, would be the real NFL, and from the start, the Jaguars' preseason doldrums disappeared.

The enthusiasm was tempered on the game's first play, when Steelers running back Erric Pegram ran 27 yards on the game's first play to the Jaguars' 40, but the Steelers' success was short-lived. They managed only 2 more yards, and punted.

Brunell, meanwhile, used the first offensive series of the season to prove his preseason slump was what he had said all along—a too-quick judgment by the media. Starting from the Jaguars' 20, Brunell sliced through the Steelers' defense, passing when he could and running when he couldn't. He passed three times for 60 yards, and ran four times for 18. The last two runs were 10- and

2-yard scrambles that gave the Jaguars a second-and-eight on the Steelers' 38. On the next play, he took advantage of Steelers cornerback Rod Woodson to give the Jaguars the lead.

Woodson, one of the NFL's all-time great corners, missed most of 1995 with a torn anterior cruciate ligament. On second-and-eight from the Steelers' 38, Jackson—the Jaguars' fourth receiver—lined up wide right. The Jaguars were in a tight formation, and the Steelers left Woodson in one-on-one coverage on Jackson. He beat Woodson with a quick inside move, and caught a slant pass from Brunell 5 yards behind him, running untouched to the end zone for a 7–0 lead.

The teams traded punts before the Steelers moved offensively. Starting at their 37 with 4:50 remaining in the first quarter, they worked again to establish the run. With the defense thinking run, Miller found tight end Mark Bruener for 17 yards to the Jaguars' 33. The Jaguars' defense stiffened, and on third-and-eight, Miller passed incomplete to Charles Johnson, forcing a 48-yard field goal by Norm Johnson. Jaguars 7, Steelers 3.

Brunell had found weaknesses in the Steelers defense, but struggled to exploit it, throwing an interception to Levon Kirkland that stalled an early second-quarter drive. The rest of the second quarter defined the game. Throughout, the Steelers struggled in the red zone. The Jaguars excelled. It was Coughlin football, and today, the Jaguars played it.

With 7:58 remaining in the half, the Steelers inched toward the end zone, with Jerome Bettis running four times for 26 yards and Miller having success, completing two of two passes for 24 yards. On third-and-nine from the Jaguars' 11, the Jaguars came up big defensively in the red zone yet again, forcing Miller to throw incom-

plete to Bruener. Johnson's 29-yard field goal made it
7–6.

The Jaguars took the ensuing kickoff with 3:12 remaining. Brunell worked quickly, peppering the defense
with slants, and running when the Steelers' quick, attack-
ing defense took away the pass. He passed 13 yards on a
slant to McCardell for a first down at the Steelers' 43,
then Stewart ran for 14 yards over left tackle to the Steelers' 29. Brunell scrambled for 7 yards, then passed to
Derek Brown for 6 yards and a first down to the Steelers'
15.

With 21 seconds remaining in the half, Brunell passed
into the back of the end zone for McCardell, who caught
it for a touchdown and a 14–6 halftime lead. The Jaguars
had been in the red zone once, and scored a touchdown.
The Steelers had been there twice, and scored two field
goals. The difference was the eight-point margin.

"You guys put some pressure on to see if he [Brunell]
could turn it on," McCardell said. "Preseason doesn't
count. This is where you make your money. When Labor
Day comes around everybody gets focused; it was time
for him to do what he had to do."

The Jaguars' offense scored two touchdowns in a half
on the Steelers' powerful defense. In the second half, it
was the defense's job to hold the lead. They did that, and
more.

The teams traded punts early in the third quarter, but
the Steelers got a break midway through when Andre
Rison turned the wrong way in a pattern. Brunell's pass
went instead to Woodson, who returned it to the Jaguars'
42. Again, the defense forced the Steelers to squander the
opportunity. With Bettis bruising the middle four times
for 10 yards and Miller passing three times for 28 yards,
the Steelers drove to the Jaguars' 5. On first down, Eddie
Robinson stopped Bettis for a 1-yard gain. Then Stew-

art—subbing on the play for Miller—was tackled for a 1-yard loss by Kelvin Pritchett. Miller passed incomplete to Andre Hastings on third-and-goal from the 5, and Johnson's 23-yard field goal made it 14–9, Jaguars, with 1:19 remaining.

The teams again traded punts before Brunell drove the Jaguars. Starting at the Jaguars' 20 with 14:05 remaining in the game, he passed 8 yards to Stewart. After a 2-yard run by Stewart on third-and-one, he passed for 12 yards and a first down to Rison at the Jaguars' 43. Brunell again converted a third-and-two three plays later, passing 20 yards to Rison to the Steelers' 29. After a holding penalty on Brown, Hollis's 52-yard field goal made it 17–9, Jaguars, with 8:25 remaining.

The Steelers needed a touchdown desperately. On the kickoff, returner Andre Hastings faked a handoff, and returned it 42 yards to the Steelers' 44. Steelers coach Bill Cowher again substituted Tomczak, the most experienced quarterback on the roster, for the biggest drive of the game.

Earlier, Miller had completed a short pass in the flat for a short gain. The play had occurred in front of Hardy, who chastised himself for not making an easy interception. On the play after Hastings's return, Tomczak dropped, then threw to his right to Johnson, the same pass Miller had completed in front of Hardy earlier. This time, Hardy intercepted. "A monster play," Lageman said. "That was the game-winning play right there."

Hardy returned it 6 yards to the Steelers' 40, and from there, the Jaguars used their pregame strategy—outlast the Steelers physically. Eighty-two degrees didn't seem hot for a late-summer day in northeast Florida, but the Jaguars trained in worse heat, while the Steelers trained in the comparative cool of Pennsylvania. Also, the Jaguars were wearing white uniforms for the opener, which meant the Steelers wore black. Usually, the black gave the Steelers an aura of intimidation. On this day, it drained them.

"We wore them down," Boselli said.

On first down after Hardy's interception, Stewart ran 4 yards, then Brunell ran for a first down to the Steelers' 28. On third-and-two from the 20, Stewart ran around Boselli for a 14-yard gain to the Steelers' 6. The Steelers called time-out. On the next play, Brunell rolled left for 4 yards, and a face-mask penalty on Steelers linebacker Chad Brown gave the Jaguars first-and-goal at the 1. Stewart, who ran five times for 27 yards on the drive, dove for a touchdown on the next play.

"We started manhandling them late in the game," De-Marco said. "Eventually, they started getting tired and backing down. You could tell at the end they were all smoked out."

On the next series, Lageman—who had three sacks while often double-teamed the year before—showed the rollicking, celebrating crowd what he had wanted to show for more than a year, beating Steelers tackle Bernard Dafney on back-to-back plays and sacking Tomczak for losses of 7 yards.

"I doubt I could have done that last year," he said. "We've got eight guys, and we were running them through the whole game. That's the way it's going to be. Nobody's pissed off about playing time. In the fourth quarter, you feel good."

All that remained was the Jaguars' jubilation, and the Steelers' frustration. The Steelers punted, and as the Jaguars milked the clock, Steelers defensive end Kevin Henry punched Boselli, and was ejected. On the sideline, Clark—a veteran cornerback who had steamed over the team's pursuit of Williams and Lyght during the off-season—reveled in the moment. "Still need Todd Lyght?" he yelled at a sportswriter. "Still need Todd Lyght? Makes a difference when you get pressure."

The Steelers' mood was far different. Far from bullying the upstarts, the Steelers left broken and injured. Greg Lloyd, their Pro Bowl linebacker, sustained a torn left patella tendon in the third quarter, and was lost for the season.

Brunell completed 20 of 31 passes for 212 yards and two touchdowns with two interceptions, and the Jaguars won by the largest margin in team history. They were unbeaten and above .500 for the first time, and they had dominated a Super Bowl team, holding an opponent without a touchdown for the first time. They also had four sacks, nearly a quarter of the 1995 total and a franchise record.

"What it means is we're 1–0, but that's as far as I'm going to go with it," Coughlin said. "I'm not trying to hold it down. It's just that it's one game."

"I know we shocked the world," said Rison, who caught four passes for 42 yards. "Nobody thinks about Jacksonville except for us. We have our own family. We're going to show the whole world we can win in any kind of fashion."

Other veterans put their twist on the significance. Searcy, who later said he played the opener "with something to prove," said afterward, "This time there can be no excuses. This time the Steelers knew what to expect, and we beat them. It's that simple."

Simmons spoke of a bigger picture. "Jim McMahon used to tell us when we were in Philadelphia that if you win at home, you can limp into the playoffs," he said after having a sack and forcing a fumble. "That's what we're trying to do. If we play this well, week in and week out, we're definitely going to be somebody to contend with. People come here, and it's going to be a battle."

On this day, however, it wasn't so much a battle as a celebration. A birthday celebration.

"It was good to get off to a good start," John Jurkovic said. "It took the pressure off. Everyone wanted to know, 'How were these guys going to be?' They had brought in some high-priced free agents. Were they going to be a better football team? Then, we came out and answered everything. We were a better football team than they were the year before. Tom was happy because the team he had prepared for six weeks came out and won a football game. The players were happy, the fans were happy. We were all elated."

In the locker-room tunnel afterward, Coughlin received a victory kiss from his wife, Judy, and a hug from Wayne Weaver. Moments earlier, he had received perhaps his biggest surprise. As he ran from the field, the fans surrounding the tunnel sang.

"Happy Birthday."

"I knew there was only one way it could be a great one," Coughlin said, smiling in the aftermath of the victory. "And this was it. This is the way to celebrate."

7
SEPTEMBER STRUGGLES

"If anything, I'm consistent. I'm the same way—or I try to be—all the time. How our football team has gotten away with not being is just sticking a dagger right in my heart."

—TOM COUGHLIN
September 1996

Tom Coughlin took pride in consistent teams. When the Jaguars beat the Steelers, they played like it, preying on mistakes and minimizing turnovers. Coughlin once called turnovers "the bane of my existence." That went for any other mistakes, too.

The *American Heritage Dictionary of the English Language* defines bane as follows:

1. Fatal injury or ruin. 2. A cause of death, destruction or ruin. 3. A deadly poison.

Throughout the three weeks after the victory over the Steelers, mistakes, penalties, and turnovers were the bane of the Jaguars' September.

The week after the Steelers game, the Jaguars were

again at home playing the Houston Oilers. The Jaguars were 1–0; the Oilers were 0–1 after losing 20–19 the previous week to the Kansas City Chiefs.

Still, the Oilers were a confident team, one improving rapidly. They went 2–14 in 1994, and 7–9 in 1995, and felt the improvement should continue. Like the Steelers, the Oilers were a rival for the Jaguars, and held a prominent place in Jaguars history. Houston had been the Jaguars' first opponent, having won the 1995 season opener, 10–3, in Jacksonville Municipal Stadium. The Jaguars' first victory came against Houston later in 1995, 17–16 in October.

To the Jaguars, the past was just that. What they were discussing as they prepared for Houston was their 1–0 start, first-place status in the AFC Central, and a defense—often maligned the previous season—that now was ranked No. 1 in the NFL. Not for long.

The Oilers had a better offense early in the season than the Steelers, and in front of 66,468 at JMS, that offense produced early and often. Oilers quarterback Chris Chandler was a journeyman, holding the job for up-and-coming quarterback Steve McNair. On this day, he was much more, completing 14 of 22 passes for 226 yards and three touchdowns, but at first, the Jaguars matched the Oilers score for score.

On the opening kickoff, Dave Thomas hit Pro Bowl returner Mel Gray, forcing a fumble. Dana Hall recovered, and three players later, a 38-yard field goal by Mike Hollis gave the Jaguars a 3–0 lead. On the first play of the next possession, Chandler passed 29 yards to Derek Russell to the Jaguars' 43. A 15-yard face-mask penalty on Jeff Lageman set up a 32-yard field goal by Al Del Greco: 3–3.

They continued trading scores throughout the first quarter. The Jaguars drove 77 yards on 10 plays on the next possession to take a 10–3 lead when James Stewart scored on a 1-yard run. On the Oilers' next possession, Gray made up for his early mistake, returning the kick 62 yards to the Jaguars' 30. Seven plays later, Eddie George's 1-yard run tied it 10–10.

In the second quarter, the Oilers turned the shoot-out into a blowout. Chandler was hot, and the Jaguars defense was getting little rush. On Houston's next possession, on second-and-seven from the Oilers' 37, Chandler rolled left, avoiding pressure. With little rush, Jaguars cornerback Vinnie Clark stopped and looked into the backfield. Malcolm Floyd ran past Clark, and Chandler passed over him for a 63-yard touchdown with 13:10 remaining in the second quarter. Oilers 17, Jaguars 10.

The Jaguars appeared headed for a touchdown on the ensuing possession as they used the middle minutes of the quarter to drive steadily into Houston territory. As happened the week before, a wrong route by Rison led to an interception—this time by Marcus Robertson at the Oilers' 5, ending a 48-yard drive. Hollis later made it 17–13 with a 37-yard field goal, but Chandler capped an 11-play, 80-yard drive with a 7-yard pass to tight end Frank Wycheck with 47 seconds remaining in the half for a 24–13 Oilers halftime lead.

It got worse before it got better for the Jaguars. Houston never really stopped the Jaguars, but mistakes hurt, and when Hollis missed a 31-yard field goal early in the second half, it wasted a 45-yard drive.

The Jaguars spent the first half watching Chandler throw touchdown passes. On the second play of the next drive, they were watching again, only this time they watched George.

On first-and-20 from the Oilers' 11 after a holding penalty, the 1995 Heisman Trophy winner took a handoff from Chandler and ran into the middle. Nothing. He bounced outside, shed two tacklers, and ran around the left end of the line.

"We didn't tackle worth a damn," Dana Hall said later.

On this play, they paid for it. George evaded several more tacklers in the open field, and kept running, finally being brought down at the Jaguars' 13: a 76-yard gain, longest against the Jaguars in either of their first two seasons.

Two plays later, they watched Chandler again—this time, he passed to Willie Davis for an 11-yard touchdown and a 31–13 lead. "We didn't tackle and that led to big plays," John Jurkovic said.

Still, the Jaguars continued to fight. A pass interference penalty on Darryll Lewis covering Keenan McCardell gave the Jaguars a first down at their 44 early in the next drive. Brunell followed that with three consecutive completions for 48 yards. The third pass was for 17 yards to McCardell, and two plays later, Brunell passed 5 yards to Jimmy Smith for a touchdown to make it 31–20 with 2:47 remaining in the third quarter.

This, though, was a game for answering a score with a score. On the next drive, starting from the Houston 20, Chandler passed three times for 41 yards to move to the Jaguars' 46, but passed only three more times on what became a 16-play drive. The quarter changed, and the Oilers—leading by 11—drained the game. George carried three times for 20 yards. Rodney Thomas carried for four times for 18. Finally, with 7:27 remaining in the fourth quarter, Del Greco's 29-yard field goal made it 34–20, Oilers.

The Jaguars' hopes seemingly ended on the following drive when Pete Mitchell fumbled after a 13-yard pass from Brunell to the Oilers' 2. The Oilers recovered with 3:08 remaining. "It's [the ball] precious down there near the goal line," Mitchell said.

Somehow, the Jaguars weren't done. The Jaguars' defense held, calling time-out after each play. Two minutes, 37 seconds remained when Chris Hudson returned a punt 46 yards to the Oilers' 3. On the next play, Brunell passed to McCardell. Touchdown. Oilers 34, Jaguars 27, and when Dave Thomas recovered the ensuing onside kick, the Jaguars had first down at their 49 with 2:28 remaining.

Now, it was far from finished.

A 10-yard pass from Brunell to Mitchell gave the Jaguars a first down at the Oilers' 41, but two plays later, Brunell passed deep and high to Mitchell. The ball bounced off Mitchell's hands and into the hands of the diving Robertson—yet another Jaguars turnover deep in Oilers territory. The Jaguars drove inside the Oilers' 20 seven times, and scored three touchdowns, but four other drives produced three points.

"You can't win games like that," Tony Boselli said.

They had three turnovers, all of which came inside the Oilers' 20.

"When you get chances, you have to convert," Brunell said.

Stewart rushed for 58 yards on 17 carries, his second solid game in as many starts. Brunell, at times, was impressive, completing 27 of 38 passes for 302 yards and two touchdowns. His two interceptions, however, gave him four for the season. The line allowed two sacks. McCardell caught eight passes for 100 yards and a touchdown; Rison caught six for 81.

On defense, the Jaguars struggled. Chandler hurt the secondary throughout, and George—in his second NFL start—carried 17 times for 143 yards, the high in the NFL that day. "If you would have told me before the game that they would have scored this many points," Hardy said, "I would have told you you were crazy. I don't feel like it was that close a game. They really took it to our defense."

And it ended the Jaguars' reign in first. The Jaguars, Ravens, Oilers, and Steelers were tied for first at 1–1, with the Bengals 0–2. "We're 1–1," Coughlin said, "and the best teams in our division are 1–1."

The Jaguars, however, knew there was more to the loss than just a loss. They had lost at home, and now faced a stretch in which they played five of their next seven games on the road. No venue would be tougher than the one to which they traveled on September 15— Oakland Alameda Coliseum against the Raiders.

The Jaguars never had played on the West Coast, and in the NFL, cross-country trips were traditionally tough. From 1986 to 1996, the record for East Coast teams playing in the Pacific time zone was 44–96, and making it more difficult was the Coliseum—famous for housing one of the NFL's dirtiest, most penalty-ridden teams.

"It's rowdy and you have to keep your helmets on," Leon Searcy said.

Searcy played there with the Steelers in 1995, but because the Raiders had returned there the previous season after 14 in Los Angeles, he was one of the few Jaguars players to have played in the Coliseum. "We had everything thrown at us—from batteries to beer," Searcy said.

The Jaguars left a day early, Friday instead of Saturday, to adjust to the time change. As they left, talk was about forgetting the loss to Houston. "Our division is looking for someone to take a lead," Searcy said.

The Raiders, meanwhile, were looking for some way to win. They were 0–2, and dating back to 1995, had lost eight consecutive games. The Raiders were desperate. The Jaguars were hungry. The result was a game typical of the Coliseum—marred by penalties, fights, and a bizarre game-deciding play in the fourth quarter.

"You suck, you suck, you suck," Raiders fans chanted as the Jaguars took the field.

And for most of the game the 46,291 were right—about both teams. Neither team looked ready. Mistakes and lost opportunities defined the game, causing frustrations to mount early—particularly for the Jaguars.

After a Raiders kickoff in the second quarter, Raiders safety Carl Kidd shoved his hand through the face mask of Willie Jackson, poking him in the eye and blurring his vision. "Somebody needs to call the league and get him fined," Jackson said later. "I couldn't see until the third quarter."

By the time Jackson regained his vision, it seemed everyone had fought. Clyde Simmons, angry at a chop block from Raiders guard Steve Wisniewski, grabbed Wisniewski's throat, and later said he would have killed him had he not been stopped. In the second half, Boselli went after Raiders linebacker Mike Jones, and had to be restrained by Raiders defensive tackle Chester McGlockton. "The guys were fighting their butts off," Boselli said, "and things happen when emotions run high."

Neither team moved offensively, but the Raiders moved just enough to take control. The game was scoreless after a quarter, but on the Raiders' second drive of the second quarter, they began at their 45, and moved to the Jaguars' 38 with a 17-yard pass from Jeff Hostetler to Derrick Fenner. Raiders tackle Lincoln Kennedy was penalized for holding, but two plays later, Hostetler passed 24 yards to Darryl Hobbs. First down at the Jaguars' 19. On the next play, the Jaguars' defense—stiff until this series—let down again, and Hostetler passed 19 yards to Tim Brown for a 7–0 lead.

The Jaguars' defense was playing well enough to win. Unlike the previous week, it was the offense that struggled. On the next possession, again the offense failed to produce a first down. After a 38-yard punt by Bryan Barker, the Raiders drove from their 49 to the Jaguars' 13, with Cole Ford's 32-yard field goal giving them a 10–0 halftime lead.

The Raiders, to this point, had been bad. The Jaguars were worse—92 yards passing and 18 yards rushing.

Not much happened in the third quarter. The teams exchanged punts, and a return by Chris Hudson of 16 yards gave the Jaguars a first down at the Raiders' 42. Natrone Means, playing for the first time since his preseason injury, carried 11 yards to the Raiders' 23. That set up a 33-yard field goal by Hollis, and the Raiders led, 10–3.

Late in the third quarter, the Raiders seemed poised to clinch victory, driving inside the Jaguars' 10. On third-and-goal from the 1, Raiders running back Harvey Williams ran into the middle, but Jaguars defensive tackle Don Davey reached out, stripping the ball. Tony Brackens recovered. Typical of the day, the Jaguars squandered the opportunity.

The Jaguars spent the fourth quarter staying close. Barely.

Early in the quarter, Hudson intercepted Hostetler, but the Jaguars stalled on downs at the Raiders' 33, the second time they moved that deep into Raiders territory.

The offense finally moved late. Taking possession at their 28 with 5:53 remaining the Jaguars moved to a first down at the Raiders' 26 with just over two minutes remaining, converting a fourth-and-five on a 5-yard pass from Brunell to Smith. "It was there for us," Boselli said.

And then it was gone.

On the next play, Brunell attempted a quick slant to Rison. Blitzing linebacker Rob Fredrickson beat Boselli, hitting Brunell as he threw. The ball popped into the air. Raiders defensive tackle Jerry Ball caught it and ran 66 yards untouched for a 17–3 Raiders lead with 2:15 remaining.

"I see Jerry's big fat ass after catching the ball, and that was it," Searcy said.

"You see the ball go up, and everything is in super slow mo," Jurkovic said. "You see Jerry Ball catch the ball, and here he comes, and there he goes."

The postgame mood was nasty. The frustration of two lost opportunities vented through the offensive line. The media surrounded Boselli's locker, and an Oakland reporter asked if he was surprised the Jaguars had a chance so late in the game. "Surprised?" Boselli said. "What the hell kind of question is that? No, I wasn't surprised."

The offensive line was a close-knit group that took criticism personally with a one-for-all, all-for-one attitude. Center Dave Widell was a veteran who was often criticized, but his younger linemates respected him. They leaned on Widell for guidance on and off the field, and rallied around him when he was criticized.

Widell wasn't the only one of the group criticized early in 1996. Few members of the line escaped it. Boselli and Searcy, who had signed contracts worth $34 million, were under pressure to fulfill expectations. DeMarco was struggling to adapt to the new role. The other guard, Ben Coleman, was cut the previous season by Arizona, and was struggling to establish himself as an NFL starter.

The frustration stemmed from what the line considered early abandonment of the running game. The unit long had been maligned for its run blocking, and against the Raiders, the Jaguars rushed for just 69 yards on 21 carries. Still, the game was close late, and because 47 of those yards came in the third quarter, linemen figured the run could have been part of the fourth quarter. Several players felt Ball's interception occurred because it was obvious the Jaguars would pass.

"Everybody in the stadium knew exactly what we were going to do," Coleman said. "Teams don't respect the run. They don't respect the bootleg. They're just rushing the passer. I don't care how good you are as an offensive line, you can't let a team from a pass-rushing standpoint tee off and just come after you."

The biggest problem for the Jaguars in Oakland was they weren't good anywhere. Brunell completed 18 of 37 passes for 217 yards, but threw two more interceptions, raising his season total to six. Worse, he wasn't getting the Jaguars in the end zone consistently. Stewart ran well, carrying eight times for 51 yards, but Means—in his first game since injuring his thumb—carried eight times for 12 yards. Holes for these two were rare.

Defensively, the team improved from the week before, but the Raiders produced 334 yards offense, often stalling from their mistakes. The loss dropped the Jaguars to 1–2, one game behind Pittsburgh and Houston in the Central. They were tied with the other two teams for last.

"We're going to grow up," Jurkovic said. "We can't lose many like this. Eventually, we have to step up and start making plays."

An opportunity was wasted, but nearly as bad were the postgame facilities. Because of a broken main outside the stadium, water was cut off during the game. Afterward, there was no hot water in the Jaguars' locker room. "You believe this?" Means said. "We play this way, and then have to take cold showers. . . .

"What a day."

Make that what a year . . . so far, at least. A 1–2 record after three games? That, Coughlin said the week after the Raiders game, might have been acceptable if not for the way the Jaguars were losing.

The offense was good at times. The defense was good

at times. The problem was, Coughlin said, they were never good together. "After a while," Coughlin said, "it's frustrating for me. I'm not interested in doing a whole lot of talking. I'd rather act, and deal with results. Again, the word is consistency."

Consistency defined Coughlin. His life was based on routine. Each day, he awoke at the same time, and arrived at the stadium at 6 A.M. Each week, the schedule was the same, and if something forced him to deviate— weather, events at the stadium, etc.—it made him testy.

The Jaguars were as inconsistent as was imaginable. The defense shut down Pittsburgh and Oakland, yet allowed 401 yards and 34 points to the Oilers. In that Oilers game, the offense played well enough to win, but against Oakland, it couldn't score a touchdown. Coughlin, who built the Jaguars in his image, didn't see himself like this.

"One of the things that's most troubling about the way we've played in the first three games is it's not consistent," Coughlin said. "If anything, I'm consistent. I'm the same way—or I try to be—all the time. How our football team has gotten away with not being is just sticking a dagger right in my heart."

Players agreed. "We have to be more consistent," Stewart said. "Until we are, we won't be successful."

Inconsistencies and nagging, ongoing problems had been the story thus far:

—Penalties. The Jaguars led the league.

—Offensive line. The post-Raiders scene was only an example of this unit's struggles. At the time, the Jaguars were 21st in the NFL in rushing with 3.3-yard-per-carry average. The league average was 3.5 yards. Making it worse for the linemen was they didn't feel they were getting a chance to improve. The Jaguars passed 58 percent of the plays in the first three games despite being close in each at the end. "If we're going to run it," Coleman said, "we need to run it and run it until they stop it."

—Brunell. The Jaguars ranked first in passing yardage, but elsewhere, Brunell was struggling. He wasn't seeing the field, ran too soon, and struggled in the two-minute offense. Before 1996, he never threw more than one interception in a game. He threw two in each of the first three games of 1996, and had four touchdown passes.

—Means. He returned from the torn thumb ligament against the Raiders, but was far from 100 percent. He had 12 yards on eight carries against the Raiders, including an 11-yard run.

—Rison. He was quiet on the field with 13 receptions for 149 yards and no touchdowns, but by Week 4, he was becoming less quiet off it—complaining privately about Brunell not throwing to him enough. Thirteen receptions in three games was hardly enough for someone who considered himself the Jaguars' "nuclear weapon."

The season was three games old, but there was a sense of urgency. Another loss would mean a 1–3 record, and a huge hole, particularly with the schedule featuring road games four of the next six weeks. The team traveled to New England the week after the Raiders game. The trip was shorter, but certainly no less strange.

Coughlin didn't want to talk mistakes, penalties, and losses as the Jaguars prepared for a September 22 game against the New England Patriots. That was fine with the media covering the team. They wanted to talk about something else. They wanted to talk Bill Parcells.

This was the pregame theme, obvious and compelling, as the Jaguars prepared for the Patriots—Coughlin versus Parcells, student versus boss, dictator versus dictator.

"When either one of them walks into a room, people automatically give them respect," Jaguars tight end Rich Griffith, who also played for Parcells in New England, said.

"Our philosophies aren't much different," Parcells said of Coughlin. "There are a lot of things we both believe to be right. I agree with a lot of the way he does things, and we have a lot in common in that regard."

What they had in common as September 22 approached was a need for a victory. Each team was 1–2. The Patriots lost their first two games, then routed Arizona the week before. The Jaguars were 1–2, losers of two consecutive games, and looking for answers and inspiration. Also, Jeff Lageman would miss at least two weeks with a sprained knee sustained against Oakland.

The Jaguars arrived at the Biltmore Hotel in Providence, Rhode Island, Saturday afternoon. A team meeting was scheduled, as always, for that night, but before that, most players went out. With Jacksonville stores often lacking the clothes styles players coveted, Saturday afternoon shopping was a big event for players on road trips. Andre Rison went out, too, and when he came back, he was in a talkative mood.

During the meeting in the Biltmore, Coughlin discussed the Patriots' personnel. Parcells had brought in several former Giants players, most of whom had been in New York with Coughlin. Coughlin spent the meeting warning the Jaguars of one of those players in particular—returner Dave Meggett, a Pro Bowl player who, although late in his career, was still a game breaker. "Watch out for Meggett," Coughlin told his team. "He can be dangerous."

Rison, until now, sat quietly in the rear, but as Coughlin continued about Megget's talents, Rison slowly stood. "Fuck Meggett!" Rison yelled. "And fuck the Patriots!"

Players smiled, looking at one another. "We don't need to worry about no fucking Patriots," Rison said. "We just need to go out and play our game."

Reaction from the players, many said later, was happiness that someone other than Coughlin was speaking. A month into the second season, his message sometimes reached uninterested ears. "At first," Ben Coleman said, recalling the incident after the season, "we thought it was Andre just trying to put life into the team."

Players realized something else soon. "We started sitting back, looking around, and we realized Andre was drunk," Coleman said. "He appeared to have had a bunch."

Rison quieted. The meeting ended without further incident, and over the next days came further evidence of a change in Coughlin, however subtle. The previous season, when Kelvin Pritchett called Coughlin a dictator, Pritchett received the punishment many feared—a closed-door dressing-down from Coughlin. Coughlin never mentioned the incident in Providence to Rison again, and the next day, as the Jaguars prepared for the Patriots, Rison was the starter.

Coughlin never mentioned knowing Rison was drunk, but early against the Patriots, he had more worries than whether a starting receiver was nursing a hangover. In front of 59,446 at Foxboro Stadium, the Jaguars got an early break, recovering a Patriots fumble on the opening kickoff. They called two run plays, threw an incomplete pass, and when Hollis missed right from 42 yards with 13:29 remaining in the first quarter, an opportunity was lost.

That was the good part of the first half. The next 28 minutes went like this:

—First quarter, 6:38 remaining. Patriots quarterback Drew Bledsoe caps a 12-play, 67-yard drive with a 5-yard touchdown pass to All-Pro tight end Ben Coates. Vinnie Clark, earlier on the drive penalized 19 yards for interference, is beaten on the play. Clyde Simmons blocks the point after. Patriots 6, Jaguars 0.

—First quarter, 1:17 remaining. After a pass by Brunell intended for Rison is intercepted by Patriots cornerback Jimmy Hitchcock, the Patriots use seven plays to drive 36 yards to the Jaguars' 5. Rookie kicker Adam Vinatieri's field goal from 23 yards is good. Patriots 9, Jaguars 0.

—Second quarter, 9:50 remaining. After Meggett recovers a fumbled punt by Hudson, the Patriots drive 25 yards on seven plays, helped by a penalty on Clark for lining up offside—his second such penalty in two weeks. Vinatieri is again good, this time from 30 yards. Patriots 12, Jaguars 0.

—Second quarter, 5:29 remaining. Meggett returns a punt 20 yards to the Jaguars' 36. Clark is pulled in favor of Dave Thomas. The Patriots drive easily, moving 36 yards in eight plays, scoring when running back Curtis Martin runs around left end for 4 yards. Patriots 19, Jaguars 0.

—Second quarter, 1:06 remaining. Meggett returns a punt 40 yards to the Jaguars' 14. Four plays later, Vinatieri's field goal is good from 29 yards. Patriots 22, Jaguars 0.

Twenty-two points, 20 minutes. The Jaguars, who entered ranked No. 1 in passing, had one first down. "It was," Brunell said, "an ugly first half."

The Jaguars got two first downs on the ensuing series, but with five seconds remaining, faced fourth-and-13 at their 49. Coughlin sent in the punting unit, but Parcells called time-out. Simmons and McCardell pleaded with Coughlin to instead try a Hail Mary pass into the Patriots' end zone. Coughlin relented.

On the play, Brunell rolled to his right and threw a high lob that came down near the New England goal line. The ball bounced from a pile of receivers and defenders, then hit the foot of Patriots linebacker Willie McGinest, who kicked it into the air. Smith, who fell initially, stood as McGinest kicked it, and caught the ball chest high. Patriots 22, Jaguars 7.

"The ball just popped up in my hands," Smith said. "I thought it hit the ground, so I was going to fake it anyway."

As concerning as the halftime score for the Jaguars was the status of middle linebacker Bryan Schwartz. The field was a source of controversy throughout the game, and at halftime, Jaguars officials were particularly angry. NFL rules mandate no events be held on natural-grass surfaces within 24 hours of a game. The night before the Jaguars-Patriots game, a professional soccer game was played, making the field nearly unplayable. The Jaguars complained to the NFL, which took no action. In the second quarter, Schwartz, trying to make a tackle, slipped. He fell awkwardly, and his leg gave. Team officials expected and feared the worst—a severe knee injury.

"Worst field I ever played on," Rison said.

"It was like we were playing on a minefield—there were so many holes," Searcy said.

The mood lightened in the second half. Rison, frustrated all season, led a Jaguars rally. On the first series of the half, he ran behind Patriots cornerback Ricky Reynolds, motioning for Brunell to throw deep. Brunell did—a high lob that Rison pulled away from Hitchcock for a 41-yard touchdown. Patriots 22, Jaguars 14.

Two possessions later, with the Jaguars trailing 25–14, Rison ran a deep slant, beating Reynolds. After Brunell hit him in stride, Rison evaded safety Willie Clay, and as Clay and Reynolds collided, Rison ran free for a

61-yard touchdown. Brunell ran for a two-point conversion with 1:09 remaining in the third quarter. Patriots 25, Jaguars 22.

The Jaguars held the Patriots, then drove 53 yards to the Patriots' 9 in 10 plays with Hollis kicking a 27-yard field goal with 8:26 remaining in regulation. Patriots 25, Jaguars 25. "There's no question about the fight in these players," Coughlin said.

"I've been involved in some screwy games in my life, but this one about took the cake," Patriots linebacker Todd Collins said afterward. "It was like a heavyweight championship fight out there where neither guy was willing to quit."

After taking the 22–0 lead, the Patriots had managed one field goal, and suddenly, a game they thought was over was tied in the fourth quarter. "They had us reeling," Collins said.

The Jaguars' defense, which struggled early, was finding itself and controlling Bledsoe. A reason was Clark's replacement, Thomas. Acquired in the expansion draft before the 1995 season, Thomas had never started an NFL game on the corner, and in the preseason, there was a feeling that Thomas—a former seventh-round draft choice of the Cowboys—might not make the team. That feeling was wrong. He was a big (6-foot-3, 215-pound), physical corner and a solid tackler who was better in coverage than many realized. Jaguars coaches considered replacing Clark with Thomas throughout the season, and against the Patriots, he showed why, breaking up two passes, and limiting Patriots rookie Terry Glenn.

With just under four minutes remaining, Thomas nearly gave the Jaguars a victory. With New England at the Jaguars' 21, Bledsoe threw in the right flat to Martin. The pass went astray, and Thomas made a diving interception at the 20, returning it 80 yards for an apparent touchdown. An illegal-block penalty on Chris Hudson negated the touchdown. "We were eating dinner at somebody else's house," DeMarco said.

The Jaguars failed to score on the drive, but as the clock moved toward overtime, a moment of drama remained. With three seconds remaining in regulation, the Jaguars faced second-and-10 at their 41. This time, no debate. Coughlin called for the Hail Mary.

Brunell rolled left, throwing high and long. Again the ball came down at the goal line. This time, no tip. Willie Jackson caught the pass one-handed, falling toward the end zone. Patriots defenders touched him as he fell at the 1, but Jackson said later he was bobbling the ball as he hit the ground. After he gained possession, Jackson said, he rolled into the end zone. Because of that, Jackson and Coughlin both later said, the play should have been a touchdown.

Officials ruled the play down at the 1. Overtime.

"Clearly, my ball was across the plane of the goal line, but you're not going to get that call away," Jackson said.

New England won quickly in overtime, but not without further controversy. The Patriots took the kick at their 29, and on second-and-four, Thomas was called for interference on Glenn.

"I thought I played the ball well," Thomas said later.

The Patriots had first down on their 47. On the next play, the Patriots all but put the Jaguars away when Bledsoe passed 32 to yards to Glenn, who caught the pass wide open on a crossing pattern. Tom McManus trailed him as the closest defender, but Hudson blew the coverage, leaving the vacant area. Four plays later, Vinatieri was good from 40 yards.

"Every loss hurts," Jurkovic said, "but this one a little more because I feel like we won it twice."

Patriots 28, Jaguars 25. Finally.

"As I was leaving the field, I glanced up at the scoreboard to make sure the score was right," Reynolds said. "It was that kind of game."

And another difficult heartbreaker for the Jaguars. Afterward, emotions were expectedly on edge. The Hail Marys were the natural topic, and players tried to remember if they ever saw two completed by one team in a game. "The odds of completing two of those in a season aren't very good," Brunell said. "Never mind two in a game."

Said Bledsoe, "I've thrown 15 or 20, and never completed one. Mark hit two in one game. Unbelievable."

The oddity didn't make it humorous for the Jaguars, particularly Brunell. Afterward, *Florida Times-Union* columnist Mike Bianchi, searching for a humorous anecdote regarding the Hail Marys, asked Brunell if, perhaps, the team should put it in the offense more.

"Are you trying to make a joke? Right now?" Brunell said.

Less of a joking matter were Jaguars penalties. Most players thought the officiating was, well . . . a joke. "They were throwing yellow flags at us like they were allergic to them," Searcy said.

The Jaguars were penalized 17 times for 148 yards, team records. Eight were against the offensive line, including six for holding. "Maybe a few of them were legitimate, OK?" Coleman said. "But it seemed like a lot of home-cooking."

Smiling faces were few. Even Rison was unhappy. He caught four passes for 115 yards, but none after his second touchdown, and afterward, he sat in his locker, head down and slouching, quietly answering a reporter's questions.

"No comment," he said when asked if he was used enough.

"No comment," he said when asked if he was surprised he didn't catch a pass after his second touchdown.

Later, as another group of reporters crowded around, he was again asked if he was used enough. Rison turned to McCardell, who dressed next to him. "Were we used enough, Keenan?" he said. They both shook their heads in disgust.

"You figure it out," Rison said.

It was easier to interpret the emotions on the other side of the Jaguars' locker room, where a day- and season-long drama played out what seemed to be its final scenes.

Clark, a veteran cornerback, had signed with the Jaguars as an unrestricted free agent in 1995 after four seasons with Green Bay, Atlanta, and New Orleans. In the Jaguars' first season, with a limited pass rush, covering receivers in the Jaguars' secondary was often an impossible task. Clark received much of the criticism of fans and media.

Still, he remained media-friendly until, in the off-season, his name was mentioned as a release possibility if the Jaguars signed a corner. He stopped talking to the media in March, and as months passed, job pressure took a toll. During training camp, he often yelled at reporters on the sidelines, once threatening to have one killed. His pass coverage was also a growing concern, and in New England, after an interference penalty, an offside penalty, and a touchdown allowed to Coates, Jaguars coaches benched Clark for Thomas.

Clark fumed the rest of the game, often kneeling alone far from his teammates. As Vinatieri's game winner sailed through the uprights, Clark stripped his shoulder pads, walking quickly and quietly to the locker room. Inside, he dressed immediately, then pulled a cellular telephone from his bag.

Tears in his eyes, he told his agent to force the Jaguars to release him.

After the call, Clark was inconsolable and uncontrollable. Teammates tried to calm him, but after sitting in a locker briefly, he moved to a corner and began shouting to several teammates, while several others tried to silence him and get him away from the media.

"If he doesn't respect me, fuck that guy [Coughlin]," Clark yelled.

At this point, Joel Smeenge tried to calm him, but he continued. "I have enough money," Clark said. "I don't need to put up with this."

Clark declined comment, but after he left the locker room, Michael Huyghue said, "He was frustrated. We'll get on the plane and he'll cool off."

He didn't. On the plane ride home, Clark sat in the rear, talking loudly, continuing his tirade. Huyghue, having spoken with Coughlin, approached Clark, and spoke with him for several minutes. During the conversation, Clark got his wish. Huyghue told him he was released.

The plane ride was less eventful, but no less disturbing, for the rest of the team. Stewart, solid in the first three games, had rushed for 5 yards on nine carries. Brunell had passed for a career-high 432 yards on 23 of 39 passing with three touchdowns and one interception, but 170 yards had come on three long passes—two of which were fluky Hail Marys.

The defense improved in the second half, but most of the team wondered what Coughlin had wondered for most of September—why so inconsistent? The Jaguars were 1–3 and, far from the first-place status of three weeks before, were alone in last. Only the Jets at 0–4 had a worse record in the AFC. The only good news was the rest of the Central had had a bye, which meant the Jaguars were a game and a half behind Houston and Pittsburgh at 2–1 and a half game behind the Bengals and Ravens (1–2). Moments after the game, DeMarco was asked if the game reminded him of anything, such as the Jaguars' first season.

"It reminded me of us playing like shit," he said.

With the most important game in franchise history in seven days, few disagreed.

8

A TALE OF TWO THEORIES

"Jacksonville has been kicked and kicked so long. It was like backing a cat into the corner and it wants to come out fighting."

—LAMAR LATHON
September 29, 1996

The Jaguars arrived home from New England around 9 P.M. Sunday. Ten hours later, Clark's release became official. He cleaned out his locker and was gone before the media arrived for interviews at 11:45.

He was, as had been the case for several months, unavailable for comment. No matter. His teammates had plenty to say.

The media-player relationship in professional sports is strained, but the postgame locker room is the most volatile forum in which players and media meet. Tensions after losses are high—even after the NFL's mandatory 10-minute "cooling-off" period. The media have fought for years to secure "open" locker-room time as quickly as possible for that reason. Comments made in a postgame locker room typically are public domain unless a player specifies otherwise, and often, the most emotional, controversial comments come from postgame locker rooms. Such was the case in New England.

Clark, despite telling reporters no comment, shouted loudly enough for the media to hear. He cried, and teammates restrained him on several occasions.

The next morning, the *Florida Times-Union* reported the incident, saying, "He spent the second half alone on the far end of the Jaguars bench. Afterward, teammates tried to calm him as he talked angrily of calling his agent and asking for his release." The story said Clark told teammates, "I have enough money. I don't need to put up with this."

Upon arriving at the stadium Monday, players read the story. Many were angry. Clark's now former teammates took the release—and the newspaper's handling of the situation—personally.

Brian DeMarco and Jeff Novak approached one reporter, yelling and accusing him of printing an overheard, "personal" conversation. The reporter yelled back, and several teammates stood near, backing Novak and DeMarco.

The two linemen repeated the scene, accusing the paper's other beat reporter of maliciously eavesdropping on Clark. "You took food off his table and out of his kids' mouths," DeMarco said. Later, on his weekly radio show, DeMarco called the reporters "maggots," yet Tom Coughlin and Michael Huyghue insisted Clark's comments in the paper had nothing to do with his release. "Not at all," Huyghue said, and in fact, Clark was released the night before on the team plane.

"It's performance-based for everybody," Huyghue added.

"We felt Dave Thomas played well this weekend, and he would be the starter this coming week," Coughlin said. "This is in the best interest of the football team."

The tension from the incident lingered, setting a tone for a week many viewed as the most important in team history. Many teammates agreed the paper handled the situation poorly, but some believed DeMarco and Novak lacked tact. Several veterans warned the younger teammates to let the situation pass without further incident.

The controversy left a citywide impression of a team thinking of anything but football the week the Jaguars would play the team most believed to be their biggest rivals, the Carolina Panthers.

The Carolina Panthers and Jacksonville Jaguars. The Jacksonville Jaguars and Carolina Panthers. Two teams . . . forever intertwined.

That's how it is in professional sports. Two teams enter a league the same season and they are forever linked. The Seattle Seahawks and Tampa Bay Buccaneers, as of 1996, had been in the NFL 20 seasons, and to some, they were still the 1976 expansion teams. Carolina and Jacksonville were the 1995 expansion teams, and their rivalry—albeit often denied by team officials, coaches, and players—ran deep. Throughout the expansion race, Jacksonville considered Charlotte its No. 1 opponent. Jacksonville media made fun of Carolina and Charlotte media snubbed Jacksonville, most notably *Charlotte Observer* columnist Tom Sorensen, who irked Jacksonville citizens with columns about the resident "Yahoos" of Jacksonville and the city's supposed problems with cockroaches.

The bitterness born in the expansion race flourished in October 1993, when Charlotte received its franchise, and TD Jax! officials were told to wait a month. Jacksonville received a franchise a month later, but Carolina was the 29th NFL team, and Jacksonville the 30th.

Always, in that way at least, Carolina would be ahead.

"As far as them being an expansion team and us being an expansion team, I don't buy that making it big," Tony Boselli said as the team's first regular-season meeting approached. "It's a media-hype thing. The fans are going to get a little excited, but as far as players, it's just one of 16 games."

That was a nice quote, and it's what players, coaches, and front-office personnel echoed before the game. It also wasn't true. Carolina and Jacksonville, entering the league in an era when expansion teams could build fast and strong, constantly were compared. Which franchise was ahead? What plan had worked? Which players were better? Which owner was smarter? Which coach was the better choice?

What team, fans of Jacksonville, would you rather have?

As game day approached, none of those questions had positive answers for the Jaguars. They were 1–3, losers of three consecutive games, and because of the Clark controversy, seemed in disarray. Carolina was anything but that.

The Panthers were the talk of the NFL. They were 3–0, and while the Jaguars were losing in Foxboro, the Panthers were dominating the mighty San Francisco 49ers, 23–7, to take sole possession of first place in the NFC West. The Jaguars spent the week again wondering what was wrong, and saying the game wasn't big, but what they were hearing was Carolina, Carolina, Carolina.

"There's no question the nation forces the issue," Coughlin said of comparisons between Carolina and Jacksonville. "You look at one, you look at the other. It's another game, but it's a big game for us. The fact that

Carolina is the opponent is another issue. It might be something to pay attention to if we had similar records, and it was a similar approach to the game. Ours is totally different. We're 1–3, and need a win. The need for a win kind of surpasses the focus on Carolina."

The Panthers and the Jaguars shared the same first season, and the distinction of overcoming the odds of being from small-market, southern cities, breaking into the high-dollar, once northeastern-dominated world of the NFL. The similarities ended there, because if anything was true of the two franchises, it was that they were different. As different as different could be.

Coach? Different.

Front-office structure? Different.

Defensive and offensive styles? Different.

Roster development? Different.

The Jaguars were new-school and forward-thinking with a college, offensive-minded coach. The Panthers were old-school, hired a coach with NFL experience, and concentrated on defense.

This tale of two philosophies began with the owners. Wayne Weaver was a rich businessman, with little desire to own an NFL team until approached by his brother, Ron, in the early stages of TD Jax! Jerry Richardson, the Panthers' owner, was a receiver for the Baltimore Colts in the 1950s and 1960s, and even before he became a multimillionaire owning Hardee's and Denny's restaurants, he dreamed of owning an NFL team.

The league's older owners viewed Richardson as one of their own. By comparison, in the final days of the expansion race, the backing for Weaver came from the NFL's new owners—men such as Cowboys owner Jerry Jones—who joined the NFL after successful business careers, and who were determined to bring that experience to the league.

The differences began there, continuing in each phase of building. "No one has patented a way to be successful," Panthers president Mike McCormack said.

When Weaver structured the Jaguars, conventional NFL wisdom was to hire a general manager, who then hired a coach. Sometimes, too, there was a third and fourth power figure—perhaps a president involved in the football operations, and/or a powerful director of player personnel.

Weaver went against that. After considering the usual way, with a GM, coach, and president, he hired Coughlin as all three. "One of the things we learned in the process of talking with a lot of football people is the flatter the organization, the more success you have," Weaver said. "You can't hold someone accountable on the field and tell them who their players are."

The Panthers, again, went the opposite way. Richardson hired a former coach and Hall of Fame offensive tackle, McCormack, the year before he was awarded the team. When Charlotte got the team, McCormack became president/general manager. Soon, he gave up the GM title, hiring for the job Bill Polian—an NFL old-schooler who had built powerful teams in Buffalo in the early 1990s.

The difference continued as the teams hired coaches. Weaver hired Coughlin 19 months before the first game and let him learn the NFL while working. Richardson had a front office and wanted a coach with limited personnel responsibility. That meant Richardson could wait until after the 1994 season to hire the coach. He then hired Dom Capers, defensive coordinator of the Pittsburgh Steelers.

"We're pretty independent thinking in terms of how we approach this," Michael Huyghue said. "Everything is different. It goes to show you there's no clear road map in expansion."

Even the coaching choices reflected a difference in philosophy. Coughlin ensured the Jaguars would be offense oriented. They drafted an offensive cornerstone, tackle Tony Boselli, with their first draft choice. Capers, who developed his reputation by devising the Steelers' zone-blitz scheme, gave Carolina a defensive focus, and the thrust of the Panthers' early building was defensive free agents.

Extra draft selections and access to the free-agent market gave Carolina and Jacksonville more access to quality personnel than their predecessors, and also gave them far more power in shaping the personality and image of their teams. The teams were seen as a case study. Everything was fresh—no problem players to be discarded, no salary-cap burden. The expansion teams could build without rebuilding, and the two franchises might eventually be looked upon as models for future organizations—both existing, and expansion.

The Jaguars built with youth, using a precise, detailed plan based upon some of the theories with which Jimmy Johnson built the Dallas Cowboys—build young, build with talent, and let those players mature into winners. The early seasons of such a plan typically would be losing ones, but the future would be bright. The Jaguars built with a three-year plan—make the playoffs in Year Three and the Super Bowl in Year Four. The core of the talent would be draftees and free agents signed from 1994 to 1996, players who would mature together through the late 1990s.

So strong was the belief in the plan that the front office put it in writing—a series of thick black notebooks, each outlining the Jaguars' goals for a given year, and how much to spend each year to attain those goals.

The plan gave the Jaguars a target age during the first several years. A player, unless circumstances dictated differently, would be 26 or under, and signed to a contract that would keep him with the team into his early 30s. Each player brought in during free agency was first examined to see if he fit the plan, and the team's three premiere 1996 free agents fit the formula:

—Leon Searcy, 26, signed a five-year contract.
—Keenan McCardell, 26, signed a four-year contract.
—Eddie Robinson, 26, signed a four-year contract.

On paper, the plan worked. Entering 1996, the Jaguars were the NFL's fourth-youngest team, with potential stars such as Mark Brunell, Boselli, Searcy, Robinson, McCardell, Kevin Hardy, Natrone Means, James Stewart, and Tony Brackens under 27. Coughlin had criteria, too. A player was never signed without a background search, and usually, a new acquisition was a Coughlin Guy— tireless in the weight room, self-made, hard worker.

The Panthers' philosophy, again, couldn't have been more different. Carolina officials believed the way to build was defense first, which in the free-agency era meant signing a slew of veterans. "We thought you could buy a defense, and build an offense with the draft," McCormack said.

Carolina signed nine defensive starters as free agents in the first two off-seasons, and the average age on defense in 1996 was 30.8. Only one defensive starter, second-year cornerback Tyrone Poole, was younger than 28, with six 31 or older. Defining the unit was linebacker Sam Mills, who signed with the Panthers in 1995 at age 35.

The Panthers had 17 players 30 years or older; the Jaguars, four. The Jaguars' oldest players, Clyde Simmons and punter Bryan Barker, were 32. Carolina had nine players 32 or older. The Panthers' 22 starters had played in 1,930 games. The Jaguars' 22 had played in 1,165. The Jaguars' philosophy came down to building for the future. The Panthers figured the future, in this era of free agency, was now.

"With free agency, teams change so much from one year to the next," Capers said. "It's virtually impossible to have all good young players."

Which way was better?

On paper, it was hard to say. The Panthers were winning, but if you looked at the Jaguars' youth and potential, and their numerous close losses, it was hard to believe they were *too* far away from the Panthers' winning ways.

"Both teams have proven they can be competitive quickly," Panthers quarterback Steve Beuerlein, who played with the Jaguars in 1995, said. "They're doing things by different philosophies. Who's to say who's right or wrong? That won't be something we can tell for 10 or 15 years when you establish some consistency and credibility over time."

As the game approached, the Jaguars' record prompted some in Jacksonville to think the Carolina way, the 3–0 way, was superior. Many league observers called that view shortsighted. Tex Schramm, architect of the most successful expansion franchise in NFL history, the Dallas Cowboys—an expansion team in 1960—called it something else. "Ridiculous," Schramm said. "What is this? Their second year? Call me in five years."

Thus far, the Panthers' philosophy *had* brought more success. The Jaguars won four games the first year; Carolina, an expansion-record seven. As September 29, 1996, approached, the Panthers were 10–9 as a franchise; the Jaguars, 5–15. Success, too, brought the Panthers respect nationally. Chris Berman, anchor of ESPN's much-watched, opinion-influencing *NFL Prime-Time*, a Sunday night highlights show, made the Panthers his pet story of the season early. Weekly, Jaguars management bristled at Berman's gushing for Capers and the Carolina franchise, but what was there to say?

The Panthers led their division. The Jaguars were last.

"The better team right now certainly is Carolina," ESPN NFL analyst Ron Jaworski said the week leading to the game.

Others weren't as convinced. "Carolina and Jacksonville are further along than anyone could have anticipated," former 49ers coach Bill Walsh said. "People had grave concerns they would struggle, but the formula [the NFL had] has allowed them to do it."

The Jaguars wanted to believe that, and as game day approached, they were discussing the difference, but the company line was, no, the Carolina game wasn't Judgment Day.

"The comparison is there, because they've had success more quickly than we have," Huyghue said. "They've done things totally different. Their team has been the oldest team in the league. Ours has been the youngest. I don't aspire to their philosophy, but it works for them. The bottom line for our organization is we believe our plan will work.

"I'm sure they believe theirs will work, too."

The problem as the Carolina game neared was that the Panthers' approach already worked. No one knew if the Jaguars' would.

Carolina, Carolina, Carolina.

This was all the Jaguars heard the week leading to September 29. The Jaguars, however, had other concerns. "We need a win regardless of who we're playing," Brunell said.

Expansion Bowl?

"It might be something to pay attention to if we both had similar records," Jeff Lageman said, "but we're 1–3 and need a win. I think the need for a win kind of surpasses the focus of Carolina. We're kind of above that, and we have to be above that."

The Clark story faded as the week wore on, and the team had worse news about which to worry: Brian Schwartz, injured in New England, was lost for the season with a torn anterior cruciate ligament in his left knee. Also, concern over three frustrating—and some thought, inexcusable—losses was growing. This was a team on which many members looked around the locker room, and couldn't see a reason why *they* weren't the talk of the league, instead of Carolina. Since the victory over Pittsburgh their season had gone like this: Three close games. Three games decided in the fourth quarter. Three losses.

"That doesn't cut it," Dana Hall said. "We're not in this game to compete. Some teams say they just want to compete. That's a bunch of shit. Guys that just want to compete don't go to the playoffs.

"I'm sick and tired of coming in here on Monday and saying, 'We played and fought hard and this is what this game is all about.' What's that mean if you lose? To have a chance to win, like we've had the last three weeks in a row, and haven't pulled it out? After a while, you start to think, 'What do we have to do to win?' "

Coughlin agreed, saying, "No question. They have to learn how to win."

Hall, acquired from the Ravens as a free agent in the off-season, spent the first three years of his career with the 49ers. A former first-round selection, he never lived up to that, but was developing into a solid NFL veteran who brought to Jacksonville the perspective of a Super Bowl ring. He had the ring from the 1994 49ers, and even at 1–3 couldn't see why he shouldn't get one again in 1996.

"In San Francisco, there was always an air that if we were within three points or within a touchdown, we were going to tie the score or win," Hall said. "Other teams knew that. That's just an air, confidence. The more you play together, the more you trust one another, the more that will come. I think that's here, too. I think guys believe we can win those type ball games."

Like Hall, most veterans were impatient for that time. "With the veterans on this team, at this point, we should have learned how to win," Don Davey said. "We should have three or four wins by now."

The game didn't need an additional story line—not with the Jaguars looking for respect, needing a victory to save their season, and the city of Jacksonville wanting to quiet the people of Charlotte. The game had an extra subplot anyway—a former starter for one team was returning to start for the other.

This, to Jacksonvillians, was ironic—Beuerlein, whom fans had grown to hate the previous year, would start for Carolina, where he had signed as a free agent.

His role was to back up Kerry Collins, a second-year quarterback, but Collins sprained his left knee in the Panthers' second game, and Beuerlein started against the 49ers the week before. He had a career game, completing 22 of 31 passes for 290 yards and two touchdowns. In the first half, while Carolina built a 17–0 lead, Beuerlein completed 17 of 20 passes against a defense ranked No. 1 in the NFL the previous season and in the same spot entering the game. A day after the 49ers game, Capers announced Collins wasn't ready.

Popular upon arriving as the No. 1 selection in the expansion draft, Beuerlein fell into disfavor early in the 1995 season with Jaguars fans, who blamed him for a then anemic offense. Fans love a backup, and in the Jaguars' case in that first season, there seemed much to love—Brunell, not yet a polished passer, scrambled for big, dazzling gains. At times, he was the team's only offense, and fans called for Brunell. This feeling rose throughout preseason, and through the first four games of 1995. When Brunell subbed for Beuerlein and led the team to a 17–16 come-from-behind victory over the Oilers for the first victory in franchise history in Week 5, Beuerlein's fate was decided. Brunell became the starter, and Beuerlein never again started unless Brunell was injured.

Beuerlein, who had eyed the Jaguars as the NFL starting opportunity he had coveted for a decade, was disappointed, but never complained publicly. Still, he was ridiculed, even in the week leading to the Carolina game in 1996. That week, as a gag, two local disc jockeys—Lex and Terry of Rock 105—distributed 35 Beuerlein Jaguars jerseys to the homeless.

This was a team, then, with plenty of incentive, and for the first time in a month, it played that way. On September 29, 1996, at Jacksonville Municipal Stadium in front of 71,537, the Jaguars didn't prove they could stay with the favored Panthers. They proved they could dominate them.

The Jaguars kicked off, and forced the Panthers to punt in three plays. Starting from their 41, the offense proved as ready as the defense. Early in the drive, Brunell surprised the Panthers, passing to tight end Rich Griffith—hardly a critical part of the deep passing game most weeks. On this drive, he was. He caught the pass for a 17-yard gain to the 31. Brunell ran 17 yards to the Panthers' 14, and after a penalty and a 2-yard sack, he again passed to Griffith—this time for 18 yards to the 3. Stewart scored on a 1-yard run two plays later. Jaguars 7, Panthers 0.

Jaguars over the Panthers? The crowd loved it. It got more.

The Jaguars forced a punt on the Panthers' next drive, and again drove—68 yards on 10 plays, and it was almost all Brunell. He passed for 46 yards. He ran for 13. The key plays were consecutive passes of 26 and 12 yards to Jimmy Smith that took the Jaguars from their 33 to the Panthers' 29. Brunell finished the series with an 8-yard touchdown pass to Smith with 1:59 remaining in the quarter. Jaguars 14, Panthers 0.

The offense was playing as well as it ever had. Brunell was sharp, and the line matched perfectly against the strength of the Panthers' defense, rush linebackers Kevin Greene and Lamar Lathon. Searcy and Boselli handled the two early, giving Brunell time.

The Jaguars' defensive scheme was working, too. Jaguars coaches knew Beuerlein's tendencies, and thought he would wilt under a heavy rush. The Jaguars blitzed more than at any time early in the season, and pressured their former teammate into early mistakes.

One mistake came on the ensuing drive. Trailing by two touchdowns, the Panthers drove 35 yards to the Jaguars' 17. On second-and-eight, Beuerlein dropped to pass. Tony Brackens knocked the ball from Beuerlein and recovered at the Jaguars' 28. "They played with a lot more emotion than we did," Mills said. "They were an excited team out there."

And one finally getting the breaks—and making some of their own.

On the series after Brackens's sack/fumble recovery, Beuerlein moved the Panthers to a first-and-goal at the 1, but botched the handoff to Anthony Johnson. Brackens again recovered. Later, in the second quarter, Panthers kicker John Kasay—who hadn't missed a field goal or extra point all season—missed wide right from 45 yards, and on the final play of the half, Hollis's 53-yard field goal made it 17–0.

"Jacksonville has been kicked and kicked so long," Lathon said. "It was like when you back a cat into the corner and it wants to come out fighting."

It was, players and coaches said, the Jaguars' best half ever. They dominated, and unlike some games in which they played well, it showed on the scoreboard. Brunell, too, had the best half of his career, completing 10 of 15 passes for 162 yards and a touchdown with no interceptions. He ran three times for 51 yards.

"We played angry, and I think that's good," Leon Searcy said. "As much talent as we have . . . and no one in the league cared about the Jaguars. People really don't have high regard for the Jaguars, and that really pissed me off. I'm not used to the lack of respect we get around the league, and from the press."

The Jaguars spent the second half punishing Beuerlein, but early, after a trade of punts, the Panthers got a break that gave them hope. On the first play of a drive that started at the Jaguars' 19, Brunell was pressured, and threw to Andre Rison. Panthers safety Pat Terrell intercepted at the Jaguars' 39. Five plays later, Beuerlein passed to Mark Carrier for 24 yards, a touchdown, and a 17–6 Jaguars lead.

Much of the rest of the third quarter was uneventful. Four punts. The Panthers gained one first down. So did the Jaguars. But with 4:44 remaining in the third quarter, the Jaguars took possession at their 20. They picked up three first downs before the quarter ended, with Brunell popping short passes to Derek Brown (10 yards), McCardell (6, 12, and 16) and Rison (6). On the last play of the quarter, Brunell passed 10 yards to Smith, who turned it into an 18-yard catch and run for a first down at the Panthers' 20 at the end of the quarter.

The Jaguars were done passing on this drive. As happened against the Steelers three weeks before, the Jaguars had worn the Panthers down physically. Six runs later, Stewart ran around left end for a 4-yard touchdown, and the drive summary looked like this:

—15 plays.
—80 yards.
—7:57 elapsed.

Jaguars 24, Panthers 6. Expansion Bowl I was all but finished.

"Jacksonville was the only team we played all year that physically whipped our ass," Lathon said after the season. "They weren't better than us, but something happened that day. We went out there thinking they were going to lay down. We started slow, and they whipped our ass. We tried to get it together, but it was too late."

If the game was a homecoming for Beuerlein, it was hardly happy. He completed 15 of 30 passes for 219 yards, but was sacked five times. Each time, the crowd rejoiced, cheering more loudly on those plays than on any others. "It seemed, under the circumstances, they all wanted to kill him," Panthers offensive guard Greg Skrepenak said. "The crowd wanted to see Steve's head on a silver platter. I think he got caught in the middle. It's not his fault he decided to play somewhere else this year."

The crowd got their wish. By game's end, he was beaten. He left with leg cramps in the fourth quarter, and long after the game, he lay in the Panthers' training room, IVs pumping fluids into him.

"Whenever you go back to where you were before, loyalties change," Beuerlein said. "That's part of the game. I was a little surprised at some of the things that were said by fans, but I'm not going to get into that. I cramped up real bad in both calves and hamstrings. I didn't want to stay down and I didn't want to come out, but I couldn't get up."

The Panthers scored a final touchdown after Beuerlein left, and the Jaguars won, 24–14. Statistics revealed a game less close. The Jaguars outrushed the Panthers 179–57 and outgained them overall, 378–271. Brunell completed 15 of 27 passes for 214 yards and a touchdown, and Stewart had his best game of the season, rushing for 96 yards and two touchdowns on 21 carries.

Defensively, the memories of the sackless, rushless days of 1995 were over. The Jaguars set a team record with five sacks. Brackens had the first two of his career. Smeenge had two, and Robinson had one, too.

Afterward, the Jaguars let the frustrations flow. Andre Rison, like Searcy, was angry not only that they were under .500 after five games, but with the lack of respect the Jaguars received when people—locally and nationally—compared Carolina and Jacksonville. "It pissed us off," Rison said. "If I was Andre Rison of old, and Tom Coughlin wasn't the head coach, I might have said something [during the week], but I'm going to just be quiet and keep it plain and simple. We were the better team. It's quite obvious.

"I think we were all angry. Not at each other, but because we knew we were better than 1–3. We should be 5–0. I don't give a damn what people say. That's a fact. It's us against the world."

Just another game? No rivalry between the Panthers and Jaguars?

"This game was more important than people let on," Davey said. "People were going to measure us on this game today."

"This team has nobody," Boselli said. "We have us. You guys didn't believe in us. The fans—they were trying to get behind us. We had the coaches and guys in this room. It was us against them."

Said McCardell, "We could sense how much this game meant to the franchise. We downplayed it to the media, because we were planning our ambush."

So important was the game that even Coughlin said so afterward, shedding the facade in an emotional post-game scene. He ran from the field to the loudest cheers he had received yet as Jaguars coach, then strode confidently into his postgame press conference. Usually, Coughlin answered questions from the start in the press conference, speaking blandly, and mostly of X's and O's and whats and whys.

After Carolina, he spoke first, specifically to naysayers and doubters:

"Let's put it right on the money. There are a lot of second-guessers, but this is a day for the loyal. I'm very happy today for our ownership and for all those people who were part of the 15-year process to bring the NFL to the great city of Jacksonville. Everyone had decided we were on the short end of the stick. To all of our loyal fans, thank you very much for hanging in there.

"And for the fickle . . . well, that's the way it is."

9
OCTOBER STRUGGLES I

"We have to live in misery for some godly reason."

—LEON SEARCY
October 1996

s September ended, so too, Jaguars players thought, had the difficult times. The team lost three games, but there were high points. They played two division leaders—Pittsburgh and Carolina—and won both games. The Jaguars, clearly, were talented enough to play with—and beat—most teams in the NFL.

That was the good news. The bad news was they were young, and inconsistent, which caused Coughlin continued headaches. The three losses were to teams with a combined 5–8 record. The two victories came against teams a combined 6–2. The Jaguars got up for good teams, but played down to bad ones—hardly a formula for the playoffs. Yet, hopes were high as October opened. Two victories and three losses were not great, but the Carolina victory was big, and it put them within a game of .500 with 11 remaining—an eternity in the NFL. Causing optimism, too, was the October schedule:

—October 6: at New Orleans.
—October 13: New York Jets, at home.
—October 20: at St. Louis.
—October 27: at Cincinnati.

The Saints, when September ended, had yet to win. Jets, either. The Rams and Bengals were 1–3. "We've got a schedule that, hopefully, we can get back into this thing," Leon Searcy said. "But we can't take anybody lightly. We have to play like we did against Carolina."

The schedule was unfavorable in one way—three of the four games were on the road. Winning on the road in the NFL, no matter the opponent, is difficult, and the Jaguars had had particular trouble. They were 2–8 away from Jacksonville Municipal Stadium, including losses in the last six road games. Too, the road games all were on turf, where the Jaguars were 1–4 in 1995.

Coughlin scoffed at such statistics. A victory was a victory, a loss a loss, and a game a game—no matter the site. What bothered Coughlin was what he saw when he put in a game tape—particularly the penalties, some of which bordered on the bizarre. Before his release, Clark was called offside twice—rare for a defensive back, where being close to the ball is not a prerequisite. The team also had an inordinate amount of false-start penalties, particularly on Searcy, who was hurrying off the ball because of the pressure of protecting Brunell's blind side, a responsibility he never had in Pittsburgh. Against Carolina, the Jaguars were called for unsportsmanlike conduct when assistant John Pease collided with back judge Duke Carroll in the sideline border. "We get some of the damnedest things you've ever seen called on us," Coughlin said. "I don't see those things getting called anywhere else. I really don't. The official falling over somebody in the white paint . . . Usually that's an advisement—next time I'll get you. We got called for that."

September was finished. The bad times, the Jaguars hoped, were past, but the only way that could be was if Mark Brunell played consistently as he did against Carolina.

So far, to the concern of many, that hadn't happened.

Mark Allen Brunell was born September 17, 1970, in Los Angeles, California, and attended high school in Santa Maria, California, where his father, Dave, was athletic director. He played football, baseball, and basketball in high school, and was a league Most Valuable Player in both baseball and football.

He passed for 5,893 yards and 41 touchdowns in three seasons, and signed with the University of Washington in 1988. He redshirted as a freshman and started as a sophomore, earning All–Pac 10 honors and being chosen the Rose Bowl MVP. As a junior, he again was expected to start, but in spring practice, he tore ligaments in his knee.

"The last thing he said before the surgery was, "Stanford,' " then Washington coach Don James said. "That was the opener."

Brunell didn't return for the opener, but he played the final eight games, including the Rose Bowl for a second consecutive year, and helped the Huskies to a share of the national title. "You couldn't have criticized him for not coming back," James said. "He made up his mind he wasn't going to miss the season."

The next year, he shared time early with Billy Joe Hobert, but when Hobert was dismissed from the team, Brunell was again the lone starter. He earned second-team All–Pac 10 again, and was drafted in the fifth round by the Green Bay Packers. As a rookie in 1993, and again in 1994, he sat behind Brett Favre. In 1994, Coughlin— scouting the year before the Jaguars' first season—saw Brunell practice in Green Bay. Coughlin wanted a quarterback with which to build. Brunell was the choice.

"Without question, of the players who might be available, he was the guy I wanted as the quarterback of the future here," Coughlin said.

In the 1995 off-season, Brunell asked his agent, Frank Bauer, to engineer a trade. Feelers came first from the Eagles, whose coach, Ray Rhodes, had worked with Brunell in Green Bay.

"The word we got was that the deal was done in Philadelphia," Coughlin said later.

Brunell wanted a three-year deal. The Eagles wanted four years. The deal fell through, and on the same day, the Jaguars offered a three-year deal. Brunell agreed, and Coughlin made his first trade—sending third- and fifth-round selections in that year's draft to Green Bay for Brunell.

Brunell was the future, but no one knew how soon the future would come. He started the season behind Steve Beuerlein, but was never far behind, and Coughlin rarely missed an opportunity to substitute the young talent for the veteran. Brunell subbed for Beuerlein throughout preseason, and again in the Jaguars' first game. Brunell's flair for the big play intrigued Coughlin and caught the fancy of the fans, who loved his running style and the spark he gave an otherwise anemic offense. Brunell played in each of the Jaguars' first four games, starting twice when Beuerlein was injured. In Week 5 in Houston, Brunell relieved Beuerlein in the fourth quarter, and his 15-yard touchdown pass to Desmond Howard gave the Jaguars a 17–16 come-from-behind victory—the first in franchise history.

The job was his.

So, for the first time since high school, Brunell was an unquestioned starter when the 1996 season began, which raised questions: Could he lead a team? With his running style, could he stay healthy in a long season? Mostly, would he become the pocket passer Coughlin wanted?

When the season began, fans talked about him being the next Steve Young. Brunell tried to temper that talk. "I haven't done anything," he said. "It's all nice, but to say I'm the next rising guy . . . I've had one statistically OK season. We won a couple of games as an expansion team, but to predict what's going to happen . . .

"I don't put a lot of faith into what people are saying."

Concerning Brunell the most was the change he was trying to undergo—from running quarterback to a mature NFL prototype. "He's trying to make a much more difficult development now, which is being the precise, mistake-free quarterback the greats are," offensive coordinator Kevin Gilbride said days before the opener. "That's a hard step. Improvement won't be as dramatic, and it won't be as discernible to the untrained eye. He's getting better, but with that—and trying to not run recklessly, and depend on the receivers to do the right thing— there will be some hesitation, and mistakes. That eventually will evaporate, and he'll raise his game, which he's trying desperately to do."

If Brunell had yet to mature on the field, he was maturing as a leader off it—in part because of his status as the Jaguars' spiritual leader. Deeply religious, Brunell considered faith an important part of his career, forming Bible study groups in the locker room. The groups had a major impact on many teammates, including Tony Boselli and Bryan Schwartz, Brunell's closest friends on the team. "For those who don't think Bible study, or standing up for God, has a place in an NFL locker room, that's too bad," Brunell said. "I'm sorry, but this is the way it's going to be, because this is how I choose to live my life. I don't try to jam anything down anyone's throat. As a Christian, you're going to be resented at times. That's the way it is."

The statement spoke volumes about Brunell. He was strong-willed, and if he believed something, he was never shy about saying it—and that extended to his attitude regarding fans.

Brunell, as 1996 began, was the most popular Jaguars player, with lucrative endorsement deals that kept him visible, but he was passionate about his privacy. Jacksonville was a small market, new to the NFL. Rarely could he go out in public without being hounded for a handshake or an autograph. "It's hard," Brunell said. "There are times you don't want to sign. Sometimes, it's more than just being moody. There's a time and a place for everything. You want to be left alone, but you realize, too, people are always going to want an autograph.

"We [he and his wife, Stacy] don't go out as much as we used to—especially during the season. I'd rather be home. It's not that people are rude. You would just rather be left alone, and the only time you get peace is when you're at home."

A month into the 1996 season, peace had yet to come on the field. Gilbride had worried that Brunell would struggle to become a pocket passer, and after five games, he was right. Brunell looked sharp against Carolina, but that was his first interception-free game of the season. He threw two in each of the first three games and another against New England. The seven matched his total for 1995.

Brunell led the NFL in passing yards, but early in 1996, his maturation was not yet complete.

If Brunell and the Jaguars had a problem early in 1996, it was an inability to produce inside the opponent's 20-yard line—known as the "red zone." This problem would come into focus in the Jaguars' sixth game of the season, October 6 in the Louisiana Superdome against the New Orleans Saints.

The Saints, for 20 years, were a league joke, a joke their fans joined in the early 1980s by placing bags over their heads and calling themselves Aints' fans. In the late 1980s and early 1990s, under coach Jim Mora, they shed that image, but now, the bags were returning. The Saints were 0–4, and Mora's job was in jeopardy. Fans were leaving, too. Only 34,231 arrived in the Superdome. Many were Jaguars fans who had made the 12-hour drive from Jacksonville.

The Jaguars, as against Carolina, dominated. The offense was sharp between the 20-yard lines, and the defense stifled the Saints. The Saints' lone drive in the first three quarters gave them an early lead—79 yards on 10 plays, ending when running back Mario Bates ran for a 1-yard touchdown with 5:35 remaining in the first quarter. On the first play of the ensuing drive, Saints defensive tackle Joe Johnson poked the ball from James Stewart. Linebacker Mark Fields recovered. Mark Brunell chased and dove, and Tony Boselli pushed Fields out of bounds at the Jaguars' 7.

Brunell injured his knee on the play. It hampered him; but he played the rest of the game. The defense held, and Doug Brien kicked a 27-yard field goal with 2:50 remaining in the first quarter. Saints 10, Jaguars 0.

The rest of the half was a strange series of Jaguars close calls. They cut the deficit, then squandered opportunities to take the lead. It was a quarter that set the tone for the game.

Brunell, ineffective early, now felt a rhythm, and

drove the Jaguars into Saints territory. The drive stalled, but it gave the Jaguars field position, and on the next series, they finally cut into the lead. Taking possession on their 41, Brunell passed three times to McCardell for 20 yards. First down at the Saints' 38. The Jaguars inched toward the goal line, and on second-and-10 from the 21, Brunell passed to Stewart, who scored on a screen.

Saints 10, Jaguars 7 with 4:42 remaining in the half.

On the Jaguars' next series, Mike Hollis hit an upright on a 48-yard field goal. No good. And then, before the half, they had another chance to tie, taking possession at midfield with 27 seconds remaining. They drove quickly to the Saints' 30 with a 9-yard pass from Brunell to Pete Mitchell. Out of time-outs, Brunell tried to get the Jaguars to the line to spike the ball and stop the clock, but officials ruled that time expired before Brunell grounded the ball. Coughlin protested, but without result.

"We had one second," Coughlin said.

Thus ended a strange half. The Jaguars dominated, but trailed by three, having outgained the Saints, 169–101. Coughlin, though, was confident. His defense was dominating, and the offensive line was strong for a second consecutive week. A three-point deficit seemed nothing, and on the first drive of the second half, the Jaguars took control, moving easily from their 20 to a third-and-four at the Saints' 5. Brunell again keyed this series with passes to McCardell, the biggest of which came on third-and-one from the Saints' 37—a 26-yard gain to the Saints' 11.

On third-and-four from the 5, Brunell threw a wide-receiver screen to Jimmy Smith, who caught it, cutting inside. He gained 4 yards, enough for the first down, but before he was ruled stopped by officials, Saints line-backer Richard Harvey poked the ball free. Defensive end Renaldo Turnbull recovered. "I was just trying to do too much," Smith said. "I was trying to make a play. I should have gone down instead of trying to stretch the ball over the goal line."

At first, the fumble seemed not to hurt much. The defense held, and safety Chris Hudson returned a punt 60 yards to the Saints' 21. Mistakes hurt again. On first down, Stewart—playing as well as he had in a season and half for the Jaguars—ran to the Saints' 2. The Jaguars, however, had lined up illegally, negating the gain. Four plays later, Hollis's 36-yard field goal made it 10–10 with 2:53 remaining in the third quarter.

Two second-half drives.

Two touchdown opportunities.

Three points.

On their next possession, the Jaguars reverted to a familiar pattern. Often in the early season, they stalled in the red zone—sometimes because Brunell made mistakes, but also because of Coughlin's insistence on a power-running game near the goal line. Coughlin, because of his experience with Bill Parcells's run-oriented Giants teams with huge offensive lines, felt good teams outmuscled opponents near the goal line. The Jaguars, in their first season, were a weak run-blocking team, and after five games in 1996, they hadn't matured. Against the Saints, after driving to a first-and-goal at the 8 from their 34, Coughlin called three consecutive runs. Stewart gained 6 yards, and Hollis's 19-yard field goal was good with 5:15 remaining. Jaguars 13, Saints 10.

Now, the second-half red-zone count was:

—Three opportunities.

—Six points.

"The red zone is where it counts," Brunell said. "That's where you win and lose games, and today, we were bad."

Since the first-quarter touchdown, the Saints managed one first down, and besides the 79-yard touchdown drive, had gained 27 yards. Now, the Saints had possession on their 19 with 5:15 remaining. "We had a lot of confidence going into that drive," safety Travis Davis said. "We were pretty sure we could stop them."

The Jaguars, though, had violated a cardinal NFL rule. Don't let a lesser team stay close—not on the road. The Saints got a first down, then another, and quarterback Jim Everett—erratic throughout—gained confidence. The Saints drove to the Jaguars' 23, and on second-and-two, he passed to receiver Michael Haynes. Dave Thomas was called for interference, and the Saints had first-and-goal on the 6. On the next play, Torrance Small lined up in the right slot as the Saints' third receiver. That matched him on Hudson. Small ran a crossing pattern in the end zone, beat Hudson, and caught a pass from Everett with 1:45 remaining. Saints 17, Jaguars 13.

"We just didn't stop them," Clyde Simmons said. "It's a shame it came down to one play, one drive—but that's the way it is in this business. That's part of the game. To win it in the fourth quarter, you've got to take advantage of your opportunities."

The Jaguars, who took possession at their 20 with 1:45 remaining and two time-outs, had struggled in the two-minute offense so far in the season. This series was no different. On the first play, rookie center Michael Cheever—subbing for injured starter Dave Widell—was called for holding, and after a pass from Brunell to McCardell gained 17 yards, the Jaguars faced second-and-three on the 27. The clock ran and 1:12 remained after Brunell passed incomplete to McCardell to make it third-and-three. A 6-yard pass to Willie Jackson gave the Jaguars a first down, but 23 seconds passed before Brunell threw a 3-yard pass to James Stewart. When the clock stopped after a holding penalty on Ben Coleman, 33 seconds remained, and the Jaguars faced third-and-16 on their 27.

That made it a 7-yard, 1:12 drive, but the Jaguars made a first down two plays later on a pass interference penalty and were at their 44 with 20 seconds remaining. Brunell passed incomplete twice, and although Joe Johnson was called for illegal contact, that only pushed the Jaguars to the Saints' 41. Two seconds remained.

Time for a Hail Mary, which fell harmlessly to the turf. End of game.

"To come out and lose a ball game like that is horrible," Dana Hall said. "Every guy needs to look in the mirror and regroup. We should win these games."

In a season of bizarre losses, this was the most so. All four losses had been decided in the fourth quarter, but none quite like this. The Jaguars outgained the Saints 382-197, had 70 offensive plays to 47 for the Saints, and held the ball for 37:19 to 22:41. The Jaguars had 22 first downs; the Saints, 11.

"The New Orleans game was a disgusting game," John Jurkovic said. "We had played good defensively, and then we gave up a drive. When we had to stop them one more time, we couldn't."

The Jaguars were 2–4, in fourth place in the AFC Central. The Steelers hadn't lost since the opener, and were 4–1, a game ahead of Houston and two games ahead of Cincinnati. Coughlin, furious, launched into a postgame tirade so loud it was heard through the locker-room walls and into the hollow cement halls of the cavernous Superdome. "How could you come over here and lose to this team?" Coughlin screamed.

His players wanted to know, too.

"We have to live in misery for some godly reason," Searcy said.

"This one will hurt," Stewart said. "This is heart-wrenching, because this is a game we should have won."

Shoulda, woulda, coulda. The Jaguars had said these words how many times? The search for answers continued—and Rison decided this was a time to start offering his opinions on the problems. He began the next day.

Rison pulled a hamstring and missed much of the Saints game. This was particularly frustrating because he was learning the offense and the team planned for him to have a major role against the Saints.

"I would have caught 13 or 14 balls," he said later.

"That's not too far off," Kevin Gilbride said.

Irritated, Rison decided to hold court. What was happening was inexcusable, Rison felt.

His teammates thought so, too.

Rison, known as a cocky flake, was more. He was adept at getting a message to his teammates, and on the Monday following the Saints loss, he wanted to use the media as a motivational tool. Many Mondays, he skipped interview time, napping in a players-only room off the locker room. Typically, if the media needed Rison on Mondays, public relations representative Dave Auchter tried to wake Rison, with varying degrees of success.

On this Monday, he was ready and waiting.

The locker-room scene was far from the despondency of the day before in New Orleans. Players were relaxed. Many younger players were as interested in the new John Madden Football '97 game for Sony Playstation as they were preparing for the afternoon's meetings. The Madden game was a favorite among players, and on the morning after the Saints game, Willie Jackson and Randy Jordan sat just in front of Rison's locker, playing the game on a TV in the main locker room.

Rison sat just behind, surrounded by reporters and

cameramen jockeying for position around the video-playing players, stretching to hear Rison's words. As in New England three weeks before, Rison was irritated at the coaching staff for emphasizing the quality of the Jaguars' opponent.

"If you go in there saying, "We're going to beat them," we're beat them," Rison said. "I would love for our whole team to have the confidence I have, because we have the talent. The leaders of this team have to stay strong like a tight-knit group, and not let the bows and arrows [of the media] come in this building, and tear us apart.

"We knew they were 0–5, but the coaches preached to us they were a better team than their record. We gave them too much credit instead of saying, 'The hell with the Saints. They're 0–5. Let's make them 0–6.' From Day One, after we beat Carolina, we should have said, 'We're going to New Orleans to kick their asses.' Instead, we went down there saying: 'Well, they're better than 0–5.' "

The urgency was shared. The September inconsistency had confused Coughlin. Now, it was an obsession. "I'm concerned we don't have a level of performance, a level of intensity, and just stay there," Coughlin said. "My concern is the consistency thing. Back and forth, back and forth. It's a concern to all of us.

"Monday is a tough day when you don't win. And it better be for them, too. Their guts better be aching, just like ours, because it's not any fun when you put yourself in a position where you can win, where you should win and you don't."

Another season-long concern—playing up or down to the level of the opponent—also was turning into a trend. "We've been on a roller-coaster ride," Natrone Means said. "If you're going to be one of the good teams, you have to be able to get here, and stay here. It's a matter of being consistent, and we haven't been. If we play an 0–5 team, we play like we're 0–5. Sometimes we come out and play like gangbusters. We say, 'This is who we are, and this is what we're about.' Then, we take steps back. We show we can play with anybody. It's just a matter of us playing at that level all the time."

"We need to set our own level," Ben Coleman said. "That's what we're searching for. Once we find that, then we can do that on a consistent basis, but right now, we question what level we can play at. The sky's the limit, but we just haven't done it week in and week out."

The next game would test that. Even a team adept at playing to its level of competition would have a hard time doing that against the Jaguars' next opponent, the New York Jets. The Jets were 0–6, and had lost 19 of 22 over two seasons. The Jets weren't a team the Jaguars should beat, but one they needed to beat.

Knowing that, Coughlin chose the day before the Jets game to reach into the world of his players—a world that, at the time, he knew was troubled. The day before the Jets game, Coughlin—sensing his players needed to know him and needed a lift—joined his players for doughnuts.

"Thank goodness he did that," one coach said later. "The players needed that. They didn't know him. He had to let them see another side of him. It was a good thing he did, reaching out to them."

Coughlin reached, but at first, his players didn't reach back. The players left him that first day he approached them in the locker room, and the next day they hardly played like a team ready to break free from a pattern of inconsistency.

The Jaguars were 2–4, but against the Jets they were favored by 8½ points, most in franchise history. The Jets were a wrecked franchise. After spending $70 million on free agents in the off-season, they were winless, and fans were calling for coach Rich Kotite's job. Their quarterback, Neil O'Donnell, had signed a five-year, $25 million contract, but would miss the Jaguars game with a shoulder injury sustained the previous week. Starting against the Jaguars would be Frank Reich, a career backup. True to the Jaguars' form in 1996, the backup played like an All-Pro.

At first, in front of 65,699 at JMS, it seemed the Jets were what everyone anticipated—the lowly, awful Jets. Randy Jordan returned the opening kickoff 73 yards to the Jets' 22. After that, however, the Jaguars became the typical early-season Jaguars. Given an opportunity, they failed to take advantage. Stewart ran for 2 yards. Brunell threw incomplete, then was forced to run for 3 yards. Opportunity wasted. Hollis's 35-yard field goal gave the Jaguars a 3–0 lead with 13:25 remaining in the first quarter.

Two drives later, Reich gave the Jets a lead, passing for a 14-yard touchdown to running back Adrian Murrell with 6:43 remaining in the first quarter. On their next drive, the Jets again drove through the Jaguars' defense, and with 14:52 remaining in the second quarter, Reich passed 12 yards for a touchdown to Wayne Chrebet. Jets 14, Jaguars 3.

This, in the wake of the Saints loss, infuriated players and coaches, but for the first time in team history, the fans were disgusted, too. Boos were heard in the first two years, but nothing like the heartfelt boos the defense heard after Chrebet's touchdown. The offense was received no better.

The Jaguars had produced 14 yards. The NFL's worst team was handling the Jaguars. In their stadium.

The Jaguars needed a big play. They got it from their top draft choice.

With 11 minutes remaining in the second quarter, the Jets faced third-and-13 from their 43. Reich passed, and

Kevin Hardy intercepted, returning it 13 yards to the Jets' 37. The Jaguars drove 15 yards in seven plays, and Hollis's 40-yard field goal with 7:27 remaining in the second quarter made it 14–6, Jets.

The Jets punted, and after the Jaguars took possession at their 7, Brunell produced the longest, biggest play of his career—a bomb to Jimmy Smith. Smith caught the pass at the Jaguars' 44, and ran 25 more yards to the Jets' 31. Four plays later, Brunell passed 15 yards for a touchdown to Smith, who beat rookie Ray Mickens on a fade in the back left corner of the end zone with 1:51 remaining. Brunell then completed a two-point conversion pass to McCardell. Jaguars 14, Jets 14.

The second half was less eventful. With 6:19 remaining in the third quarter, Brunell threw a 10-yard slant-in to Willie Jackson, who turned it into a 41-yard catch-and-run touchdown. Jaguars 21, Jets 14.

The Jets made it 21–17 with a 20-yard field goal by Nick Lowery with 10:59 remaining in the fourth quarter. After that, they twice missed chances to make it closer or take the lead. Lowery missed a 36-yard field goal with 4:13 remaining, and on the Jets' final drive they moved to the Jaguars' 31 with just over a minute remaining. Reich threw four consecutive incomplete passes.

The Jaguars had escaped—all that could be said for the day. Stewart carried 12 times for 55 yards. Brunell had one of his best games of the early season, completing 14 of 23 passes for 248 yards and two touchdowns with no interceptions. Smith, too, was emerging as a surprise player, and against the Jets, he had his first career 100-yard receiving game—five receptions for 135 yards and a touchdown.

The game, though, was too close—not only for the fans, but for the players. The defense allowed Chrebet a career game—12 receptions for 162 yards—and at times, made Reich look like a Pro Bowl player. He completed 23 of 42 for 276 yards and two touchdowns. The Jaguars, though, had won, and seemed to have new life. They were 3–4, a half game ahead of the Bengals and the Ravens, still trailing the Steelers (5–1) and the Oilers (4–2).

"It wasn't pretty," Wayne Weaver said, hugging Coughlin afterward, "but we'll take it."

Nothing was uglier to Coughlin than the Jaguars' continued penalty problems—15 for 123 yards against the Jets, including a holding penalty on Brian DeMarco that negated their prettiest play of the season to date—an 86-yard touchdown pass from Brunell to Smith.

The Jaguars led the NFL in penalties: 73 for 636 yards. The issue became such a hot topic that Coughlin's wife, Judy, offered advice. Coughlin reviewed game tape each week, sending the NFL a list of questionable calls for review. The practice was encouraged by league rules. In theory, Judy wondered if the league's referees weren't punishing her husband for it. "My wife said, 'You better stop sending that in.'" Coughlin said. "I can't tell you there isn't a little retaliation for sending it in sometimes."

Even in victory, the Jaguars felt persecuted, and even victories hardly seemed like victories in what had become another long, frustrating month.

10
OCTOBER STRUGGLES II

"We don't know him [Coughlin]. There's a relationship, but there's an intimidating relationship. . . . There's no love. It's like we're scared."

—ANDRE RISON
October 27, 1996

$\mathbb{J}$acksonville Municipal Stadium was an unhappy place in mid-October 1996. Players were frustrated, unsure why success was sporadic. Days before, players had walked away from Tom Coughlin, and if players were upset, fans were irate.

The off-season acquisitions meant lofty expectations, and the Jaguars had improved drastically—everywhere but the record. They were the NFL's No. 28 offense in 1995. After seven games of 1996, they were No. 4, No. 1 in passing. Still, in October, the hot topic wasn't the wonderful offense, but the College Coach and his Run-and-Shoot Offensive Coordinator.

"When is Kevin Gilbride going to realize this isn't Pop Warner?" reader Mike Mayland wrote in the *Florida*

Times-Union's "Monday Morning Quarterback" column the day following the Jets victory.

"The coaching is the worst in the NFL," reader Terry L. Martin added. "Inane play calling with no discipline will lead to losses every time. Let's get smart and get rid of Coughlin and Gilbride. Coughlin was just a so-so coach at Boston College, and we know Gilbride's problems in Houston."

The "Monday Morning Quarterback," at first, was noticed little each week. In the first season, with criticism from fans and media rare, the feature's comments were tame—and players rarely mentioned it. In the second year, with the losses, the Jaguars became more sensitive.

The criticism wasn't fierce—Jacksonville is a small market, and with few exceptions, the media were among the NFL's least critical—but criticism was growing. The "Monday Morning Quarterback," which some players considered an avenue for "ignorant" fans to voice unwarranted criticism, added tension.

Jaguars players weren't thrilled with the four-point victory over the Jets, but they were surprised reaction was so negative.

"The Jaguars are a sorrily coached 'Gang' (not team) of expensive babies who make All-Stars of the league's worst every week—my tickets are for sale cheap," reader Carroll G. Teague wrote.

"With Gilbride at the controls, he is trying to better his own welfare rather than the team's," reader Bill Urbanski wrote. "Coach Coughlin is blind to this fact because he doesn't know enough about running a team to begin with. You can see this in his or Gilbride's play calling. Coughlin can't motivate himself, let alone a team. It's time for a change. The talent is there, but the coaching isn't. Jacksonville deserves better than this garbage."

Gilbride had built his reputation in Houston with the

run-and-shoot. Once trendy, by 1996, it had lost its luster. When Jaguars fans had a criticism of the offense, usually it was Gilbride and the run-and-shoot reputation they mentioned. The run-and-shoot, detractors said, had trouble in the red zone, and now, the Jaguars were struggling there, which loudened the criticism of Gilbride. "I guess they're not happy with the No. 2–ranked offense," Gilbride said, sarcastically. "The improvement is so mind-boggling—it's unbelievable. I don't think anyone in their right mind could have anticipated that kind of improvement, but the bottom line is they'd all trade any of those numbers for a few W's."

And it was hard to find fault in the coaching of the Jaguars' offense. The fans' criticisms, in essence, was this: Too conservative. No imagination. Not wide-open enough.

The run-and-shoot—not *wide-open* enough?

The run-and-shoot was an innovative, imaginative offense that revolutionized NFL passing. If Jaguars fans thought the Jaguars too conservative, the run-and-shoot hardly could be blamed.

Jaguars players were incredulous. Mistakes, they felt, not play calling, caused the struggles. Play calling didn't explain losing to New Orleans, or the too-close victory over the Jets. Or close losses to Houston, New England, and Oakland in September

"I'm annoyed by it," Mark Brunell said. "I don't understand why people have problems with our play calling. That's not close to being our problem. Good offensive teams find a way to make the play work no matter what play is called."

Such was the burden of expectations. The Jaguars were 3–4 and their offense was producing yards in a way they couldn't imagine a year before. They were competitive, and with a few breaks, could have been 7–0. Instead, JMS was an unhappy place in mid-October 1996.

The Jaguars' October 20 game was to change the mood. The site was the Trans World Dome in St. Louis, and Jeff Lageman—a spiritual leader on the defense—would return after missing four games. The opponent was the Rams, considered a playoff contender before the season, but now struggling worse than the Jaguars at 1–5.

Their quarterback from the previous season, Chris Miller, had retired because of repeated concussions, and two games into the season, coach Rich Brooks benched his replacement, Steve Walsh. That left rookie Tony Banks starting, and Banks wasn't ready in his first four starts. He wasn't ready for the Jaguars, and neither were the Rams. The Jaguars and Rams played in front of 60,066, and rarely in NFL history has one team so dominated another.

The Jaguars produced a team-record 538 yards offense. The Rams had 204.

The Jaguars produced a team-record 36 first downs. The Rams had nine.

The Jaguars had possession 41:34. The Rams had it 18:26.

Mistakes again hurt the Jaguars. Brunell, who never had thrown two interceptions in a game, threw five—all inside the Rams' 15. Rams cornerback Anthony Parker returned one 92 yards for a touchdown with 9:20 remaining in the first quarter, and the Rams' other touchdown came on a 29-yard third-quarter pass from Banks to rookie wide receiver Eddie Kennison with 6:44 remaining in the third quarter.

The Rams' other points came on a 25-yard field goal by Chip Lohmiller, set up by the Jaguars' sixth turnover, a fumble by returner Kendricke Bullard. That field goal came with 6:08 remaining in the first quarter, and gave the Rams a 10–0 lead and a momentum advantage the Jaguars spent the rest of the game trying to eliminate.

In the second quarter, the Jaguars took possession at their 29 after a Rams punt with 14:03 remaining. On the first play, Brunell passed to McCardell on a play that worked all day with record success—a slant for 13 yards. The Jaguars moved easily, with Brunell passing twice more to McCardell for 15 and 7 yards. The last pass to McCardell gave the Jaguars a first down at the Rams' 1. Stewart ran for a touchdown on the next play. Rams 10, Jaguars 7.

The Jaguars took a 14–10 lead when James Stewart scored on an 8-yard run—his second touchdown of the game—with 11:26 remaining in the third quarter. This was a rare Jaguars drive on this day that produced points. The Jaguars had seven drives of more than 50 yards but continually stalled in Rams territory. The long drives shortened the game, and with 2:38 remaining, the Jaguars trailed, 17–14.

The offense, again struggling in the two-minute drill, needed 1:44 to move from their 6 to their 34, where they faced second-and-five with 54 seconds and two time-outs remaining. Brunell passed 22 yards to Keenan McCardell for a first down at the Rams' 44 and 42 seconds remaining. Jaguars time-out. A pass from Brunell to Andre Rison gained 5 yards, after which the Jaguars used their final time-out with 26 seconds remaining.

With 22 seconds remaining, after an incomplete pass, Brunell threw to Willie Jackson on a slant pattern. Jackson broke free from Rams cornerback Jeremy Lincoln and headed for the end zone. Rams cornerback Todd Lyght, however, caught Jackson from behind at the 5 with 14 seconds remaining.

"I felt I was going to score," Jackson said. "I just knew

the one guy was going to tackle me, but when I broke the tackle, I thought I was home free. I didn't see the guy [Lyght] until late, but I didn't turn up the speed until it was too late."

The clock ran.

The Jaguars rushed to the line of scrimmage. Jackson dropped the ball rather than hand it to an official, and officials had to retrieve it, using valuable seconds. The Jaguars lined up, intending for Brunell to spike the ball to stop the clock in time for a field-goal attempt. Center Dave Widell pulled the ball from the hands of the referee, who took it back.

"No, no, no," he told Widell.

Widell finally got the ball, but the Jaguars failed to get off a play. That's what the officials ruled—eventually. Before that final ruling, there was controversy. Several players said back judge Tim Millis told them there would be one more play. Many players already were leaving the field, but Coughlin—told what Millis had told the players—brought the team back.

"I was told there would be one more play," Coughlin said.

The officials continued to huddle, finally getting away from yelling Jaguars players, and ruled the game over. Rison chased Millis into the tunnel, shouting, "This game is not over!"

"That was home cooking," Searcy said. "He was afraid to make the right call in St. Louis. I don't know if he was afraid of getting attacked after the game or what."

Searcy wasn't alone in his anger. The postgame locker room was as intense as any in team history, with players shouting at media, directing their aggression in that direction. "We were screwed," Tony Boselli said. "Put that in the paper. We were 100 percent screwed."

The offensive linemen who minutes before shouted at

officials continued venting at reporters. As they did, from one side, Rison—until now sitting quietly in full uniform in front of his locker—began to talk loudly.

"Tell 'em the real story, Dave," came Rison's voice. He was speaking to Widell, and continued, "Tell 'em how the officials lied to me—just flat out lied to my face. That official told me we would have one more play, then he took it away. You heard him, didn't you, Dave? Everybody heard him. It's a damned joke. I wanted to hit him."

The controversy overshadowed a game best described as bizarre—a fifth loss in a season that could also best be described as bizarre. The Jaguars dominated, and lost. The passing offense, effective all season, was dominating besides Brunell's interceptions. Stewart had his best NFL game, rushing for 112 yards and 2 touchdowns on 29 carries. Brunell completed 37 of 52 passes for 421 yards, but led drive after drive inside the 20 with no touchdown passes, and five interceptions. "He's down on himself," Searcy said of Brunell, "but I told him, he gave us the opportunity to come back, and that's all we can ask for. I told him to keep his head up."

"I feel real responsible for this one," a testy Brunell said afterward. "A quarterback's job is not to throw interceptions, and those took place."

On another side of the locker room, a player sat answering questions about a performance lost in the controversy, a performance that nearly put him in the NFL record books.

McCardell had caught 16 passes for 232 yards. The receptions were two shy of an NFL record for a single game. The yardage was the most any receiver would have in a game all season. The loss, McCardell said, ruined all that.

"My job is to go out and catch the ball," he said. "It was just another day at the office."

* * *

Keenan Wayne McCardell was born January 6, 1970, in Houston, Texas. He played football and basketball, and ran track at Waltrip High School in Houston, but few thought McCardell's football career would get even that far.

McCardell's story was one of perseverance, one of work making a dream come true. "That boy did it the hard way," Elton Conger, an assistant at Waltrip, once said.

McCardell—then thin and small—didn't make the Waltrip junior varsity team as a ninth grader. The varsity coach at Waltrip thought he was too small, and kept him off the jayvee team until late in the season.

In that off-season, McCardell grew, and he started at wide receiver as a junior and senior. After his senior year, he and Conger drove to Prairie View A&M University— Conger's alma mater and that of McCardell's father, Arthur—in Prairie View, Texas, for a basketball game. At the game, Conger introduced McCardell to Conway Hammond, then Prairie View's football coach, and C. L. Whittington, the team's defensive coordinator. "They looked at Keenan, and looked at me like I was crazy," Conger said.

Conger told the men he had secured a grant for McCardell, and they wouldn't even have to give him a scholarship if they wanted him. Sorry, they said. On the drive home, McCardell "shook it off, like he always did" when disappointed, Conger said. "You know something about Keenan?" Conger said. "The man upstairs must be working for him because every time he falls flat on his face, he lands in a better place than he left."

The place was the University of Nevada at Las Vegas. A UNLV assistant came to Waltrip the summer after McCardell's senior year. The coach watched film and offered scholarships to two players named Damon Kenner and Jason Davis. Bill Barron, Waltrip's coach, told him about McCardell. "He said, 'Well, if I don't get this kid in Detroit, I'll come down and sign Keenan,'" the assistant said. The kid from Detroit said no. A day later, UNLV signed McCardell, who became the school's all-time leading receiver.

The Washington Redskins drafted McCardell in the 12th round in 1991 after 335 players were chosen. He spent that season on injured reserve, then signed with Cleveland as a Plan B free agent. The Browns released McCardell three times that year, re-signing him to their practice squad each time. The next year, they released him again. This time, they didn't re-sign him.

Six weeks later, he signed with the Chicago Bears, who placed him on the practice squad. Three weeks after that, he re-signed with the Browns. This time, they didn't release him.

McCardell caught one pass for 8 yards in 1992, and 13 for 234 yards and four touchdowns in 1993, his second season with the Browns. He caught 10 passes in 1994 for 182 yards, but in 1995, he emerged as one of the NFL's up-and-coming receivers, catching 56 passes for 809 yards and four touchdowns. He became a free agent after that season, signing with the Jaguars, the first team in his career that really wanted him. This was his chance to show he belonged, to be an integral member of a team. He became a team leader and a trusted player on third-and-long situations.

He wasn't a blazing deep threat and didn't score many touchdowns, but he was a reason the Jaguars' offense was vastly improved—evidenced by 16 receptions and 232 yards against the Rams. He led his new team with 55 receptions for 727 yards and two touchdowns.

"It's about what kind of heart you've got," McCardell

said. "This, being in the NFL, is something I had to earn, and I did earn. It's a big part of my life—knowing I earned an opportunity to play in this league. Every time I go out on the field, I remember where I came from and what it took for me to get where I needed to be."

The Jaguars could be thankful for one thing as they left St. Louis. They wouldn't play in a dome for two months. The Rams game was a second Dome Debacle in three weeks—no player on the team remembered being on a team that had so dominated two opponents in so brief a time and lost. The mood was sullen again, angry. A season was slipping away, and players didn't know why.

The offense was powerful, the defense was stopping opponents, but always, it seemed, a mistake, a turnover, a penalty, an official's call. . . .

The Jaguars Jinx reappeared in a new, stranger form almost weekly.

Since beating Pittsburgh, the Jaguars had lost five of seven games, with the only highlight being the adrenaline-packed home victory over the Panthers. The Jaguars were 3–5, and what followed the St. Louis loss was a week preparing for a road game against the Cincinnati Bengals—the most tension-filled week in the team's brief history.

Brunell was again the target of criticism, and was testy. Asked after the St. Louis game if he recalled a game as weird, one in which his team had so dominated and lost.

"New Orleans 1996," he said, curtly.

His mood got no better the following night. Lex and Terry—the same two disc jockeys who gave away the Beuerlein jerseys to the homeless—turned their wits on Brunell, sending one of their assistants to his weekly television show. The assistant carried a box of six jelly-filled "turnovers," one for each of Brunell's interceptions, and another for the fumbled kickoff.

The audience laughed. Brunell didn't. Upon receiving the box, he looked unamused. Forcing a smile, he threw one of the turnovers at the assistant. The assistant threw it back, getting jelly on Brunell's shirt. That set the tone for the week.

Fans, by now, were near mutiny. "The Jacksonville Jugheads should be arrested for impersonating a professional football team," reader Tony Fleming wrote in the "Monday Morning Quarterback."

"Mr. Weaver, wake up," reader Linda Brim advised. "You need to consider the fact that coach Coughlin, as good a friend as he may be, is not a proven coach. Mark Brunell is putting up impressive numbers, but is he color blind?"

Added reader Pete Ratto, "When the pressure isn't on, Mark Brunell is a fine quarterback. Come crunch time, when it counts, CHOKE." That morning, as Coughlin readied for his Monday press conference, a fan marched outside JMS with a bag over his head, holding a sign. "Coughlin Must Go."

Again, Rison tried to provide a lift. The locker room was quiet and depressed the morning after the Rams game. In contrast to the scene after New Orleans, when the team considered the loss a fluke, players were concerned. A few spoke quietly with the media, but generally, the room was empty. And then Rison's voice was heard.

He appeared in a doorway on one end of the room, fresh from a nap. Disheveled, he looked at the gathered media and began to shout.

"I guarantee you we beat Cincinnati! Write that in your papers."

He wasn't finished. He left, then quickly reentered. "I

know you all know the referees cheated us," he yelled, referring to the end of the Rams game.

He left, then entered again, this time with the Bengals still on his mind. He repeated the guarantee, saying the Jaguars would win in the Bengals' "crib." When he finished, there were a few more smiles in the room.

Smiles, otherwise, were scarce that week. A repeat of a 4–12 season seemed more and more a possibility. Some players decided something—anything—must be done. That meant a meeting with the boss. Not Coughlin.

The other boss, Wayne Weaver.

Throughout the first season and a half, players routinely visited Weaver, who had an open-door policy. And unlike Coughlin, not only was Weaver's door always open, his mind was, too. It was part of his business philosophy to listen to employees. This week, he listened to six or seven of his employees discuss Coughlin.

Coughlin had changed since 1995. Practices were easier, and rules were less strict, but it hadn't been enough. Morale was as low as the victory total, and players felt further change was needed. They told Weaver this. "I wanted to know what was on their minds," Weaver said later. "I wanted to hear from them in a candid environment. In all those conversations, I didn't hear criticism of Tom Coughlin the man. I heard, 'Boy, it would be nice if we didn't work so hard on Friday, if we didn't beat ourselves up.'"

Weaver was concerned. He believed in Coughlin, and believed discipline and order was the right way. Yet, he had built his fortune listening to employees, and his employees were sending a clear message. Weaver, team sources said later, spoke to Coughlin that week, suggesting he reach out to his players, lighten practice, and let them see the personal side. "He got it from above," a coach said later.

Weaver denied such a pointed discussion occurred, as did Coughlin. "Tom and I always have had honest conversations about how things go," Weaver said.

The Jaguars traveled to Cincinnati with Weaver backing his coaching staff. Anything else would have been shortsighted, he felt, and untrue to the self-imposed three-year plan. An hour before kickoff that Sunday, while eating a hot dog in the press box at Cinergy Field and watching the team warm up, he discussed his coaches.

"I'm extremely pleased. Tom is a brilliant X's and O's coach. I think it's all coming together."

Asked about the fans' impatience, particularly the bag-headed fan, he said, "I think that's an uneducated fan. How do you move the football the way we do and blame Tom Coughlin? That's plain dumb.

"The season is going well," he continued. "It's been up and down. We're still making mistakes, but, overall, I'm pleased. In terms of talent and being competitive, we're probably ahead of schedule. We just haven't played well together. It's frustrating to a layperson like myself to understand why we haven't been winning. When you start off the way we started off, really dominating a team like Pittsburgh, all of our expectations were probably higher than they should be.

"The way I look at it is it's a young team. It's not that these guys have a lack of discipline in knowing what they're doing. They're uptight, and they're learning to play together. I think too many times we've been playing not to lose versus to win. When you do that, you make more mistakes. We proved that we have a football team that can be competitive. You can play all the what-if games and their team could be 5–3 easily.

"So, I think now what we have is a new season. We

Jaguars Coach Tom Coughlin. Took the job in 1994 and three years later had his team in the AFC championship game

Courtesy of Jacksonville Jaguars, Ltd.

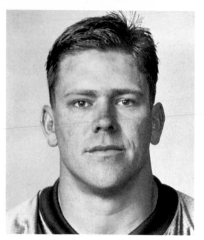

Mark Brunell. The Franchise
Courtesy of Jacksonville Jaguars, Ltd.

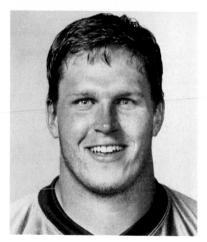

Tony Boselli. Team's first ever draft pick
Courtesy of Jacksonville Jaguars, Ltd.

Kevin Hardy. Second overall pick in 1996
Courtesy of Jacksonville Jaguars, Ltd.

Tom McManus. Former bartender who went on to be the team's starting middle linebacker
Courtesy of Jacksonville Jaguars, Ltd.

Dave Thomas. His injury, a fractured femur, helped change Coughlin
Courtesy of Jacksonville Jaguars, Ltd.

Jeff Lageman. Key
early free-agent
acquisition who
became a team leader
Courtesy of Jacksonville
Jaguars, Ltd.

Keenan McCardell.
His 16 receptions for
232 yards against the
Rams were NFC in 1996
Courtesy of Jacksonville
Jaguars, Ltd.

Clyde Simmons. 1996 free-agent acquisition who was the first to believe this team could make the playoffs
Courtesy of Jacksonville Jaguars, Ltd.

Brunell. His dramatic improvement in 1996 mirrored the team's rise
Rick Wilson, *The Florida Times-Union*

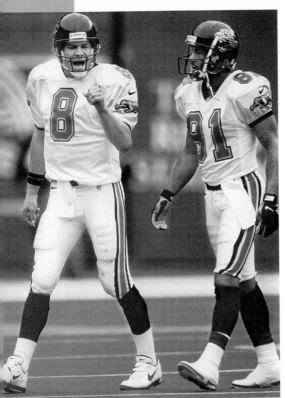

Brunell and wide receiver Andre Rison. Brunell chastises Rison for a wrong route in Pittsburgh. The next day Rison was released
Rick Wilson, *The Florida Times-Union*

Jimmy Smith. After Rison's release, Smith emerged and led the AFC in receiving yards
Rick Wilson, *The Florida Times-Union*

Morten Andersen's missed 30-yard field goal put the Jaguars in the playoffs
Rick Wilson, *The Florida Times-Union*

Tony Boselli v. Bruce Smith in playoff victory over Buffalo. Boselli dominated Smith, giving him national recognition
Rick Wilson, *The Florida Times-Union*

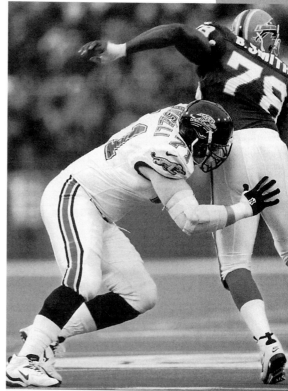

Natrone Means ran for 175 yards in the
upset victory over Buffalo
Rick Wilson, *The Florida Times-Union*

Don Davey, Keenan McCardell, and Travis Davis greet
some of the 46,000 who packed JMS at 1:00 A.M. after
the upset of Denver
Rick Wilson, *The Florida Times-Union*

End of a dream. Boselli walks dejectedly from the field while Leon Searcy hangs his head late in the loss to the Patriots in Foxboro
Rick Wilson, *The Florida Times-Union*

have eight games to play. I think we're going to win a lot of football games the second half of the season."

Early against the Bengals, in front of 45,890, it seemed the winning would start immediately. October road games had had a pattern. The Jaguars played well early, but didn't score to take advantage of it. Against the Bengals, they played well, and it was the same story. Neither team scored in the first quarter, and finally, late in the quarter, the Jaguars began to drive. After an 11-play drive, with 12:30 remaining in the second quarter, Brunell scrambled 11 yards for a touchdown. Jaguars 7, Bengals 0.

The Jaguars' defense, tough until the offense scored, then allowed the Bengals to drive. Jeff Blake passed 11 yards to Carl Pickens, tying it 7–7. That's how the half ended.

The Jaguars' defense, however, was strong. Besides the Blake-to-Pickens touchdown, the defensive line was beating on Blake, and would sack him five times, eventually knocking him from the game. While the defense held, the offense was sporadic, but late in the third quarter, the Jaguars drove 75 yards on seven plays. With 2:41 remaining in the third quarter, Natrone Means scored the first touchdown of his Jaguars career, an 11-yard pass from Brunell.

Jaguars 14, Bengals 7.

A pattern inexplicable to Coughlin then continued— the Jaguars squandered a fourth-quarter lead. This time, they lost it early. The Bengals drove late in the third quarter, with Blake completing passes despite the punishment. On the first play of the fourth quarter, he capped a six-play, 67-yard drive by passing to Pickens for a 10-yard touchdown and a 14–14 tie. Both teams then failed to move, but the Bengals again pushed toward the goal line midway through the quarter, scoring on a 1-yard run by Ki-Jana Carter with 6:10 remaining.

Bengals 21, Jaguars 14.

The Jaguars still had a chance. They weren't excelling in the two-minute drill, but with six minutes remaining, that wasn't a factor. Plenty of time remained, but on the first play after the kickoff, Brunell's pass was deflected at the line of scrimmage, and bounced high in the air. Bengals safety Bo Orlando made a diving interception at the Jaguars' 22. Jeff Lageman knocked Blake from the game on the ensuing series, but a few plays after that, Carter knocked the Jaguars out of the game, scoring on a 4-yard run. Bengals 28, Jaguars 14.

The Jaguars outgained the Bengals, 338–267, and had more first downs, 19–16. They outrushed the Bengals 149–60. Again, none of it mattered—not on the road in October of 1996.

The Jaguars did drive 79 yards on nine plays on the ensuing series, with Jimmy Smith catching an 11-yard pass from Brunell to make it 28–21, but 1:35 remained afterward, meaning if the Jaguars didn't recover the onside kick, the Bengals would win.

The Jaguars, in their brief history, had had an uncanny knack for recovering onside kicks. Much of the success was because of Dave Thomas, an athletic, physical player who outmuscled opponents for loose balls. In Week 2, when the Jaguars recovered an onside kick against the Oilers, Mike Hollis bounced the kick and a wall of Jaguars players blocked the Houston recovery team, allowing Thomas to leap and recover. The Jaguars tried the same tactic against Cincinnati, but three defenders hit Thomas. Dana Hall, lined up next to Thomas, sensed the collision, and stuck a shoulder in to protect Thomas. A loud, sickening crack was heard throughout the stadium.

The Bengals recovered. As players unpiled, Thomas and Hall lay motionless. Ten minutes passed. Then five more. Players from each team stood near, silent.

Included in the group was Bengals coach Bruce Coslet, who stood near Jeff Lageman and Paul Frase. This was a frightening déjà vu for the group, who as Jets players and coach five years before had watched Dennis Byrd lie paralyzed in a similar circumstance.

One person not on the field was Coughlin.

This disturbed many Jaguars players. "He's gotta go out there," one player said to a coach on the sideline. "He's gotta go out there. What's he doing? He's gotta go out there."

Finally, he did, and a few minutes later, Thomas left on a stretcher. Minutes later, so did Hall. The Bengals ran out the clock. Any player thinking Coughlin was unconcerned about the injured players need only have seen him minutes later, as he spoke with the media. Visibly shaken, he said the game was unimportant, and that all that mattered was the health of Thomas and Hall.

At last, Coughlin spoke of the game, saying, "I told the players as we prayed in the locker room that we pray for Dana and Dave, but we also need to find the courage to win a ball game when it's on the line."

Coughlin considered the statement an important message, and said later it was the first time he had spoken to Jaguars players in such a way. Players didn't understand.

"I don't know what that statement means," Ben Coleman said. "Maybe he does. Maybe that's beyond my comprehension a little bit. Find the courage to win. I don't know what that means. We just have to win."

Coughlin's courage statement did nothing to lessen the rift between him and his team, which now was wider than ever before. Later, in the shower, two players were complaining about Coughlin. A teammate barely had time to warn them before Coughlin entered.

One player had no intention of keeping quiet on the matter of Coughlin. As the media entered the locker room, a reporter approached Rison's locker. Before the reporter could speak, Rison said, "You're not going to write the real story."

"What is it?" the reporter said.

"You know."

"What? I can't write it if you don't tell me."

"You won't write it. You know what it is."

This continued for several minutes before the reporter left to interview several other players. Soon he returned, and Rison continued, "You won't write the real story." Several teammates had joined Rison, and were agreeing with him. None of the others wanted to speak publicly, but to Rison's credit, he did.

The real story, the players said, was Coughlin.

"There's no love," Rison said. "We don't know him. There's a relationship, but there's so much of an intimidating relationship. It's almost like if I go out and do good, it ain't going to matter anyway. If I go out and do shitty, I might be gone. We have chatter among ourselves, but when we all group up, and we're surrounded by the generals who really run the ship, everybody condenses themselves. They go into a little box, and play tight. We play emotionless. We're going onto the field, and it's like we're playing X's and O's. We have no relationship with what's going on emotionwise. There's no love. It's like we're scared."

This was a low point. Players had said this, but never publicly. Instead of finishing October on a high, they were 3–6 with a bye week now—two weeks to sort the mess that had become the 1996 season.

11
AN UNLIKELY LEADER

"It doesn't matter if you're an offensive player or a defensive player, people cling to Andre. To many of us, he's a leader on and off the field."

—ROBERT MASSEY
November 1996

Jaguars players, at last, had reason to be happy Monday, October 28. The NFL had given them the final bye week, and after six losses in nine games, they needed rest. A day after the loss to the Bengals, players talked anxiously of getting a day or two to relax.

Relaxing for Coughlin wasn't easy with Andre Rison around. Rison, as he had promised, had been tamer than with previous teams, but a coach was never sure what he would say. Unlike the incident in New England, or the comparatively mild comments following the New Orleans loss, it would be hard for Coughlin to ignore his comments in Cincinnati. These were directly about Coughlin, and they were on the sports front of that morning's *Florida Times-Union*.

151

At last, the rebel and the taskmaster were clashing.

As players arrived at the stadium that morning, they wondered . . .

Would Rison be released? Or fined? Would Coughlin, as in New England, ignore the issue? This was what the media wondered, too, awaiting Coughlin's Monday press conference. Coughlin handled these as weekly State of the Jaguars addresses. Films were reviewed by now, and during game weeks, the task was to put to rest the previous game and set a theme for the following week. This morning, the only theme was Rison.

At 12:15, Coughlin strode into the room, stood behind the podium, and faced a cluster of cameras.

"With regard to the articles this morning in the newspaper, let me say, I'm the head coach of the Jacksonville Jaguars, and the blame for any loss goes directly on my shoulders, period," he said. "That's just the way it is. There's no passing the buck, pointing to players, coaches, or situations. It's my responsibility, and I accept it fully. It doesn't have to go any further than that. Secondly, we have a rule around here that indicates that I don't want people sending messages through the media. If someone has something to say, they're more than welcome to come down and spend time with me in private and tell me what their thoughts are, and I will respond."

Coughlin understood his players' feelings toward him, and he understood his change was taking time. Doughnuts only did so much, and he had only started sitting with the players on Saturdays three weeks before. He didn't expect players to accept the change immediately—and at 3–6, he expected raw nerves. Coughlin, however, believed nothing was gained talking about problems in the media.

What bothered Coughlin most was Rison's timing. Coughlin hadn't gone onto the field quickly the day before when the players were injured, but his voice afterward indicated he was shaken. Coughlin said the game meant nothing in the wake of the injuries—a major admission for a coach as obsessed with winning as Coughlin. Yet, moments after the players were wheeled away, Rison was in the locker room, spouting to the media about "no love."

"The issue wasn't that he said what he said," Coughlin said after the season. "That was out of place. There's a place for everything, but at that time, those two kids were laying right in that auxiliary room off the locker room."

Jaguars players were divided over whether Rison should have spoken at all. The losses were ridiculous, but a team divided? A team against its coach? "Nobody on this team questions each other," James Stewart said. "We still believe in each other. The coaches coach and we play. You can't fault anybody for what's going on. It's a team concept. We're all losing, and when we win, we're all going to win."

Don Davey agreed, saying, "Maybe I read the team differently, but I don't see something going wrong. That stuff happens when you lose. We're 3–6, and every team I've ever been on, when the teams start to lose, someone starts to point fingers, and someone starts spouting off. When you win, those things never come up."

The Jaguars weren't winning, and "those things" were coming up more and more.

The bye couldn't have come at a better time.

Coughlin, at last, had reason to be happy Monday, November 4, though optimism seemed illogical. Dave Thomas had remained in Cincinnati the previous Monday and undergone surgery on a broken left femur, and was out for the season. Aaron Beasley, a rookie, would start on the corner.

There was, however, good news. Dana Hall, also injured in Cincinnati, would play Sunday against the Baltimore Ravens in Jacksonville Municipal Stadium. Coughlin felt good about something else, too. He saw something in his team the week before. He saw life.

"When we got to the bye week, I laid out objectives and our guys practiced with great attitudes," Coughlin said after the season. "I'm looking at this thing and saying to myself, 'This is not a bunch of people who aren't interested in what they're doing here. These guys are excited, and they've got one thing in mind. They feel like they're pretty damned good out there. There's not anything to show for it, but they feel like they're pretty good.' That really picked me up. With the way that week went and the weekend off, I felt pretty good.

"I know the difference between a player and a coach. I know how players are, but I really felt the majority of the guys were serious. It was very important to them, and they were going to do whatever they could to straighten it out."

Two days after the players returned, bad moods did, too—as did a feeling that no matter what Coughlin did to change, maybe he couldn't. A chief complaint of players was Coughlin's insistence on practicing in pads with full contact. Many teams did this in training camp and early in the season, but most coaches lightened practices as the season continued to reduce wear on the body, and the chance of injuries.

On Wednesday, four days before the Ravens game, the Jaguars were running a nine-on-seven, full-contact drill when a practice-squad player fell on the left leg of Brian DeMarco—a durable player who had started all 25 Jaguars games.

The impact of the collision caused a slight tear of the medial collateral ligament, and word spread that De-

Marco was expected to miss at least a month. "Guys are pissed that it happened," one player said.

"Something like that shouldn't happen this late in the season," another said.

To Coughlin, football was contact—in practice or a game—and the only way to prepare was to hit. Asked if the injury might not have occurred had players not been in full pads, Coughlin said, "It doesn't make any difference. What are we going to do, stand around and play two-hand touch?"

A story on the matter appeared in the *Florida Times-Union* the next day. Coughlin, furious, asked players if the reporter or the players initiated the story. Players said the reporter pursued it. Coughlin stewed early that Friday, confronting the reporter in the locker room near noon. Coughlin pulled him aside, berating him near the area in which the receivers and running backs dressed.

The reporter and coach argued several minutes, and then Coughlin left. As he did, several players—mostly receivers—smiled and shook their heads.

"You got some, too?" Rison said to the reporter, laughing.

Rison laughed often that week, a week he had anticipated since the Ravens released him that summer. The previous off-season, he had signed a five-year, $17.075 million contract with the Browns—as the team was then known—that included a $6 million signing bonus. That money, he said, alienated him from his teammates.

"I was never received well in the locker room," he said. "They had a lot of jealous-head punks on the team who were more concerned with what I was taking home than what I was doing for the team. We're on the team together. They couldn't get that understanding. They were more, 'Here comes Andre Rison. Bad Moon. With a lot of

luggage.' What luggage do I got? You ain't seen no luggage down here since I've been here."

Rison, apparently forgetting the baggage left in Cincinnati two weeks before, also was angry at being blamed
for the Browns' problems that year. Owner Art Modell
said the 1995 move to Baltimore was necessary because
of his poor financial situation, much of which he blamed
on Rison's contract. "The finger was pointed at me,"
Rison said. "I don't think people knew how big that was.
I wasn't in the front office saying we're going to move. I
wasn't the one saying. 'We're going there.' I have to ride
the ship. Wherever the ship sails, I have to ride.

"I don't give a damn who you are. If you're Charles
Barkley. If you're Michael Jordan, or if you are God—
you'd be hurting. I'm not saying I'm God. Heck, a little
child would be hurt. Anybody would be hurt if you're not
wanted."

Rison eyed the game as an opportunity. "I've got my
mind back straight," he said. "I've got my priorities in
order. When they start throwing me the ball, you'll see
some big plays. I just have to get the ball."

Rison was cocky. He was ready. This would be his
breakout game. Finally.

Look at me. Look at me.

By now, Jaguars fans had heard those words again
and again. And again and again.

Andre Previn Rison was born March 18, 1967, in Flint,
Michigan. He attended Michigan State University, where,
despite a run-oriented offense, he became a first-round
draft choice of Indianapolis in 1989. He spent a year with
the Colts, who then traded him to the Falcons in a deal
that eventually sent the Colts the rights to quarterback
Jeff George.

Rison was an All-Rookie selection with Indianapolis,

but it was with the Falcons that his career—and his bad-boy reputation—developed.

He spent five seasons in Atlanta, catching 423 passes for 5,635 yards and 56 touchdowns and catching at least 81 passes each season. Only once in Atlanta did he not have at least 1,000 yards receiving. He reached 400 receptions faster than all but two players in NFL history, and set league records for most catches (308) in his first four seasons, and five seasons (394). He averaged 10 touchdowns a season in his first six seasons, the second-best ratio in NFL history. His numbers were those of a player potentially destined for the Hall of Fame.

In the 1995 off-season, he became a free agent, and was one of the market's most coveted players. Several teams, including the Green Bay Packers, Philadelphia Eagles, and Cleveland Browns, bid on him. He signed with Cleveland, where his career sustained a lull. He caught a career-low 47 passes for 701 yards and three touchdowns.

The Browns moved to Baltimore in the off-season. Once there, to alleviate salary-cap problems, they released Rison, who then signed with the Jaguars.

Rison arrived with his reputation tarnished by his subpar Cleveland season, and by a league-wide belief he was a "run-and-shoot" receiver, having had his best seasons in the oft-criticized offense in Atlanta. The run-and-shoot is pass-oriented, and many believe receivers' statistics in the scheme are less impressive than those of receivers in conventional offenses. His quest to prove his critics wrong obsessed Rison.

"I was made out to be a receiver who can't play in a certain style of offense," he said.

Particularly bothersome to Rison was a refusal by people to consider him at the same level as the receiver regarded as the best of all time, Jerry Rice of the 49ers.

Several weeks into 1996 training camp, discussing his statistics, Rison reached to a top shelf in his locker, shoved several items aside, and retrieved a stack of his football cards. Rison turned the cards to his statistics on the backs, pointing at them. "I got numbers," he said, cackling.

And he did. His receptions, yardage, and touchdowns were comparable to those of Rice from 1991 to 1994:

—Receptions; Rice, 374; Rison, 341.
—Yards: Rice, 5,409; Rison, 4,425.
—Touchdowns: Rice, 52; Rison, 46.

"I used to look at the numbers," Rison said. "I'd throw up Jerry's numbers, throw up Michael's [Irvin of the Dallas Cowboys] numbers and see where I would compare. I'm always there, but for some reason—I guess you could say in the writers' eyes—there's no way. My accomplishments have been thrown into the dirt. Jerry played with Joe Montana and the powerful 49ers. I played with the Atlanta Falcons. He had Ronnie Lott, along with four or five All-Pros on the defensive line to get him the ball back, and I had no All-Pros on the defensive line. I just had Deion [Sanders], and at one point, he [Rice] even had Deion.

"Those are a lot of intangibles that present you opportunity to catch the ball because you get the ball back. Then, you talk about the greatest quarterback, arguably of all time, in Joe Montana. Then, he leaves, you get MVP of the league at quarterback in Steve Young. I'm steady having makeshift quarterbacks. That adds up to him winning and me not. That's a big difference.

"What if me and Jerry had switched teams? Jerry would have those same numbers, even more probably, but I wonder if they would talk about him the way they talk about me. Would they throw his numbers in the dirt?

Probably not, yet for some reason I'm made out to be a villain, and I'm not."

One reason was that Rice was perceived as one of the NFL's classiest players. Rison's image was far from that. Throughout his career, he had bickered with coaches, complaining publicly about quarterbacks not throwing to him enough. Rison's personal life, too, caused image problems. He reveled in a street-tough, hood persona, hanging out with rap artists, and had produced a rap album on which he sang. His relationship with TLC singer Lisa "Left Eye" Lopes made national news in 1994 when she set fire to his house. They married two years later, in the summer of 1996. If Rison was made out to be a villain, he fostered much of the image.

His problems were more than image. He disdained discipline, and in his last season in Atlanta, he missed 19 team meetings. He missed the bus to the season opener, and did not start. His tardiness in Cleveland, too, was well documented.

The Jaguars' signing of Rison was easily questioned, and through 10 games, open to debate. He had caught 32 passes for 444 yards and two touchdowns, but hadn't made the impact Coughlin anticipated. Ironically, Rison made his biggest positive impact in Jacksonville not on the field, but in the locker room.

Rison, by Game 10, was a strange sort of team leader. Not all players loved his style, and many later said they were aware he was drinking and partying more than most players, but he brought a cocky, confident edge. This aura, from a four-time Pro Bowl player, earned respect from young players, as did speaking out in New England. Anyone standing up to Coughlin was OK by many veterans and rookies alike.

"Dre opened some eyes for everyone," Keenan McCardell said.

He was fined at least 30 times in his first three months with the Jaguars, but to write Rison and his words off as a bad boy and his drivel would be unfair. Part of Rison desperately wanted to win, and wanted to win because of strong feelings for his teammates. Those feelings overshadowed any ill feelings toward the front office and coach.

"A lot of people on this team look up to Andre," Jimmy Smith said.

"He's a guy who has had great success and who believes in himself," Coughlin said. "He's helped others believe in themselves. There's no question that has become a positive."

Andre Rison? Team unifier?

"It doesn't matter if you're an offensive player or a defensive player, people cling to Andre," Massey said. "To many of us, he's a leader on and off the field."

That was how it was on the Jaguars as Rison's ex-team came to town—Rison, troublemaking Andre Rison, was a team leader.

On November 10, 1996, Ravens players reading the *Times-Union* learned their team was full of "jealous-head punks." That's what their ex-teammate thought, anyway.

Rison provided the Ravens incentive. Not that they needed it. This was a matchup of two of the three last-place teams in the Central. Each was 3–6, as was Cincinnati. The Oilers were 5–4. All trailed the 7–2 Steelers. If the Jaguars or Ravens had a chance to catch the leaders, it had to start now.

The Ravens, too, had the incentive of pride, never having beaten the Jaguars. As the Browns, they lost twice to Jacksonville the previous season. Early on November 10, it appeared that would change.

First, the Ravens got an early laugh when a quick pass

from Brunell bounced off Rison's hands to Ravens safety Eric Turner, who intercepted at the Jaguars' 45.

On came Vinny Testaverde. In the middle of his best NFL season, Testaverde was a Pro Bowl candidate, and along with Brunell was a surprise among the AFC's leading passers. On the Ravens' second drive against the Jaguars, he continued his hot hand. Starting from the Jaguars' 45, he passed three times for 27 yards, setting the tone for a big yardage day, and Bam Morris bruised the Jaguars' middle five times for 18 yards. On the ninth play of the drive, Testaverde passed 5 yards to Michael Jackson for a touchdown with 6:15 remaining in the first quarter. Ravens 7, Jaguars 0.

A 23-yard field goal by Mike Hollis made it 7–3 with 6:33 remaining in the half, but the Jaguars' offense was stagnant, managing four first downs in the half. The running game was ineffective, with 30 yards on nine carries in the half. Testaverde, meanwhile, maintained his early hot streak, and on the possession after Hollis's field goal, he threw short to Morris. The play caught the Jaguars in an all-out blitz, and Morris turned it into a 52-yard catch-and-run touchdown with 5:39 remaining in the second quarter. Ravens 14, Jaguars 3.

On the Jaguars' next possession, the Ravens held. After a punt with 4:02 remaining in the half, Baltimore drove slowly from its 40, running to use the clock and scoring on a 21-yard field goal by Matt Stover with five seconds remaining in the half. Ravens 17, Jaguars 3.

In the locker room, "Coach Coughlin cussed us out," Rison said.

The Jaguars were struggling, and the Ravens were having fun—mostly at Rison's expense. Throughout the first half, Ravens defensive backs taunted him. "They were telling each other to hold me up, so they could get some shots," Rison said. "I got a bloody lip, but it was no big deal."

Said Ravens safety Bennie Thompson, "They said some things in the newspaper that fired us up. It was my motivation. There's no love when the whistle blows."

"I didn't name any names," Rison said afterward with a smile and a shrug.

In the second half, the Jaguars' offense improved, but at first it only matched scores with the Ravens. The Jaguars opened the second half on their 16, and on third-and-seven from the 19, Brunell passed deep to Pete Mitchell for a 30-yard gain. On the next play, Rison gained revenge on his former team—and the defensive backs who had bloodied him in the first half. He slipped behind the secondary, and Brunell threw deep. Donny Brady interfered for a 41-yard penalty to the Ravens' 10. Two plays later, Stewart scored on a 10-yard run with 12:53 remaining in the third quarter to make it 17–10, but Stover kicked another 21-yard field goal on the ensuing possession.

Ravens 20, Jaguars 10 with 7:01 remaining in the third quarter.

The Jaguars cut the deficit, but squandered chances to take a lead. Late in the third quarter, Kelvin Prichett recovered a fumble by Testaverde at the Ravens' 19, but three plays failed to produce a first down, and Hollis's 33-yard field goal made it 20–13 with 4:05 remaining in the third quarter.

On the Jaguars' next possession, they drove from their 4 to a first-and-goal at the Ravens' 4, one of their most impressive drives of the season. Brunell, who had become effective with middle-range passes in recent weeks, keyed the drive early with 14-yard passes to Jimmy Smith and Rison. Four plays later, Brunell again provided the big play, scrambling 33 yards to the Ravens' 18. After a

14-yard pass to Mitchell, the drive stalled, and Hollis's field goal from 24 yards made it 20–16 with 11:11 remaining.

The Jaguars had rallied, but it seemed not to matter. On the Ravens' next possession, they started at their 12, and with Testaverde riddling the Jaguars' secondary for 68 yards on four completions, drove quickly. On second-and-15 from the 21, Testaverde passed to Derrick Alexander for a touchdown with 6:23 remaining. Ravens 27, Jaguars 16.

If the Jaguars had any chance at a comeback, it had to start now. On the next drive, it did. Brunell completed his first three passes—25 yards to Willie Jackson, 13 yards to Keenan McCardell, and 11 yards to Rison.

First down at the Ravens' 41.

After an incomplete pass, Brunell completed three more—15 yards to Rison, 6 to Mitchell, and 15 to McCardell. First down at the Ravens' 5. After a sack, Brunell threw a screen pass to James Stewart, who scored on an 8-yard catch and run with 3:50 remaining. Brunell threw incomplete on the two-point conversion. Ravens 27, Jaguars 22.

The Ravens needed to run the clock. Instead, Testaverde threw incomplete on second and third down. These were two of the most inexplicable plays of the Jaguars' season. On second down, the Ravens called a screen—a safe pass, in theory. Testaverde threw a horrible pass at the feet of Morris. On the next play, Testaverde threw incomplete. The two incomplete passes saved the Jaguars at least a minute. After a Ravens punt, the Jaguars had first down at their 34 with 2:31 remaining. Suddenly, there was plenty of time.

The two-minute offense, for a quarterback, can define a career. Two-minute heroics made Joe Montana, John Elway, and Dan Marino legends. Brunell's two-minute drives, in two seasons, weren't the stuff of legend. His clock management in losses to the Rams and Saints was one reason the Jaguars desperately needed a clutch drive now. This time, he shone.

First, he passed to Mitchell for 13 yards. After an incomplete pass, he threw a sideline route to Jimmy Smith, who turned it into a 25-yard catch and run to the Ravens' 28 at the two-minute warning. "We looked at each other and said, 'We're going to win, period,'" McCardell said. "There was nothing that was going to stop us. We had been in that position so many times before. This time was going to be different."

The Ravens, throughout the Jaguars' rally, stayed in zone coverage—even after the two-minute warning. Zone coverage took away long plays, but allowed shorter plays in front of defenders. Brunell, at times in 1996, was impatient in such situations. Not today. A play after the two-minute warning, he passed incomplete, but on the next play, he threw in front of the defense for an 8-yard gain to Mitchell. "I really felt we would score," Coughlin said. "I really did."

On the next play, Brunell passed to McCardell across the middle. Moments earlier, on the first play after the two-minute warning, McCardell had run a similar route, sustained a vicious hit from Browns safety Vashone Adams, and dropped the pass. On this play, McCardell was hit hard by Browns safety Eric Turner but he held the pass for a 13-yard gain to the Ravens' 7. After a quarterback draw to the Ravens' 1, the Jaguars called their final time-out. Forty-six seconds remained.

Gilbride called for a naked bootleg to the left with one receiver, tight end Rich Griffith, in the pattern to that side. Brunell rolled left, and the safety had a choice—cover Griffith or chase Brunell. The safety tangled with Griffith, and Brunell scored easily, running untouched into the end zone. He raised the ball with one hand, and his finger to the sky with the other. Forty-one seconds remained.

His two-point pass to McCardell was good. Jaguars 30, Ravens 27.

"It was Mark being Mark," Rison said later. "That's why he's the best quarterback in the league."

The victory caused optimism. "This is huge," Coughlin said. "This is what it's all about. This is what we've been missing. With all the disappointments we've had, it was nice to share that kind of win. That's the kind of thing that can help the meeting together of this team."

Never had Brunell engineered such a comeback—two scores in the final four minutes. "It was one of those wins that can really put gas in the tank," Coughlin said. The best rally in team history?

"We won," Gilbride said. "That makes it the best."

The happiness increased immediately afterward when Coughlin, for the first time in his two seasons, gave the players Monday off from practice. "Every now and then, he has to throw us a bone," Dana Hall said.

"Guys were elated that day after he said, 'Get your lifts and conditioning in, and go home,'" John Jurkovic said later. "We had all Monday and Tuesday to relax, and that was a good feeling. The mind is a crazy thing. Any time the mind tells you things are going good, that the coach just basically gave us Monday off, your psyche is a little up, your biorhythms are up. You come back Wednesday, and you're ready to attack.

"You know you have to be mentally prepared because you only have Wednesday, Thursday, and Friday. That brought an urgency to the end of the week, and to the end of the season."

The euphoria of the victory, and a day off, made for a confident, relaxed team. That Wednesday, came another unexpected lift. Coughlin, for the first time players could remember, lightened practice, and the players worked without pads.

Coughlin denied a major transformation. As with the off day two days before, Coughlin said the lighter practice was part of his overall plan. If part of that plan was to endear himself more to his players, it worked. Many perceived it as a positive step for Coughlin.

The question was what it would mean on the field. The changes—easier practices and relaxed, rested players—were designed to help in the second half of the season, which is far different in the NFL than the first. Players consider the final eight games "money time." The intensity of preparation, focus, and hitting rises exponentially each week. A good team, the theory goes, improves in the final half of the season.

Disturbing to Coughlin in the Jaguars' first season was a seven-game losing streak in the final half. That exposed a lack of depth, experience, and focus. The Steelers, the previous season, were opposite, overcoming a slow start to win the division and the conference. In 1996, as the Jaguars prepared to face Pittsburgh a second time, the Steelers again were surging.

Since the opening loss to the Jaguars, the Steelers were 7–2, and they led the division with a 7–3 record, partly because coach Bill Cowher settled the quarterback situation immediately after the opener. Jim Miller was benched, Kordell Stewart's future at quarterback was put on hold, and Mike Tomczak—a 12-year veteran—was made the starter. Most importantly, running back Jerome Bettis—acquired in a draft-day trade from the Rams— was the power back the Steelers' system required. Bettis led the AFC in rushing, entering the Jaguars game with 1,064 yards and nine touchdowns.

"They showed their heart and soul each week," Coughlin said.

"I knew when they lost to us, they would turn things around," Searcy said. "It's no big surprise to me."

This Jaguars-Steelers game, then, had the same theme as the opener. The Steelers were mighty again, and the Jaguars—at 4–6, having lost six of nine since the opener—were trying to earn respect.

"Sometimes I feel they don't really respect us," Clyde Simmons said. "They think we beat them down here and it was a fluke. A lot of guys were saying, 'Wait until we get you back up in Pittsburgh.' So, we have to prove it wasn't. They're a team you have to keep hitting in the mouth. They're not going to lay down for you. You have to keep hitting them, and hitting them. You have to make them respect you. Respect is not given. It's earned."

Respect, in this case, depended upon the venue. The Jaguars had beaten the Steelers twice in three meetings, but both victories were at home. The Jaguars' one game at Pittsburgh was a 24–7 loss in October of 1995 in which the Steelers punished the Jaguars physically. "When we come to play at both locations, then it will be a rivalry," Coughlin said.

The events of November 17 did nothing to change Coughlin's mind.

The Jaguars weren't as overmatched physically as the previous season. Instead, in front of 58,879 at Three Rivers Stadium, they reverted to their mistake-prone ways of October. The defense was tough, stuffing Bettis, but after a scoreless first quarter, the Steelers drove 44 yards in eight plays, taking the lead when Tomczak passed 12 yards to Yancey Thigpen with 13:11 remaining in the second quarter.

On the Jaguars' next possession, lack of depth on the offensive line hurt the Jaguars for the first time in 1996. Rich Tylski, a practice-squad player in 1996, was starting at guard in DeMarco's absence. Tylski had proven a more-than-worthy replacement, but on the kickoff following Thigpen's touchdown, he sustained a neck stinger. Jeff Novak, a reserve guard/tackle who had yet to play this season, replaced Tylski. On second-and-nine from the Jaguars' 14, Jason Gildon beat Novak, sacking Brunell and forcing a fumble. Steelers nose tackle Joel Steed recovered at the Jaguars' 3, and Bettis scored on the next play. Steelers 14, Jaguars 0.

The Jaguars steadied. The offense was still struggling, but the defense hadn't played poorly, and it continued to keep the Jaguars close. Defensively, the Steelers were stuffing the Jaguars' running game and forcing Brunell to throw too soon. Finally, on the last drive of the half, Brunell gained confidence. He completed five passes for 50 yards, keying a drive that left the Jaguars on the Steelers' 22 with four seconds remaining in the half. Hollis's 40-yard field goal on the next play made it 14–3, Steelers.

The Jaguars opened the third quarter more confident than in any of their previous six quarters at Three Rivers. Finally, there was life. The Jaguars took the kickoff, driving from the 23 to the Steelers' 7, where they faced third-and-two.

The Jaguars, despite recent criticism, had improved offensively in recent weeks. One reason was a willingness by Coughlin to use more four- and five-wide-receiver sets, sometimes in situations where most coaches wouldn't use them, such as first downs and short yardage. On third-and-two against the Steelers, Coughlin called for five receivers.

The advantage of the formation was to spread the defense, putting more receivers in the pattern than quality cover defenders. The disadvantage was it left only the five offensive linemen protecting the quarterback, making it vulnerable to blitzing defenders.

As the Jaguars prepared to snap, Steelers safety Carnell Lake—who usually lined up in blitz packages outside defensive end Brentson Buckner—lined up between Buckner and nose tackle Bill Johnson. This was a new blitz scheme, one the Jaguars hadn't seen on film.

Typically, when faced with a new defense, a quarterback calls time-out, or checks out of the play. Brunell did neither. Left tackle Tony Boselli's assignment was to block Lake, the closest defender to the ball. Instead, Boselli blocked outside on Buckner, leaving Lake a clear path to Brunell. Lake reached Brunell as he prepared to throw to Rison on a slant. The ball bounced away and to Brunell's right. Lake picked up the fumble and returned it 85 yards.

Steelers 21, Jaguars 3.

"A huge, huge emotional letdown," Coughlin said. "It was a drastic change in the scoreboard."

Of the third-and-two call, he said, "I'll take the fall."

"What's really killing us this year is our inability to protect the ball," Brunell said. "In every area, there are way too many breakdowns that are causing us to turn the ball over."

"It was still early, but it temporarily takes the wind out of sails," Dana Hall said. "When something like that happens, immediately you can't believe it happens. It's a shock."

The shock all but ended the Jaguars' chances. An interception by Deon Figures set up a 27-yard pass from Tomczak to Thigpen with 56 seconds remaining in the third quarter that gave the Steelers their final margin of victory, 28–3.

"Had we scored on that first drive of the second half,

I believe it would have been a different ball game,"
Coughlin said.

Figures's interception came on a play on which Brunell threw a deep slant to Rison. Instead of making the
cut, Rison continued straight, raising his hand as Figures—filling the space where Rison should have been—
made the easy interception.

In his season and half with the team, Brunell had
never berated a teammate, or criticized one, publicly. As
the offense left the field after Figures's interception, Brunell walked quickly toward Rison. He then walked the
final yards to the sideline with the receiver, yelling and
pointing to the spot of the interception—an altercation
caught by NBC's cameras.

The game ended without further incident between
quarterback and receiver, but now, the Jaguars knew, the
situation was dire. The Steelers were now 8–3; the Jaguars were 4–7, tied with Cincinnati for fourth in the AFC
Central, two games behind Houston. Of 15 AFC teams,
10 had better records than the Jaguars, and only two
teams trailed them in the race for six playoff spots. "We
just have to go out and win the rest of these games," Don
Davey said. "We're not going to quit."

As for the Brunell-Rison blowup, Brunell pushed
aside questions. Rison was more volatile, shouting at the
publisher of the team newspaper, Vic Ketchman, over a
question. Later, Rison calmed, but denied friction between himself and the quarterback he once called "the
best in the NFL."

"It was no big deal," Rison said. "Me and Mark are
cool."

12
A GOOD-BYE
AND A MIRACLE

"These guys are shitting their pants [in Baltimore on November 24]. The guys are like . . . 'Holy Jesus.' We can't do anything right. Now we're in a major, major bind."
—TOM COUGHLIN
February 1997

ndre Rison's locker was busy the first two and half months of the 1996 season. After games, and throughout each week, reporters and cameramen crowded near "Bad Moon." On November 18, it was crowded again, but not with media, who that morning walked into a locker room as strange as any in team history.

Rison's locker, in the front right corner as one entered the room, was surrounded by teammates. Rison sat slumped in his chair, watching ESPN highlights from the previous day. On his right sat Mickey Washington and Keenan McCardell. Tony Brackens lay in front. To Rison's left sat Natrone Means and Robert Massey.

Many appeared ready to fight. Those not angry looked

171

depressed. Around this group sat younger teammates. Some spoke, some were silent. A few minutes after the media entered at 11:45, Leon Searcy walked into the group, sat, and talked to Rison for several minutes.

"What's going on?" someone asked a player.

"You haven't heard?" the player said. "They released Andre."

The media inched nearer, hoping to discuss it with Rison, who clearly was being guarded by the players, some of whom were among the team's more media-wary. No players moved.

"It's not nice to stare," Washington said to one reporter.

Moments later, Washington motioned the reporter toward him.

"Don't you guys know what's happened?" Washington said. Told yes, Washington frowned, and said, "What are they telling you guys—not to ask any questions?" Rison seemed to pay no attention, staring up at the television from behind his teammates. No, the reporter told Washington, the Jaguars had told the media nothing. Yet. Staying away, the reporter said, was a way of respecting Rison's privacy. Washington thought for a moment, and said, "That's the best thing."

This was an emotional moment. Despite difficulties with Coughlin, Rison valued friends made in Jacksonville. Being released by a franchise with which he had sought to rebuild his career and his image hurt. Besides, he liked playing in Jacksonville. "I've never played in a stadium where there were signs hung up for me," he had said the previous week. "That's happening here. I love being on this little island of Jacksonville. I love the weather. I love the trees. I love the fresh air. I love the ocean. I love my role as a leader on this team. I love setting an example for the younger players. I made some promises to the Jacksonville Jaguars and I plan to carry out those promises."

Now, promises were off, and the lovefest was finished. Soon, Rison became less interested in the TV, laughing and joking with teammates. He remained seemingly oblivious of the media, and the group remained tight around their ex-teammate. "We're showing support for our friend," Massey said.

When interview time ended, Rison was where he had been a half hour before—surrounded and uninterviewed.

When he released a player, Coughlin typically opened the day's press conference with a thought-out statement regarding the player. The day he released Rison, he did the same. Coughlin knew speculation about the move would be widespread. This was a player who had challenged him publicly, notably in Cincinnati three weeks before. Many assumed then Rison's future with the team was uncertain, and now that he was released it was easy to assume Rison's mouth was why. The post-interception argument with Brunell the day before raised a new question regarding Rison: Was there a feud between quarterback and receiver that prompted the move? Coughlin said neither were reasons.

"It was performance based," Coughlin said of the decision.

"We thought Andre would come in and be a lot more productive," Wayne Weaver said.

The release hurt Coughlin more than many realized. He saw Rison as troubled, but hoped he could revive his career with the Jaguars. Coughlin loved Rison's potential, and it frustrated him not to bring it out, but there was more. Coughlin, sources later said, was concerned about Rison personally—his drinking, tardiness, and mood swings—which many believed was why Coughlin gave Rison more chances than he might have given another player.

Rison, in many ways, was an enigma. He could be engaging, not only with friends, but with coaches. Coaches dreaded days when he was surly, late, and inattentive, but looked forward to days when Rison was in a good mood and enthusiastic about football. On those days, they felt no player was as positive an influence.

"He's Jekyll and Hyde," one coach said. That frustrated Coughlin, and finally, he released him.

"Most of you who know me know I like Andre," Coughlin told reporters. "We had our differences. We worked them out. I did not bring Andre here with the intent to have this happen. The fact of the matter is progress has got to be made."

Few felt Rison had progressed since his arrival. Jimmy Smith, until now the No. 3 receiver, had outplayed him, and was the team's best deep threat. Smith also had a tireless work ethic and a model attitude. The more coaches compared Rison and Smith, the more they felt it unfair to play Rison.

The problem wasn't physical. Rison could still get open deep and make big plays, but much of the Jaguars' system required receivers to read defenses during plays, and adjust routes according to coverage. Extensive study during game week was required to become familiar with the opponents' defenses. Rison rarely took his playbook home, coaches said. He ran numerous wrong routes, which led to turnovers. When Rison was released, Brunell had 20 interceptions. One coach said Rison had caused at least 12. "I would be less than honest if I didn't say there were some errors and missed assignments going on," Coughlin said.

Brunell denied any role in Rison's release, but team

sources said he had asked that something be done about Rison.

After Coughlin discussed the release, reporters hurried to the parking lot to catch Rison. Moments later, he emerged into the sunlight, sunglasses on, heading for a waiting car. He spoke to the driver of the car, but again ignored the media. As he passed, he was asked if he had anything to say. As usual, he did, but not much:

"I had a nice time, met a lot of nice people, nice teammates."

He opened the door, got in, and was gone.

In November 1995, the Jaguars released Ernest Givins and James Williams. In September of 1996, they released Vinnie Clark. In November, it was Rison. All had something in common: They spoke publicly against Coughlin or the organization. But all had something else in common, too. All were black.

The day after Rison's release was a Tuesday, the players' off day, and the release was the talk of the town.

After the releases of Williams, Givins, and Clark, there were whispers of racial motivation among fans. Rison's release turned the whispers into a roar. Was Rison released because he was an outspoken black player? That was what callers to radio shows, the newspaper, and even the team office wanted to know. Players moved quickly to discount such thoughts. "I don't think it had anything to do with his release," Clyde Simmons, black, said. "In today's society, race plays a major factor. You have people trying to take affirmative action away, but it has nothing to do with football, and it shouldn't have anything to do with football.

"It should be based upon whether you're a quality football player. That's it."

"Anybody bringing up whether it was a racist move is

totally off-the-wall," John Jurkovic, white, said. "You hear something like that, and you shake your head and go on."

Coughlin never discussed the issue, feeling to do so would give credibility to a subject that deserved none. There had been as many incidents of black players speaking out and remaining with the team as blacks speaking out and being released. The previous November, Kelvin Pritchett—black—called Coughlin a dictator, yet retained his starting job. During the 1996 training camp, second-year wide receiver Curtis Marsh—black—complained about how he was being used, saying, "I don't know if it's Tom Coughlin, Michael Huyghue, but somebody's doubting me. How dare you doubt me like that?" Although Marsh was no guarantee to make the team, he did so. And in the spring of 1996, guard Shawn Bouwens—a white player—complained that he had lost his job because of an injury. Bouwens was released in training camp for the same reason as Rison, Givins, Clark, and Williams: His performance no longer justified his salary.

Still, some in the organization worried it might cause problems. Coughlin worried, too—not that players would think the decision race-related, but that they might not understand the move. He met with the team the morning he released Rison, stressing the move was made because Rison was not performing. "I made sure they understood exactly why that decision was made," Coughlin said. "I made them understand what the word "performance" meant, what "accountability" meant, and they understand. They're not blind."

Even so, Rison was a strong locker-room presence among young black players. The crowd surrounding him the morning of his release was black, causing speculation that a locker room without Rison would soon divide.

Most players, however, realized Rison had not played to expectations. "He could have prevented being cut," Smith said. "He could have stayed here. They worked with him a lot."

Teammates agreed, and moved to repair any division from the release. Veterans wanted younger teammates to realize it was OK to miss a teammate, but not at the expense of the team. This was professional football: Any division needed to undivide quickly.

"I think there is a little rip in there, but now and then, you need a little rip to make you stronger," Simmons said. "You have to let it go. If you talk about it, it's going to keep living on and living on. It's not something you're going to get past. You have to let things go sometimes. One day, we're all going to be released."

Rison left without comment, but didn't stay quiet long. On the Wednesday after his release, he signed with the Green Bay Packers. Once there, he said, "It was personal, but I'm not going to go into it. Everybody can read through it. Everybody watched the games. [The Jaguars said], 'I didn't do this, and didn't do that.' . . . I watched film, and I graded out every weekend like 90 percent."

This amused many within the Jaguars' organization. Many liked Rison, but Rison rarely graded out so high.

Brunell, aware of rumors he had instigated the release, did not discuss the matter. "I'd rather go on," he said. "Let's talk about something other than Andre. We can't dwell on past games or past players. I don't think there's any division. It's part of the business. You just have to move on."

Coughlin again had set a tone of "produce or leave," and showed it applied to all players—no matter how big the name. The release had another aftereffect: The team, more than ever, was Brunell's. He might or might not have caused Rison's release, but he was a major influence—the Jaguars' first instance of a player having a major say in a personnel move.

Brunell remained, Rison was gone, and although the latter would be missed, most knew it was time to let the past be the past. "Andre was a personality in this locker room," Simmons said. "He kept it loose. I'm going to miss him. But it's one of those situations, where Tom decided he had to make a decision based on performance. That was the decision that was made."

Rison's absence left a leadership void. Many looked to Simmons.

Clyde Simmons was born August 4, 1964, in Lanes, South Carolina, but his family moved to Wilmington, North Carolina, where he had a first brush with future greatness. In Wilmington, he played Babe Ruth League baseball with a kid who would one day play in the NBA. The kid's name was Michael Jordan.

Simmons grew into an athlete, too, playing football, basketball, and baseball at New Hanover High School in Wilmington, but until his senior season in college, few thought he would become one of the NFL's all-time leading sack specialists. Even at Western Carolina, most doubted he could be an NFL player. The Philadelphia Eagles selected him in the ninth round, 234th overall, in the 1986 draft. He played primarily special teams as a rookie, but in 1987, he became a starter, playing opposite Reggie White.

The Eagles in the late 1980s and early 1990s were one of the NFL's toughest defenses, with a line—Simmons, White, and tackles Jerome Brown, Mike Golic, and Mike Pitts—considered among the most dominant in NFL history. Brown and White were the biggest names, but Simmons was as effective, and in 1992, he led the NFL with 19 sacks, three shy of the all-time record for a season.

Simmons had 76½ sacks in eight seasons with the Eagles, and in 1994, when Buddy Ryan—his coach in Philadelphia—took over as coach in Arizona, Simmons signed as a free agent there.

Simmons, for the first time in his career, faced the pressure of being a high-priced player. Ryan promised Cardinals fans dominating defense and quick success, and Simmons was one reason why. He had just six sacks in his first season in Arizona, and although the total improved to 11 in 1995, he was criticized in Arizona for not living up to his salary. "I finished with 11 sacks, and still got criticized," Simmons said.

As the 1996 season approached, his status grew uncertain. The team drafted end Simeon Rice, and re-signed tackle Eric Swann to a big contract. That forced the Cardinals to release Simmons, scheduled to earn $2.5 million that season. Simmons lived in Ponte Vedra Beach, just outside Jacksonville. When the Jaguars called, he listened, and signed.

"I want to come here for a fresh start," Simmons said when he signed. "If I bring the things I think I can bring to this team, I think we'll be a good defense. After all the stuff I've been through, this is the healthiest I've been in three—maybe four—years. I haven't been aching. I feel good. I feel healthy. I feel strong. I'm happy."

That happiness was evident in Jacksonville. Simmons began the season as a backup, which broke a streak of 140 games starting. At another time in his career, not starting might have been a problem, but not now.

"I'm at a different time in my life now," Simmons said.

That attitude endeared him not only to coaches, but to teammates. He joined Lageman as a leader on the defense. While Lageman led by being outspoken, Simmons led quietly—a gentle giant. Simmons influenced the development of rookie defensive end Tony Brackens, spending much of the first half of the season tutoring the younger player.

"Clyde was a guy who would sit, and look for younger players to take in," Coughlin said.

Simmons's senior-spokesman status grew weekly. He filled the void left by Rison with a different twist. He was calmer in demeanor than Rison, but more responsible, too—adept at discussing controversial issues or positive ones.

His presence improved a pass rush that was weak the previous season. More than a locker-room presence, Simmons was a relentless rusher, who never seemed to have an off day, or off play. He had a sack in the opener against the Steelers, and throughout the season, when the Jaguars needed a big play—a sack, a pressure, a forced fumble, a blocked kick or punt—Simmons provided it.

"Clyde's a player," Coughlin said after the season.

A player who knew what it took to play in the NFL, and didn't mind telling his teammates.

"Being a pro is what this business is all about, and that means coming to play, every game," he said. "You don't come in as an amateur. You come in, get paid, and do a job. If you don't get it done, forget it. You have to go out every week and prove yourself worthy."

Ten games into 1996, Simmons had done just that. In and out of the locker room.

The mood was desperate, the season had gotten long, and a friend was gone. Making matters worse for the Jaguars was this: They had to play a game on the road.

That meant spending a week listening to theories on why they couldn't win there. The road is a difficult place in the NFL, but it had been particularly difficult for the Jaguars.

Oakland, New England, New Orleans, St. Louis, Cincinnati, Pittsburgh . . .

The Jaguars' worst memories of 1996 were of when they left JMS, and now, on November 24, 1996, they had to go on the road again, to Baltimore. The Ravens had reason for revenge, and reason to be confident. They had outplayed the Jaguars for 55 minutes in JMS just two weeks ago, only to lose when the Jaguars scored two touchdowns in the final five minutes.

There was a twist to that road trend for the Jaguars, but one some players were starting to notice. Yes, they had lost six on the road, but they only had lost one at home.

So, the theory went . . .

Win out at home . . .

Sneak one or two on the road . . .

Do that, and a .500 season—Coughlin's preseason goal—wasn't a ridiculous notion. "To be a good team, you have to win on the road," Tony Boselli said.

Yet, beyond abstract, long-term scenarios, there was a reality to the week leading to the Ravens game that concerned Coughlin—although they matched up well with the Ravens and never had lost to the franchise. The Jaguars were 4–7. What incentive was there? "We have this situation in front of us," Coughlin said. "We're playing a division football game and we haven't won on the road. That's plenty of motivation."

"Every time you go out on the field you're playing for pride," Dana Hall said. "No matter what your record is, you have to continue to take pride in what you're doing."

The road had been unkind to the Jaguars. Early in front of 57,384 at Baltimore Memorial Stadium, it got plain cruel—so cruel Coughlin even managed to see humor in a difficult situation.

The Jaguars were tight, even scared. Coughlin saw it

from the beginning. The key early in such a game was to stay close, and wait for the players to calm. Then, 2:30 into the game, Brunell threw to Jimmy Smith. Ravens linebacker Mike Caldwell intercepted, and had a clear field. He returned it 45 yards for a touchdown and a 7–0 lead. Forty-two seconds into second quarter, Matt Stover kicked a 21-yard field goal. Ravens 10, Jaguars 0.

Coughlin, now, was as close as at any time in the season to admitting the cause was lost. The frustrations had built, and now, his team was on the road—not only losing, but barely putting up a fight.

"We started the game just like we started a lot of games," Coughlin said later. "We couldn't even take the snap. That was the first time I actually stood on the sidelines, and kind of smiled to myself, and I said, 'How is this coaching? How does coaching help this group?'"

The crowd bothered the players. The Ravens' defense confused Brunell and the rest of the offense. The Jaguars were jumpy, drawing penalties, and the team, to Coughlin's embarrassment, didn't look well coached—three false-start penalties in the first quarter. "They [the Jaguars] were moving around, he [Brunell] throws an interception for a touchdown," Coughlin said. "These guys are shitting their pants."

Coughlin, recalling the event shortly after the season, lifted his hand, and shook it, trembling. "The Tylskis of the world are like this," he said, laughing at the memory. He shook his head, and added, "The guys are like, 'Holy Jesus. We can't do anything right.'"

Coughlin paused, then added, "Now, we're in a major, major bind."

Coaches cajoled the players after each series. "We're like, 'Settle down, for God's sake,'" Coughlin said. "'Settle down. Get yourselves under control. Play the game. It's a long game, fellas. Play the game.' Then we started to play a little bit, but I tell you what: We were pathetic offensively, early on."

The Jaguars struggled through the first three quarters. Their lone touchdown of the first half was set up by a 53-yard pass-interference penalty against Donny Brady covering Keenan McCardell. The penalty gave the Jaguars a first down at the Ravens' 18, and three plays later, Stewart scored on a 1-yard run to make it 10–7 with 13 minutes remaining in the second quarter. The teams traded field goals, then the Ravens got another: a 41-yarder from Matt Stover with six seconds remaining in the half for a 16–10 Ravens halftime lead.

The Ravens drove 54 yards at the start of the second half, an eight-play drive capped by Bam Morris's 1-yard run. The two-point conversion failed with 10:39 remaining, and the Ravens led 22–10. With 1:25 remaining in the quarter, Stover kicked a 33-yard field goal. Ravens 25, Jaguars 10.

Late in the third quarter, James Stewart severely injured his toe, forcing Natrone Means into his most significant action of the season.

The Jaguars were a quarter away from 4–8, and elimination from the playoffs, but on the opening drive of the fourth quarter, they drove 74 yards on 12 plays, a drive capped by an 11-yard touchdown pass from Brunell to Pete Mitchell. Ravens 25, Jaguars 17.

The Jaguars' hope heightened when they forced a punt on the following series, but what followed was curious strategy from Coughlin. The Jaguars took possession at their 20 with 8:56 remaining, but Brunell used a time-out before the first play. Afterward, the Jaguars drove slowly. . . .

Very slowly.

They drove 13 plays, reaching the Ravens' 30 as the clock moved past four minutes. Instead of calling plays at the line, they huddled before each play, wasting seconds. They were hoping for not only a touchdown, but the two-point conversion. Since the NFL's two-point conversion rate was less than 50 percent, it was quite an assumption, particularly considering that if they had moved more quickly, they would have increased their chances to have two possessions—and therefore, two chances to score.

As the clock moved past three minutes, the Jaguars faced fourth and one on the Ravens' 25. Before the play, Boselli was penalized for a false start. On fourth-and-six, Brunell threw incomplete to Mitchell.

Coughlin's strategy had failed. The Ravens led by eight, needing only to run the clock.

Then, a miracle.

On first down, Ravens quarterback Vinny Testaverde mishandled the snap and the ball bounced in the backfield. Testaverde dove, and missed. So did Kevin Hardy. Finally, Eddie Robinson fell on the loose ball at the Ravens' 19 with 2:43 remaining. "You don't see the ball out there like that in that type of situation," Robinson said.

"We got a freak play to go our way," Simmons said.

Six plays later, on third-and-goal from the Ravens' 7, Brunell passed to Willie Jackson for a touchdown with 1:24 remaining. On the two-point conversion, Brunell ran left, and dove through several defenders into the end zone.

Jaguars 25, Ravens 25.

The Ravens moved to the Jaguars' 31 in the minute and a half remaining, but Stover missed a 49-yard field goal. Overtime.

The Jaguars received the overtime kickoff, but quickly punted. The Ravens drove from their 6 to the Jaguars' 37. On first-and-10, however, Hardy tackled Earnest Byner for a 1-yard gain. Byner fumbled, and Kelvin Pritchett recovered.

Means, subbing for Stewart, had had little chance in the fourth quarter. The Jaguars were rallying, so the running game was an afterthought. Now, the Jaguars were even, and it was Means's time.

Two weeks before, Means had talked about seeking an off-season trade. In overtime against the Ravens, he got enough use to feel comfortable running again. Means carried three times for 21 yards, power running.

"Pound it in there, Nate," players yelled on the sideline.

"Go, baby," another yelled. "All right."

The Jaguars drove 48 yards in 5:05, winning when Mike Hollis's 34-yard field goal sailed just inside the left upright. "We had weird games all year go the other way," Dana Hall said. "This one went our way."

"I have to give credit to our guys," Coughlin said, "for scrapping and fighting and finding a way to win. We didn't quit."

Later, Simmons walked from the locker room. He had seen weird games, but no one on the Jaguars remembered many like this. Shoulder bag on one arm and turkey sandwich in the other hand, Simmons was asked for perspective on the victory. Simple. It meant the season wasn't over. "We have four games left," Simmons said. "We can finish 9–7. That could get us in.

"Anything is possible."

13
JOINING THE HUNT

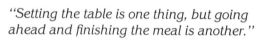

"Setting the table is one thing, but going ahead and finishing the meal is another."

—TOM COUGHLIN
December 1, 1996

In Week 15 of 1995, the Jaguars lost to the Detroit Lions, 44–0. The Lions, at the time, were in the middle of a seven-game winning streak to end the season. After nine games, the Lions had been 3–6. They made the playoffs.

On the day after the dramatic overtime victory in Baltimore, Jaguars players' thoughts wandered to that Lions team. If they could do it, the thinking was, why not us?

"Stranger things have happened," Dana Hall said.

A look at the Jaguars' remaining four games made the scenario seem strangely unstrange. Three of four were at home, where the Jaguars had lost just once. The road game was in Houston, where the Jaguars won the year before and the Oilers were drawing small crowds and struggling. The combined record of the foursome—

Cincinnati, Houston, Seattle, and Atlanta—was 18–30. None had a winning record.

"I don't think it's out of the realm of possibility," Tony Boselli said. "I think we're going to win them all, but we have to be careful. In the past, we've started looking too far ahead."

Nine and seven was the goal, but it appeared that might not be good enough. Five AFC teams appeared to be locks for the playoffs—Denver (11–1, having clinched), Pittsburgh (9–3), Buffalo (9–3), New England (8–4), and Kansas City (8–4). That left one spot for an eight-team cluster including the Jaguars (5–7), San Diego (7–5), Miami (6–6), Indianapolis (6–6), Houston (6–6), Cincinnati (5–7), Oakland (5–7), and Seattle (5–7). Giving the Jaguars cause for optimism was the fact that three of the teams—Cincinnati, Houston, and Seattle—were on the Jaguars' schedule.

Jaguars victories would help their cause twofold—they would keep them alive, and would hurt the other team. "I don't know if the young guys realize it, but the way things happen in the NFL, it's possible," Don Davey said. "If we're 9–7, I think we'll get in."

Coughlin thought so, too. After the Ravens game, he stood outside the locker room and said, "We have a chance to pull this thing together. Who knows? You never know. One game at a time."

A few minutes later, a reporter pulled Coughlin aside. His words, Coughlin was told, sounded as if he was talking playoffs. "Don't start that," Coughlin said.

Thus began Coughlin's personal no-playoff-talk rule. His philosophy was to consider each game as it came. This team hadn't won back-to-back games this season, and they had done it just once in franchise history. Did Coughlin dare think of a five-game winning streak?

"We've had enough of that kind of stuff," he said,

asked again the next day. "I'm not interested in that at all."

What remained to be seen was how interesting this could get.

Early Wednesday, November 27, Bobby Monica was excited. This was one of his favorite days of the year, the day before Thanksgiving.

Monica, the Jaguars' equipment manager, was the team jokester. Rarely a day passed that he didn't pull a gag or tease a player. Wednesday, before Thanksgiving provided one of the season's best prank opportunities.

On Tuesday, Monica made up memos on the stationery of a local Winn-Dixie supermarket, telling players complementary turkeys would be available there Wednesday. On Wednesday morning, in a team meeting, Coughlin displayed the memo on a screen. "Now, you rookies make sure you go get the ones for the older players," Coughlin said.

Jaguars video director Mike Perkins arrived early at the Winn-Dixie, setting up a camera to film the players asking a store manager for the turkeys. Kevin Hardy, Michael Cheever, Tony Brackens, Aaron Beasley—all showed at the Winn-Dixie. The manager gave them a box with a small Cornish game hen inside. No turkey. As players became aware of the gag, they became aware, too, that Perkins was filming the whole scene.

They saluted Perkins with a one-finger peace sign.

At a Friday morning meeting, Coughlin had Perkins put in a special tape. On the screen flickered the images of Cheever, Hardy, Beasley, Brackens, and the other rookies at the Winn-Dixie. Players and coaches roared with laughter.

Laughing loudest was Coughlin. "We all got a big laugh, and he was right in the middle of it," Don Davey said. "That tells you something about how much he's changed."

The Jaguars were having fun, but every game was a playoff game now, and on December 1, in Jacksonville Municipal Stadium, they played the Bengals, who—also 5–7—were approaching the game the same way. "If you lose this game," Bengals coach Bruce Coslet said, "it's probably not going to happen. There is some significance to this game."

Significant to the Jaguars was that the Bengals were the only AFC Central team they had yet to beat. The Bengals, like the Jaguars, felt they were better than their record, and when the Bengals talked playoffs, they were serious. They had won four of five since Coslet took over as interim coach from Dave Shula, fired seven games into the season.

"It's definitely a big game," said Natrone Means, who would make his first Jaguars start, replacing the injured James Stewart. "This is the biggest game in franchise history. If we win, we have a lot of options still open for us. If we lose, it's pretty much, 'What can we do next year?'"

Said Jeff Lageman, "To be playing for something in December is exciting. I've been down that road when you aren't playing for something in December, and it stinks."

The excitement showed. The Jaguars couldn't get a break in the early season. Early in a driving rain in front of 50,408 at JMS, they made their own. The Bengals drove from their 16 to the Jaguars' 25, but on fourth-and-five, Clyde Simmons blocked Doug Pelfrey's 42-yard field goal attempt. The ball bounced to the left, where Mickey Washington picked it up at the 35 and returned it 65 yards for a touchdown with 11:28 remaining in the first quarter. Jaguars 7, Bengals 0.

Mike Hollis kicked a 25-yard field goal for a 10–0 Jaguars lead with 6:24 remaining in the first quarter. On the ensuing kickoff, Bengals returner David Dunn returned it 56 yards to the Jaguars' 43. Kicker Mike Hollis made a touchdown-saving tackle. After Garrison Hearst ran three times for 15 yards, Bengals quarterback Jeff Blake faked a handoff into the line and passed 23 yards for a touchdown to Carl Pickens with 3:26 remaining.

Big plays and quick drives were the norm today, and the next series was no different. On first-and-10 from the Jaguars' 15, Brunell threw deep to Jimmy Smith, who caught the bomb for a 49-yard gain to the Bengals' 36. Three days later, with 2:05 remaining in the quarter, Hollis kicked a 46-yard field goal for a 13–7 Jaguars lead.

The Jaguars lost the lead in the second quarter. Pelfrey kicked a 22-yard field goal to make it 13–10 with 11:25 remaining in the half. The Bengals forced a punt and started from their 20. On second-and-10 from the 35, Blake again beat the Jaguars deep with a 48-yard pass to Darnay Scott to the Jaguars' 17. Tony Brackens was called for roughing the passer on the play, which gave the Bengals a first down at the 8. On the next play, Blake again hit Pickens for a touchdown that made it 17–13, Bengals, with 7:27 remaining.

Neither team again scored until Brunell drove the Jaguars 48 yards in 34 seconds, setting up a 40-yard field goal by Hollis with five seconds remaining in the half. Bengals 17, Jaguars 16.

The Jaguars were lucky to be close. The Bengals were moving at will, with 273 yards. The Jaguars were moving, too, but stalling near the goal line, and had 195 yards.

The Jaguars' offense continued to work in the second half. They drove 47 yards on their first possession to a 39-yard field goal by Hollis, his team-record fourth. The Bengals retook the lead, 20–19, on their next possession, when Pelfrey kicked a 34-yard field goal with 4:42 remaining in the third quarter.

Neither defense, at this point, was holding the opponent. The Jaguars, on their next possession, again drove, and moved to the Bengals' 48 in the final two minutes of the quarter.

There, they stalled, and faced third-and-10 with 1:40 remaining. Brunell, having one of his best games, was forced from the pocket, scrambling left and avoiding two defenders. He stopped, and as he was hit by Bengals defensive end John Copeland, threw a long lob down the left sideline. McCardell was open behind his defender. He caught the ball near the sideline and tightroped in for a touchdown. After a two-point conversion pass to Willie Jackson, the Jaguars led, 27–20.

The Jaguars had only stopped the Bengals without a score or an attempted field goal three times. The Pickens-Blake combination, which had produced four touchdowns in three previous meetings, was again in tune, and Pickens already had two touchdowns. On the drive after McCardell's touchdown, the Bengals drove easily, starting at their 28 late in the third quarter, and moving in six plays to the Jaguars' 27.

On first-and-10, Blake looked for Pickens in the left side of the end zone. Aaron Beasley, who covered Pickens most of the day with varying success, leapt high, and pulled the pass away from Pickens for his first career interception. "We were in a deep zone, and Blake threw it up so high, I knew he [Pickens] was going to push me," Beasley said. "So, I positioned myself in front of him."

Beasley's interception symbolized a reversal. In New Orleans, St. Louis, and Cincinnati, the Jaguars outgained opponents, but made too many mistakes and lost. Now, the Bengals were outgaining the Jaguars, but Beasley's interception was their second of the game, and they had returned the blocked field goal for a touchdown. As a result, they had possession and a seven-point lead with

12:57 remaining despite being outplayed much of the game.

"It's nice to get one of those games where everything went our way," John Jurkovic said. "The tipped balls went our way, the turnovers went our way. It's about time. You'd figure over the course of the season, the law of averages would work out. It finally did."

The Jaguars had momentum. After an exchange of punts, they took possession at their 24 with 7:48 remaining. This was a situation in which the Jaguars had rarely had success in their first two seasons, which irritated Coughlin.

Good teams, he felt, could engineer long, time-consuming drives in such situations. The Jaguars had done this against Carolina and Pittsburgh in victories, and scored, but Coughlin felt to win, the team had to do this consistently. Against the Bengals, with 7:48 remaining, the Jaguars used eight plays to drive 70 yards to a first-and-goal at the Bengals' 6. Two runs by Means gained 4 yards, and on third down, Brunell threw incomplete to Jimmy Smith.

On came Hollis with 2:08 remaining.

Hollis, a second-year kicker, had had difficult times in Jacksonville. He signed before the first season as an undrafted rookie from Idaho, and at first, was merely competition for Scott Sisson, who most thought would win the job. Hollis impressed coaches with his strong leg, winning the job. Hollis made 20 of 27 field goals in the first season, including two of 50 yards or longer.

Fans, however, constantly asked whether the Jaguars were going to replace Hollis with a bigger name, mostly because he struggled on kickoffs at times, his kicks often falling short of the end zone. But Coughlin believed in Hollis—even as he struggled in the 1996 preseason.

Many speculated then Hollis might be released, but

again, he proved doubters wrong, and as he lined up for a game clincher against the Bengals, he had made 20 of 24 field goals on the season—including four of four against the Bengals on a muddy, sloppy turf. His fifth, a team record, came from 20 yards away. Jaguars 30, Bengals 20.

The Bengals scored a final touchdown, a 25-yard pass from Blake to Pickens, with 21 seconds remaining, but an onside kick went out of bounds. End of game.

The Jaguars had won a close game, and hadn't had to rally. The overriding trend for the Jaguars had been to play a close game, and lose—the rare exceptions being the rallies against the Ravens and the hold-on-for-life victory over the Jets. They dominated Carolina and Pittsburgh at home, but had trouble winning a game that was close throughout the fourth quarter. Now, they hoped, that trend was broken. "We made enough plays," Beasley said. "We stopped them when we had to. We fought them off all the way."

Much of the credit went to Brunell. During much of 1996, even when he had big yardage games, he included an interception or two. Against the Bengals, he was as close to flawless as at any time in 29 games with the Jaguars, completing 21 of 34 passes for 356 yards and one touchdown. Most importantly, he did not throw an interception, his first game without an interception since Carolina. Late against Cincinnati, when the Jaguars needed touchdowns—and then completions to keep drives alive—Brunell completed 16 of his final 19 passes. "That's just the maturing of a great quarterback in the making," said Jimmy Smith, who had a second consecutive 100-yard receiving game in Rison's absence.

The Jaguars, at last, had won two consecutive games—not a big streak, but it lifted a burden, and with that burden lifted, they turned their attentions elsewhere.

The scoreboard. The team ran jubilantly from the field to the cheers of the wet, happy fans. Players high-fived, smiling and laughing.

"Pittsburgh lost, right?" Dave Widell said as he ran through the tunnel. "And who does Houston have today?"

The Jets, he was told.

"The Jets? What time?" he said, running to the locker room.

This was new. This was exciting. This was playoff talk.

"It's in our hands," Keenan McCardell said. "If we win our games, you never know. The crystal ball may come up and say, 'Jaguars.' Who knows what's in the future? We have a carrot dangling in our minds as players, because we know what kind of reward we have at the end of the carrot. That's the playoffs."

Coughlin, of course, wasn't talking carrots—or playoffs. He was talking, as usual, in themes and sayings.

"It's crystal clear," he told the players.

Crystal Clear.

"We know exactly where we stand, and we know what the circumstances are, and what can be accomplished," Coughlin said. "Setting the table is one thing, but going ahead and finishing the meal is another."

Crystal Clear.

"It is crystal clear," John Jurkovic said, repeating the words later. "There's no gray area. You have to win the game you're preparing for the next game to matter. That's the way it's been the last two weeks, and that's the way it's going to be the rest of the way."

This was a shining moment, not only for the Jaguars, but for two players once considered the Jaguars' "other" receivers, McCardell and Smith. McCardell caught the long pass that gave the Jaguars the lead, and was getting more consideration for Pro Bowl honors each week. Smith caught seven passes for 162 yards, his second 100-

yard game in as many starts since Rison's release. The game capped the best week of Smith's NFL career. Earlier that week, the team announced he had signed a two-year contract extension worth $1.086 million a season—a pleasant happening for a player who once wondered if he would ever play in the NFL at all.

Jimmy Lee Smith Jr. was born February 9, 1969, in Detroit, Michigan, and attended Calloway High School in Jackson, Mississippi. His father, Jimmy, Sr., attended Jackson State, and attended training camp with the Bengals. Smith, Jr., also attended Jackson State, and in 1992 was chosen in the second round, 36th overall, by the Dallas Cowboys.

Smith, at 6 feet 1, 200 pounds, was the sort of receiver Cowboys coach Jimmy Johnson loved—big, physical, and fast—but he broke his leg in training camp as a rookie, returning to play seven of the last 12 regular-season games, also playing in the playoffs and Super Bowl. The next season, Smith was the team's leading receiver in the preseason with 13 receptions for 197 yards and won the No. 3 receiver position behind Michael Irvin and Alvin Harper.

During the week of the final preseason game, however, he had an emergency appendectomy. The Cowboys, he said, rushed him back, wanting him to play 10 days after the operation. There was an infection, and four abscesses formed. The Cowboys placed him on the "reserve non-football injury list." Smith didn't agree, and filed a grievance to get his full salary, and credit toward his pension. "It wasn't something I wanted to do," Smith said. "The only thing I wanted to do was play football, just like every other player."

Smith won the grievance and received credit for his pension, and the NFL made the Cowboys pay him

$350,000, but Cowboys owner Jerry Jones told Johnson to cut Smith. This was in the summer of 1994. Johnson later said he had no desire to waive Smith, who later that summer signed with the Eagles. The Eagles released him, and in January 1995, Smith hadn't played a regular-season game in more than two years.

"I prayed I would someday get a chance to get back to the NFL," Smith said. "After being out for two years, and playing behind Michael Irvin, and then you have some injuries . . . you start to think, 'Maybe, I'm not cut out to be in the NFL.'"

In January of 1995, Jaguars pro personnel director Ron Hill called Smith. Hill was from Mississippi, and knew Smith from Jackson State. Hill wanted to sign him, but Smith balked, waiting for offers from more established teams. Finally, Hill convinced him, but even upon first joining the Jaguars, the NFL wasn't kind.

Smith was out of football shape when the Jaguars began their minicamps in 1995, and by the first training camp, he still wasn't at the level of the team's veterans receivers. He made the team, but was an afterthought and played sparingly, not catching a pass in the first eight games. Smith improved late that first season, catching 22 passes for 288 yards and three touchdowns in the final eight games. His career game came against the Broncos in Denver, when he scored three touchdowns in three ways—a pass reception, a blocked-punt recovery, and a kickoff return.

Entering 1996, the Jaguars decided Smith was a receiver for the future. His improvement late in the first season made them think, perhaps, he could develop into a solid player, and as training camp neared, he was one of the team's top two receivers along with Keenan McCardell.

When the Jaguars signed Andre Rison two days before

training camp, Smith slipped to third. "As a receiver corps, no one liked it," Smith said. "We knew the playing time we were expecting to get wasn't going to be that great."

After seeing Rison play, Smith realized—even if coaches didn't—that the four-time Pro Bowler was no better than he was. "I thought I was right there with him, step for step, as far as production," Smith said, "but we have things we don't have any control over. I don't cop an attitude because they bring in a Pro Bowl receiver."

Still, with the Jaguars often using three-receiver sets, Smith got as much opportunity as many NFL starters, playing extensively in the first half of the season.

When Rison was released, he took advantage. In his first two games as a starter, he had 100 yards receiving, and when the Jaguars prepared to play the Oilers December 8, few in Jacksonville thought about Rison anymore.

The Jaguars were in the playoffs. No one else had them there yet, but with three games remaining, players knew every game was a must win—in essence, a playoff game.

The players knew the chances were remote. Although they had won two consecutive games, they never had won three in a row—much less the five needed for a chance at the postseason. "Most definitely, it's a playoff game," McCardell said. "If we don't go 3–0, it won't matter."

"We've got a little streak going," Brunell said. "It's a little one, but it's a streak."

All that mattered to the Jaguars was winning in Houston, and history indicated that wouldn't be easy. The Jaguars were 1–6 on the road this season, and their two worst memories of the season had been in domes in St. Louis and New Orleans. Houston, however, was a different situation. The St. Louis crowd supported the Rams, and while the crowd in New Orleans was sparse, the atmosphere was Mardi Gras compared to the Astrodome on December 8.

The Oilers were 7–6, a game ahead of the Jaguars, but the Oilers' season had been a reversal of most NFL teams. Typically, a home game means an advantage, but when the Oilers announced plans the previous season to move to Nashville in 1998, fans turned against the team. The Oilers had games in which 50,000 people attended, but those were rare, and the lack of support showed in the Oilers' 2–4 record at home to date.

"We went into that game with a quiet confidence," John Jurkovic said. "The biggest thing is they beat us here. All week on film, we saw the way they handled us. If anything, revenge was a motivating factor."

The site of the game brought back memories, and revealed vividly just how much the Jaguars had changed in just over a year. In an October 1995 game in the Astrodome, the Jaguars won for the first time, 17–16. The heroes of that game, besides Brunell, were Desmond Howard, who caught a 15-yard touchdown from Brunell for the game winner, and safety Darren Carrington, who recovered two fumbles and had an interception. Now, Howard and Carrington were with Green Bay and Oakland, respectively. They were only two examples of the change. Sixteen starters from that game wouldn't start in the return to the Astrodome. Only Tony Boselli, Le'Shai Maston, Dave Widell, Don Davey, Jeff Lageman, and Mickey Washington were repeat starters.

That 1995 team won just three games after beating Houston. The team playing in the Astrodome in 1996 was talking playoffs. Denver and Pittsburgh were all but in as division winners, and either New England or Buffalo (both 9–4) would win the East. The other would be a wild-card team, with the Chiefs at 9–4 seemingly in control of a fifth slot. That left the Jaguars (6–7) competing with Houston (7–6), San Diego (7–6), San Diego (7–6), Indianapolis (7–6), Oakland (6–7), and Miami (6–7) for the final playoff spot.

"The biggest mistake you can make in playing the big game is to treat it unlike any other game you've played," Widell said. "The last thing I want is guys who are tight. You have to stay loose."

Which was why Coughlin *still* wasn't talking playoffs.

He was saying everything else, but by now, his reluctance to say the "p-word" was becoming a running joke among players and the media. He would say it was a big game. An important game.

Any kind of game—but a playoff game.

"To stay in this mode with positive reinforcement on Sunday afternoon is a great thing," he said. "It's a game that allows us, if we win, to move up another notch in the division, and keep all other aspects of opportunities to play, even beyond the season."

There was playoff talk there somewhere, but it was hard to find—as was a playoff atmosphere in the Astrodome. The Oilers' crowd was as expected—20,283, the second-lowest crowd ever in the Astrodome, and at times that day, the crowd was so quiet Brunell had to whisper the plays in the huddle. The key, however, was not Brunell, but the other quarterback, Steve "Air" McNair of the Oilers.

McNair, a second-year quarterback from Alcorn State, spent much of his first two seasons behind Chris Chandler. McNair was the quarterback of the future, but the Oilers wanted McNair to be ready before they made him the starter. Chandler was injured entering the Jaguars game, and McNair would get the start. He was a talent, but an inexperienced talent. The Jaguars' plan, then, was simple: Dare McNair.

That meant blitz, and blitz often, and stop rookie running back Eddie George, who ran for 143 yards in the teams' first meeting.

On the opening drive, the Jaguars drove 73 yards in 11 plays. Means, making his second start, scored on a 1-yard run with 8:56 remaining in the first quarter, but in the second quarter, Oilers linebacker Joe Bowden hit Means, forcing a fumble that Barron Wortham recovered at the Jaguars' 26. Three plays later, running back Ronnie Harmon beat Eddie Robinson for a 23-yard touchdown pass from McNair with 11:33 remaining in the second quarter. Mike Hollis's 34-yard field goal with 1:49 remaining gave the Jaguars a 10–7 halftime lead.

Gradually, the Jaguars took control in the second half. The offense did little, but the defense was strong. McNair was ineffective, and the Jaguars' offense was moving just enough.

With 5:31 remaining in the third quarter, McNair overthrew Harmon and Chris Hudson intercepted, returning it 21 yards to the Jaguars' 47. The Jaguars drove 53 yards on nine plays, and when Means scored on a 5-yard run with a minute remaining in the third quarter, they led 17–7.

On the next drive, the Oilers drove 53 yards on five plays, with the key play a 41-yard pass from McNair to Chris Sanders to the Jaguars' 6. George ran for a touchdown on the next play with 13:11 remaining.

Jaguars 17, Oilers 14.

The Jaguars were in danger, and they had been here before—outplaying a team on the road only to let the opponent have a chance late. This had been a formula for heartbreak, and now, the Jaguars were in a three-point game.

This time, the Jaguars showed poise. They didn't move on the drive after George's touchdown, but the defense held, and on the next drive, the Jaguars drove 37 yards in eight plays for a 38-yard field goal by Hollis and a 20–14 lead with 6:13 remaining.

On the Oilers' next drive, Tony Brackens sacked McNair, forcing a fumble. Don Davey recovered at the Houston 32 with 3:21 remaining. Enter Means.

Coughlin loved to run in this situation. Finally, with Means, he could. He ran five consecutive plays—6, 8, 6, 2, and then minus-3. Hollis's 31-yard field goal provided the Jaguars' final points with 1:56 remaining.

The Oilers drove, then added a late 27-yard field goal by Al Del Greco for the final margin. Jaguars 23, Oilers 17.

The Jaguars were 7–7 and starting to look like a play-off team. They ran late to secure the victory and didn't make mistakes—except the Means fumble. This time, in a close game, they made plays. They hadn't dominated, but they forced four turnovers. They held George to 45 yards on 16 carries, and won. On the road.

"The Houston game is the one that gave us a little legitimacy," John Jurkovic said later. "If you look at one game where we finally said, 'We're a pretty good football team,' it was after the Houston game. Now, we were a team that could do something."

The Jaguars, in the early season, were a team of big statistics. Now, they were a team capable of victory when they didn't play their best.

And nowhere was this reversal of the early season as obvious as in the play of Brunell.

Early in the season, Brunell threw for big yards and made mistakes. Those mistakes were the memorable plays from losses to Houston, Oakland, Cincinnati, and St. Louis. Brunell threw for at least 200 yards in each of those games, as he did in the first 13 games of the 1996 season, a streak that was at 15 including the last two games of the 1995 season. When people nationally thought of Brunell, they thought of the AFC's leader in passing yards, and the streak. Once, a few weeks before, that had been the right image, but Brunell improved drastically in those weeks in ways Coughlin wanted— that is, he was making smart decisions, and making plays enabling the Jaguars to win even when he didn't throw for big yards.

His 200-yard-game streak was broken against Houston. He completed 15 of 25 passes for 172 yards and no touchdowns.

"If you would have told me last week that we would hold Brunell under 200 yards and lose, I would have slapped you," Oilers linebacker Micheal Barrow said. "Now, somebody should slap us."

Barrow was one of the NFL's best quotes, but that one was misguided. The Jaguars long had needed to reach the point where they could win without Brunell throwing for big yardage. Many of Brunell's high yardage totals early in the season had come in Jaguars losses, and they came because the Jaguars had to pass, hardly a recipe for consistent success in the NFL, and hardly a recipe for making—or winning in—the playoffs.

One reason for the improvement, Brunell felt, was his health had improved. Before the bye week, he was bothered by a minor knee injury sustained against the Saints. That hampered his mobility. Since the bye, he had improved dramatically. Ironically, though, it was during October—when bothered by the knee—that he may have made his biggest strides. Brunell hadn't missed a snap all season, which Coughlin called a tribute to his toughness, but playing while immobile, he said, improved him.

"When you don't have the ability to run, you force yourself to stay in the pocket and find a receiver," Brunell said. "When you take off too soon, you blow some opportunities in the passing game, so it's helped a little."

His downfield reads, a weakness early, also improved dramatically. "Last year, it appeared he was in a hurry to pull the ball down and run," Oilers coach Jeff Fisher said. "He's doing a good job through his progressions. Now all the time on film, you don't see him reading the entire field. He'll stay with the progressions. Most of the time, it's to one side of the field, but he's making the right decisions."

The mature quarterback was now running a team on a big roll—and one that was starting more and more to believe what it was saying about the playoffs. "We're in it," Tony Boselli said. "We win out, and we have as good a chance as anybody. If we go 9–7, we'll take our chances. We're playing with confidence."

And yes, they were scoreboard watching—and liked what they saw. The Chargers and the Dolphins lost, further helping their chances. "Late in the game, we looked at the scoreboard," Coleman said. "We were watching the teams that needed to lose. San Diego lost [to Pittsburgh], and the Giants beat Miami. That was big for us."

But not big enough for Coughlin to say the p-word. "You're not going to get me to say it," he said. "How about just talking about winning? If that happens, we're in it." His players were starting to believe—and sensing even their coach couldn't hold out much longer.

"He can't deny we're in the hunt," Means said.

14
ONE STEP
CLOSER

"I can smell it."
—KEVIN HARDY
December 9, 1996

The Jaguars had arrived. No longer were they fighting to reach .500. No longer did they find ways to lose on the road. No longer did they wait for something bad to happen late in a game. Most importantly, no longer were the playoffs in the abstract.

The chance was real. The time was now.

The days of September and October were far behind, and finally, the Jaguars were on a winning streak—three games, longest in team history.

The Jaguars returned from Houston Sunday night. Monday morning, as players sat in their lockers, they watched ESPN's NFL highlights and noticed something they hadn't seen before. No more were they an afterthought. Jaguars highlights were shown prominently, and afterward, anchors flashed charts of the AFC's playoff situation.

The Jaguars were not only included—they were moving up. Next up was an ESPN Sunday-night game against the Seattle Seahawks, and although the Jaguars needed help, it appeared with a victory in that game, the season ender against Atlanta the following week could have very important implications.

"We're feeling a surge right now," Mark Brunell said.

Anyone doubting that surge need only have been present a few moments later. Down the hall, Tom Coughlin held his Monday conference. His game-week moods were predictable. Typically, on Mondays, he was cautious and analytical. Tuesdays, he was rarely seen, preparing the game plan, and by Wednesday, the Monday mood— sullen after a loss, happier after a victory—was gone: He recharged, and all thoughts were of the coming game. Thursdays, there was a bounce to his step, and by Friday, the game was so near he could feel it. All was right in the world.

On this Monday, he was giddy. This was why he coached, why any coach coached: late-season games with postseason implications. At his press conference, he fielded questions, again avoiding talking playoffs. Finally, David Lamm, a local radio-show host, asked Coughlin, "Why can't you say it, Tom? Why can't you say playoffs?"

Coughlin smiled.

"The media has made that up," he said. "I can actually say the word. I can almost spell it."

Then, say it.

"Playoffs," he said, laughing.

The playoffs were the team goal, but as the Jaguars prepared for the Seahawks, much of the talk was about what players considered the most important personal goal.

Of any individual honor, the Pro Bowl was the most coveted—partially because of the selection process: fan voting counting a third, coach's voting a third, and league-wide player voting a third. Making the Pro Bowl put a player among the elite. No Jaguars player made it in 1995. Now, with several candidates—including Keenan McCardell, Brunell, Tony Boselli, and Jimmy Smith—the question was: Who would be the first?

Most of the fan ballots were in, but on Tuesday, players and coaches cast their votes. Announcement day was Thursday, and while several Jaguars players were having Pro Bowl–type seasons, the selection process had a popularity-contest element likely to hurt Jaguars players. Not being on national TV would hurt, as would Jacksonville's status as the NFL's second-smallest market. Also, the Jaguars were a second-year team, and until the Houston victory, few paid them much attention.

Carolina was expected to have numerous players voted to the NFC team, but Carolina had been a season-long success story. The Jaguars, as always was the case, were the new kids. "So much of it is the fans," Brunell said. "We don't get the exposure that some teams get as a new team."

No one was more likely to be hurt than Brunell.

Brunell led the NFL in passing yardage with 3,914, but had only 17 touchdown passes and 20 interceptions. He was a candidate because of his yardage, and in the final few weeks, he was playing at Pro Bowl level, but his early-season struggles likely would hurt his chances. Hurting further was the presence of Broncos quarterback John Elway, who was having a career year; Ravens quarterback Vinny Testaverde, also having a career year despite mishaps against the Jaguars; and Patriots quarterback Drew Bledsoe. All had better touchdown-interception ratios and higher passing ratings.

Boselli was also a candidate, but likely would be hurt by lack of recognition. Pro Bowls were often overloaded with big names who made it on reputation. At no position was that as true as offensive line. Considering performance, Boselli was worthy, but he didn't have the name or experience of some AFC tackles. Against Panthers linebacker Lamar Lathon—who had 12 sacks after 14 games—he was dominant, not allowing a sack. As players and coaches voted, Boselli had allowed one sack this season.

Smith was a possibility, too. Since Rison's release, he had been one of the most dangerous receivers in the AFC, and with two games remaining, he had 70 receptions for 1,045 yards and five touchdowns.

The most likely candidate seemed to be McCardell. Although many felt Smith equal to McCardell, it was McCardell who had started all season—and it was McCardell who was among the AFC's reception leaders throughout the season. He had 78 receptions for 1,059 yards and three touchdowns, but for McCardell, the question, too, remained: Were any Jaguars known enough to make it?

"You can't worry that you play in Jacksonville," he said. "You hope you get enough media attention and your skills on the field get you the attention and the notoriety.

"It would be nice to be the first person," he added. "I think Mark feels that, too, and he deserves it. He's having a great year, but I'm not going to lose any sleep over it."

Instead, he went home Wednesday night and put up a Christmas tree with his wife and daughter. When McCardell arrived at the stadium the next day, he had jitters. The Pro Bowl was every player's dream, but for the former 12th-round selection who had been cut four times, attaining the dream would be particularly sweet.

That morning, at a team meeting, Coughlin told the team McCardell had made the Pro Bowl. No other Jaguars were named, but the entire team stood, giving

McCardell an ovation. "I didn't know what to say," Mc-Cardell said. "I was at a loss for words. My heart was beating fast. It was a dream of mine to show folks I can be one of the best in this league. It's good to know your peers respect you like that."

The others weren't ignored. Brunell was second alternate behind Testaverde, Elway, Bledsoe, and Dan Marino (first alternate). Boselli was first alternate behind Broncos tackle Gary Zimmerman, Patriots tackle Bruce Armstrong, and Dolphins tackle Richmond Webb. Leon Searcy was the second alternate at tackle.

Brunell and Boselli still had a chance to go to Honolulu, Hawaii, site of the game. Older players often skipped the game, and it was believed Elway, Marino, and Zimmerman would do so. "Maybe I'll have to hire someone to take a baton to their knees to get there," Brunell said, laughing.

This was a disappointing days for many Jaguars, but the time when Pro Bowl day was anything less than a celebration in Jacksonville seemed likely to end soon. The Jaguars roster, far from the hodgepodge group of the previous season, now looked like an NFL roster—and a good one.

Brunell was a rising star. Boselli and Searcy were among the best at their positions. McCardell was a Pro Bowler, and Smith was close. Natrone Means and James Stewart each had big-time ability, and that was just on offense. Defensively, Clyde Simmons, Eddie Robinson, and Jeff Lageman were better than the players playing those spots in December 1995.

Simmons, Robinson, and Lageman, however, were veterans. The Jaguars expected them to perform and they did. Causing the most optimism as 1996 neared an end was the development of three rookies—a defensive rookie class many considered the best in the NFL.

                                * * *

In early April 1996, it was evident on paper that the Jaguars were improved on offense from the previous season. McCardell, Searcy, and Means had been added in recent weeks, which team officials felt marked a significant upgrade to an offense ranked 28th in the NFL the year before. The Jaguars had yet to improve significantly on defense.

Robinson signed from the Oilers, Jurkovic from the Packers, and Hall as a street free agent; but the areas the team most wanted to improve—cover cornerback and pass rusher—still were weak. So, here's what they did:

—First round, No. 2 overall: Kevin Hardy, linebacker. A solid run-player, good pass-rush guy with the ability to cover backs out of the backfield.

—Second round, No. 33 overall: Tony Brackens, defensive end. A pass-rushing specialist and a player of unlimited potential, coaches felt.

—Third round, No. 63 overall: Aaron Beasley, cornerback. A big, physical player who coaches felt could develop into a solid cover corner.

They were three players at different positions from different backgrounds, but formed a rookie core many in the Jaguars organization thought could be the base of the defense for years.

Kevin Lamont Hardy was born July 24, 1973, in Evansville, Indiana, and played football and basketball and ran track at Harrison High School. There, he was a basketball teammate of future Indiana University star Calbert Cheaney and future University of Kentucky star Walter McCarty, but Hardy starred in football, and signed with the University of Illinois.

At first, Hardy was hardly a star. Illinois, at the time, was Linebacker University. Dana Howard, John Holecek, and Simeon Rice all started, and received more publicity than Hardy early. As a junior, though, Hardy made All–Big 10, and considered turning professional. He stayed, and as a senior, his NFL stock rose. Rice, a pass-rush specialist, received most of the preseason recognition, but Hardy had 11 sacks, 15 tackles for loss, and three interceptions, and won the Butkus Award, given annually to the nation's best collegiate linebacker.

The Jaguars chose Hardy with the No. 2 overall selection, and immediately made him a starter. He had trouble, at first, adapting to the NFL, but trouble was relative. He improved the Jaguars drastically, and he was a friendly, mature, good-natured locker-room leader. After 14 games, he had 117 tackles, second on the team.

He also had five and a half sacks and two interceptions, and no one around the Jaguars regretted their 1996 No. 2 overall selection.

"Kevin's Kevin," Tom McManus said. "He has amazing ability. He does amazing things."

Tony Lynn Brackens Jr. was born December 26, 1974, in Fairfield, Texas, where he played football and ran track at Fairfield High School. He played defensive end and tight end in football, and won the state championship in the shot put. Brackens grew up on an 800-acre cattle ranch, competing in rodeos throughout high school before signing with the University of Texas.

Brackens was a born pass rusher. At Texas, he earned All–Southwest Conference honors as an 18-year-old freshman, when he had a team-high 10 sacks. In his first college game, he sacked Colorado quarterback Kordell Stewart twice. He had 24 sacks in three seasons, and after a seven-sack junior season he declared his eligibility for the draft.

Many analysts expected Brackens to be a top 20 selection, but on draft day, he slipped. He sustained a knee injury in his final season at Texas, and teams were concerned about lingering effects. Coughlin, however, loved him, and at a private workout, Brackens dazzled the coach with his strength and quickness. Jaguars doctors examined the knee and it checked out. When Brackens was available in the second round, Coughlin chose him.

"He was in the middle of the first round on our draft board, which means, in effect, we were able to come away with two first-round picks," Coughlin said.

Brackens, the only underclassman selected in the Jaguars' first two drafts, arrived in the NFL unintimidated. On the third day of his second minicamp, he brawled with second-year guard Brian DeMarco, and from the start, carried himself with a cocky, arrogant air. Part of that arrogance came from his strength. He bench-pressed 450 pounds, third most on the Jaguars—strength, he said, that came from lifting 50-pound sacks of seed 50 times a day and tossing around 80-pound bales of hay on his family's ranch.

Still, the NFL was an adjustment. Brackens was young—not yet 22 when the season began. At times, he was immature and surly, alienating teammates and coaches, but particularly the media, of whom he was especially wary. Most of Brackens's early struggles on the field were temporary. He was quick, but not excessively big for a defensive end. His potential was obvious. His four and half sacks led the AFC in the preseason, but when the regular season began, he struggled against first-team offensive tackles. Still, he had two sacks against Carolina, a game teammates said showed his ability. "The kid has unlimited potential," McManus said.

"Tony's going to be a great pro," Clyde Simmons said. "He just needs to decide when he wants to be great. Once he decides, people are going to realize how talented this young man is. He's got a lot of talent and ability. When he decides Tony Brackens is going to be the best, he's going to be great."

He had a sack in the Week 9 loss to the Bengals, and in Games 10–14, had three more. As the nationally televised game against Seattle approached, he was starting to play to that potential.

Aaron Bruce Beasley was born July 7, 1973, in Pottstown, Pennsylvania, and played football at Pottstown High School. He then attended Valley Forge Military Academy, where he had the distinction of being the only one of his future teammates to have said no to his future coach.

Coughlin recruited Beasley while at Boston College, but Beasley signed with West Virginia. "I surprised them," he said, laughing. "I changed my mind."

Beasley started at West Virginia from 1993 to 1995, and was the Big East's all-time career interception leader with 18, returning three for touchdowns. In 1994, he led the nation with 10 interceptions. The Jaguars, needing a cover corner after losing Williams, Lyght, and Vincent in free agency, decided to take one with their first selection of the third round. As the selection approached, the Jaguars coveted Ray Mickens, a cornerback from Texas A&M. One selection before the Jaguars, the Jets chose Mickens, and the Jaguars chose Beasley.

Early in training camp, it became apparent the Jaguars had selected a smooth, physical corner who fit their needs better than the smaller Mickens. Beasley struggled to pick up the Jaguars' system, but carried himself with a cocky air needed in a corner—and he showed enough flashes that Jaguars coaches planned for a lineup that would include Beasley at some point in the season.

That plan was delayed in the second preseason game against St. Louis, when he fractured a shoulder blade.

Team officials said it was a 10-day injury. It turned into two months.

Beasley returned in the loss to St. Louis October 20 and made his first NFL start against the Ravens November 10 when the Jaguars started in the nickel alignment. Dave Thomas was injured against Cincinnati, and Beasley became the starter two weeks later against the Ravens. Through November and early December, he gave the Jaguars the physical cover corner for which they had been searching.

The trio, however, was more than three rookies. They breathed life into a defense, gave it youth, and made it a better unit than it was in 1995. "That's a pretty good draft by ol' Rick Reiprish [director of college scounting]," Lageman said. "That's a nice bunch there, when you consider it."

And as the first nationally televised game of the season approached, the one thing about these rookies that stood out most was they weren't really rookies anymore. "They had the benefit of playing early in the season," Coughlin said. "That's part of learning in the NFL."

As November began, the Jaguars probably figured they would be off January. In mid-December, the Jaguars had hope—and it didn't seem so slim anymore.

The Jaguars weren't alone in their playoffs thoughts. Thirteen of 15 AFC teams had them, but as one studied scenarios, strange as it seemed, the Jaguars getting in seemed logical.

"I'm more aware today than I was last week," Coughlin said. "It's a tremendous feeling to be in the hunt at this time of year."

Solving the playoff picture, annually, was a nightmare for the NFL office. With three or more teams, the possibilities seem endless. With 13 involved, the NFL hadn't

figured all scenarios by midweek, but many were so unlikely it wasn't necessary. By midweek, most players focused on three primary Jaguars-make-the-playoffs
scenarios, all of which depended upon them winning
their final two games:

—Scenario 1: One loss each by Oakland (7–7), Indianapolis (8–6), Houston (7–7), and San Diego (7–7) would
get the Jaguars in as the third wild-card team, sixth overall AFC team.

—Scenario 2: One loss each by Houston, Oakland,
and San Diego, and two losses by Buffalo (9–5).

—Scenario 3: One loss each by Houston, Oakland,
and Indianapolis, and a continued point-differential advantage in conference games over San Diego, which was
currently at plus-5.

"The only thing I know is if we win this week and the
following week, we'll enhance our chances," Coughlin
said. "I'm not trying to make a mystery out of this. I really
believe in my coaching life, if you take care of your own
business and be aware of what situations have to take
place in order for the end result to be playoffs, you go
from there."

Players were less wordy. To them, after being 3–6 and
4–7, this position late in the season was a wonderful gift.
"I can smell it," Hardy said.

"It gives you a spring in your step," McManus said.
"The excitement is there, but as a team you can't think
like that. You have to take it one game at a time."

Adding to the excitement was this: The game was nationally televised, and although players tried to downplay
the significance, a national-TV game was big. Monday
nights were biggest—a player knew all of his peers were
watching—but Sunday nights were a close second, and
this was the Jaguars' only prime-time game of the season.

"You forget the TV audience, you forget the extra coverage, once you take the field," Brunell said. "You don't think about that stuff if you take the right approach."

Coughlin also didn't want the team thinking play-offs—not too much. At a Saturday night team meeting, he warned players to "take care of business" and not to worry about the rest of the league. Above all, no TV the next day. If the Jaguars didn't win, what the other teams did didn't matter.

Not watch?

The excitement of the playoff chase made it impossible. When the day began, Jaguars players knew if everything broke right, they might take the field that night knowing if they won their final two games, they were in the playoffs. Things didn't break *that* right, but it was close.

The Jaguars needed the Raiders, Colts, and Oilers to lose Sunday afternoon. If that happened, two victories got the Jaguars in the playoffs. Two early games involved the Colts and Oilers. Houston lost to Cincinnati. Indianapolis beat the Chiefs. The Jaguars peeked at the locker-room televisions at those games as they arrived to prepare for the Seahawks game.

As they dressed for the game, they watched the Broncos-Raiders. This presented a problem because Coughlin entered the locker room periodically. "We had to make sure the TVs were off when Coughlin came in, but we were watching," Means said later. "But we knew, like he said, if we didn't take care of our own business, it wouldn't have mattered."

The Raiders lost to the Broncos, and that meant as the Jaguars took the field against the Seahawks, their playoff scenario looked like this: Beat the Seahawks, have Miami beat Buffalo the next night, and beat Atlanta the following week, and the Jaguars were in—as long as Kansas City and Buffalo didn't tie in Buffalo in the season finale.

The enthusiasm carried into the game for the Jaguars. As 66,134 looked on in JMS, the defense was tough against the Seahawks (6–8 entering the game) early. Late in the first quarter, Means began to bruise and brawl. And Brunell began to pass. And run. Brunell passed 48 yards on the drive. He scrambled 17 yards for a first down to the Seahawks' 15. Means ran for 19 yards on four carries. With 2:05 remaining in the quarter, the Jaguars took a 7–0 lead on a 12-yard pass from Brunell to Smith.

After that, however, the pressure of the playoff chase took a toll. The Seahawks made it 7–3 on a 27-yard field goal by Todd Peterson, and with 40 seconds remaining in the half, they took the lead with a 10-yard touchdown pass from Rick Mirer to Ricky Proehl. Mirer, who had lost his job early in the season only to regain it when John Friesz was injured, wasn't looking like a player the franchise had abandoned. At halftime, he had completed 10 of 15 passes for 105 yards. The Seahawks led, 10–7.

Neither team was effective offensively early in the third quarter, but then the Seahawks began to drive. Joey Galloway, a second-year receiver, had blistered the Jaguars the year before with an 86-yard touchdown run on a reverse in a 47–30 Seahawks victory at JMS. That play made most of the NFL highlight reels for the season, and with the Seahawks leading 10–7 in the third quarter, he again burned the Jaguars, running a reverse 51 yards for a first down to the Jaguars' 17.

The Seahawks continued to push toward the goal line. Mirer passed 9 yards to Carlester Crumpler, who was pushed out of bounds by Robert Massey for a first-and-goal at the 1.

The Seahawks were a yard away from a 10-point lead, and with the Jaguars' offense struggling for two quarters, a 10-point lead was a big lead. The playoffs, for the Jaguars, again appeared to be what many had thought all along—a distant, unreachable goal. The defense needed a big play—three or four of them, actually.

On first down, they got one. Seahawks running back Chris Warren ran over right guard, and McManus stuffed him for no gain. On second down, Seahawks running back Lamar Smith ran over right tackle. Smith began to break outside, but as he did, reserve linebacker Brant Boyer—a key player on short-yardage and special teams all season—made his biggest play of the season, knocking Smith sideways for no gain. Third-and-goal from the 1.

Again, the Seahawks tried Smith, this time in the middle, but Lageman hit him first, followed by Brackens and the rest of the Jaguars' defense. No gain. Fourth-and-goal from the 1.

The Seahawks had little to lose. Out of the playoff chase and in a spoiler's role, they went for it on fourth-and-1. The crowd at JMS, never having seen the Jaguars muster such a goal-line stand, was caught up in the moment. This was playoff football. Mirer dropped to pass and threw over the middle, but Brackens leapt and batted it away. The Jaguars had held, but wait . . .

Penalty.

Against the Seahawks—false start, nullifying the play. Fourth-and-goal from the 5. With the odds greater than from the 1, the Seahawks kicked a field goal. Seahawks 13, Jaguars 7—a six-point deficit rather than 10 with 1:54 remaining in the third quarter.

"That goal-line stand turned the whole game around," Kelvin Pritchett said.

"That got everybody pumped," Massey said. "Not only in the stands, but the players. You look at the sideline, and you see everybody cheering. There were guys that don't even raise their hands to the crowd raising their hands in the huddle. Defensively, we got a little more confidence out of it."

On the next possession, a 34-yard kickoff return by Bucky Brooks gave the Jaguars first-and-10 at their 43. Means ran twice for 5 yards, then Brunell scrambled for 6 yards and a first down before Stewart ran 7 yards to set up second-and-three from the Seahawks' 39 on the last play of the quarter.

The goal-line stand kept the Jaguars in the game. The first play of the fourth quarter gave them the lead. Brunell dropped, and passed long down the left sideline, into the end zone toward Smith.

Smith, Seahawks cornerback Fred Thomas, and Seahawks safety Darryl Williams all leapt for the pass. A penalty flag flew, and the ball bounced from Thomas's hands. Smith, as he landed, reached and caught the pass, and when he looked around, he was standing in the end zone. The penalty was interference against Williams.

Touchdown. Jaguars 14, Seahawks 13.

Brackens, during the second half of his rookie season, had matured fast, and for the last month could be counted upon for at least one big play—a sack or a forced fumble—per game. Against the Seahawks, it seemed he could be counted upon for one every series.

On the series following Smith's touchdown, instead of rushing, Brackens dropped into coverage. Mirer passed to the right for Galloway, but Brackens intercepted at the Jaguars' 39, returning it 27 yards to the Seahawks' 34 and setting up a 19-yard field goal by Mike Hollis. "The turning point of the game," Dana Hall called it.

Hollis later added a 39-yarder for a 20–13 victory.

Yet, this night belonged to Brackens. ESPN analyst Joe Theismann called it one of the best defensive performances he had ever seen. Rookie or veteran. Brackens was dominant. He was in the Seattle backfield throughout. "Every time you looked up, he was making plays," Hall said.

He finished with 12 tackles, one sack, one interception, three tipped passes, and four pressures.

"That's exactly the sort of thing he can do," Clyde Simmons said of his protégé. "When he comes to play and decides he wants to make plays, he can make big-time plays. Tonight was big-time, big-time, big-time."

Brackens, wary of the media after what he considered undue criticism during his early struggles, stayed in the shower long after the game, wanting to avoid postgame interviews. Director of Communications Dan Edwards convinced Brackens to speak, telling him to enjoy the moment. When he spoke, he was quiet. "I just read the quarterback and broke on the ball," he said of his first career NFL interception. "I was right there."

Most important, of course, was this: The Jaguars were more than alive. They were thriving, and the playoffs—with a very reasonable break or two—were realistic. "Our football team has risen to the circumstances," Coughlin said. "Every game is a huge game."

And the biggest players on the team were coming up big. Brunell was flawless, completing 19 of 26 passes (73.1 percent) for 231 yards and two touchdowns with no interceptions. He also ran seven times for 34 yards. Smith, who caught both touchdown passes, caught eight passes total for 124 yards—his fourth 100-yard game of the season, third since Rison's departure.

And almost imperceptibly, Natrone Means—once an afterthought this season—was becoming a factor. Means hadn't played extensively since Week 9 of the previous season in San Diego, and in his first two starts for the Jaguars, he showed rust, rushing for 56 yards on 21 carries against Cincinnati and 67 yards on 25 carries against Houston.

Coughlin loved Means's straight-ahead style, and felt his presence made defenses honest and forced them to play the run, opening up passing opportunities. So he continued to call plays for Means, and against the Seahawks, the former Pro Bowl player looked like a Pro Bowler again, rushing 23 times for 92 yards, a 4.0 yards per carry average. But afterward, Means was talking the same talk as everyone else in the Jaguars' locker room.

Playoff talk. Legitimate playoff talk.

"Guys really don't know the pressure we have put on ourselves," Means said, "but it's a good feeling."

"Four weeks ago, I wasn't very aware of the playoff picture," Brunell said. "Now, I'd be lying to you if I said I wasn't looking around, seeing what everyone else is doing."

And few felt better than Lageman. This was why he had come to Jacksonville—to build a winner, escape the doldrums of New York, and play in the playoffs. Now, it was one game away. He was happy, yet it was a cautious optimism. As the final seconds ticked, he saw his coach on the sideline, scowling. Lageman told Coughlin to smile. For his teammates, however, he had a different message, and delivered it walking up and down the sideline, poking several teammates hard in the chest with his finger.

He then walked the sideline alone, finger pointed in the air in front of him.

"One more, one more, one more," he said.

15
A MIRACLE MISS

"That's automatic. You just knew he was going to make it, but I guess you have to believe in destiny when something like that happens."

—JIMMY SMITH
December 22, 1996

The night after the Seahawks game, Jaguars players gathered around Jacksonville for *Monday Night Football*. This was a weekly ritual, but this week, it had added importance. The Miami Dolphins were playing the Buffalo Bills in Miami. If Miami won, the Jaguars were in the playoffs if they beat Atlanta—provided Buffalo and Kansas City didn't tie the following Sunday.

"I'm rooting for [Dolphins players] Richmond Webb and Dan Marino and all the guys," Tony Boselli said.

The Bills-Dolphins game was on everyone's mind at Jacksonville Municipal Stadium that day. Suddenly, the playoffs seemed real. The Jaguars had won four consecutive games—this from a team that couldn't win back-to-

back until this streak. The tough times were on Coughlin's mind that day, too:

—Oakland, 17–3.
—New England, 28–25 (OT).
—St. Louis, 17–14.
—New Orleans, 17–13.
—Cincinnati, 28–21.

"You appreciate heaven a little bit more if you spend
some time in hell," Coughlin said.

And this . . . this was heaven?

"It's not yet," Coughlin said, smiling, "but the scorch-
ing on the bottom of the feet is not as bad right now."

Coughlin's feet felt better that night. Coughlin, the ultimate creature of habit, was in bed at 10:10 every night.
No matter the circumstances. Even his team's playoff
chances being decided on TV didn't vary the schedule.
Coughlin was in bed that night when his daughter, Katie,
came into the room.

"Dolphins 16, Bills 14," she said.

One week remained.

The players were off Tuesday. Wednesday, they arrived knowing they controlled their destiny. There was
the matter of a Bills-Chiefs tie, but there hadn't been a tie
in the NFL since 1989. In October, fate might have
worked against the Jaguars enough to have two teams do
something that hadn't happened in seven seasons. Not
now.

"Stranger things have happened, but we're in a good
situation," Ben Coleman said. "Win, we're in. We lose,
and we go home. What other scenario could you ask for?
If you would have told someone that in the last game of
the year, the Jaguars would be fighting for a playoff spot,
people would have laughed you out of football."

Success did something besides stop the laughter. The Jaguars' coaching staff, intact since March of 1995, was for the first time the subject of job speculation around the country—and, irony of ironies, it was the once-hated Gilbride getting the most attention.

The improvement from 1995 to 1996 made the former run-and-shoot coordinator a hot prospect. Particularly helping Gilbride was the Jaguars' late-season surge. They were a more efficient offense now, and the improvement in that area was because of better communication between Gilbride and Coughlin.

Gilbride-Coughlin, at times during two seasons, had been an uneasy alliance. Gilbride, while trying to shed his run-and-shoot image, did believe in the principles of the run-and-shoot—and believed in spreading the field and passing early to set up the run late. Coughlin liked to pass, too, but, with his Giants background, believed a team had to run first to set up the pass. The two argued about philosophy at times, but in the first season and a half, an argument with Coughlin only had one winner—Coughlin.

This caused the offense to look confused and ineffective at times, and in the second half of the season, Coughlin realized this and let Gilbride truly coordinate the offense. When Coughlin left Gilbride alone, an offense already ranked No. 2 in the NFL became one that not only produced yards, but produced points in critical situations.

If Jacksonville's fans didn't yet appreciate Gilbride, others did. In December, he interviewed for the head coaching job at Boston College, but he pulled his name from consideration, hoping for an NFL head position later. As the month wore on, and the Jaguars improved, he was mentioned more often as a candidate for one of the numerous NFL positions opening after the season.

Defensive coordinator Dick Jauron and secondary coach Randy Edsall were also drawing interest. Edsall, a 38-year-old coach many believed would be a successful college and perhaps NFL coach someday, interviewed for the BC job, too, but did not get it. Jauron, the Jaguars' defensive coordinator, was less of an NFL candidate than Gilbride, but only because of a lack of coordinator experience. Gilbride, including four seasons in Houston, had been a coordinator six seasons; Jauron's only coordinator experience was two seasons with the Jaguars. Jauron, aloof and quiet, seemed an unlikely head coach, but he was considered one of football's top young defensive minds. Players—dating back to his tenure as defensive backs coach in Green Bay—swore by his player-friendly style.

His alma mater, Yale, pursued him heavily in December of 1996, but he declined the offer, and like Gilbride, he was mentioned as a possible NFL head coach—if not the next season, soon.

The coordinators' status had risen during the late-season streak—and there was a reason. The Jaguars were playing, and talking, like a different team. A playoff team. Clyde Simmons, who had started the playoff talk more than a month before, said, "It's a nice feeling knowing that what somebody else does can't hurt you."

It was a good feeling, but not too much different from the last month in one way—the Jaguars had been playing do-or-die since the second Ravens game. So far, they weren't dead.

"It's the same," Brunell said. "I can't express enough that it's the same as it has been the last few weeks. There's nothing new. If we do the things we've done the last few weeks, we'll be fine. We don't need any extra team meetings, or work, or anything. Or to have guys come together and talk about how important this game

JAGS TO RICHES 225

is. We know how important it is. We just have to go win it.

"I hope guys don't take a different approach to this one. There shouldn't be more pressure. If we keep doing the same things, and we don't get too tight, or too nervous, we'll be fine."

That wouldn't be easy.

Of 53 players on the roster, 24 had playoff experience—110 total games. That meant 29 players never had played in a playoff game, and most never had played in a game with implications as serious as those against Atlanta. And among those 29 was a small group who at various times in their careers certainly never expected to be in such a game at all.

When most people think NFL they think of high-priced superstars and high-drafted rookies. The league is stars and millionaires, and the Jaguars built through that route. Their foundation was high-profile draft choices such as Tony Boselli, Kevin Hardy, and Tony Brackens, and high-profile free agents such as Leon Searcy and Jeff Lageman.

That's one side of the NFL. The other side is lesser known—the minimum-salary players, usually drafted in the low rounds, or not at all; players given little chance to make a team. The Jaguars had several such players, and they were hardly minimum-contribution guys.

One was an expansion draftee. One was a street free agent.

One was acquired in a trade. One was acquired off the waiver wire.

They came to the Jaguars in every nonglamorous, ego-deflating way possible, but each carved a niche, and was crucial to the 1996 success.

Le'Shai Edwoin Maston was born October 7, 1970, in

Dallas Texas, and played for Dallas Carter, which annually produces some of the top high school talent in the country. Maston's high school team was particularly talented, including future NFL players such as linebacker Jessie Armstead and cornerback Clifton Abraham.

Maston played football and ran track for Carter, then signed with Baylor University as a safety, moving to linebacker in his second season. Maston made All–Southwest Conference at linebacker as a junior and senior, and signed with the Houston Oilers as a free-agent fullback in the summer of 1993.

He played a season as a reserve running back. In 1994, he made his first start, but after that season, the Oilers made him available in the expansion draft.

The Jaguars chose him 35th overall.

The February 15, 1995, expansion draft was supposed to be a boon. The NFL made available better talent than in past expansion drafts, but the reality of the expansion pool was—like past expansion drafts—the lesser players were still the lesser players, and few draftees made an impact. That was particularly true in Jacksonville.

Several expansion draftees, including safeties Harry Colon and Mike Dumas, wide receivers Cedric Tillman and Desmond Howard, and quarterback Steve Beuerlein, started early, but gradually, they assumed less significant roles, replaced by younger players with more potential.

In 1996, expansion draftees grew rare. Only Jeff Novak, Paul Frase, Willie Jackson, Dave Thomas, Derek Brown, Maston, and Brant Boyer remained at the end of the season. Only Maston had been a full-time starter in each year.

Maston wasn't a Pro Bowl fullback, but he improved each week, and against Seattle, when Natrone Means rushed for a season-high yardage total, coaches credited Maston. The expansion draft wasn't the boon many expected, but it gave the Jaguars a solid fullback for two seasons.

Richard Lee Tylski was born February 27, 1971, in San Diego, California, and played football at Madison High School in San Diego. Lightly recruited out of high school, he played at Utah State, where he was All–Big West in 1993 before signing with the New England Patriots as a free agent.

Tylski spent that year on the Patriots' practice squad, and was waived the following summer. The Jaguars claimed him, and he spent that season on the Jaguars' practice squad. That ended his practice-squad eligibility, meaning as 1996 training camp opened, he had to make the active roster or be waived.

"I've always considered myself someone who did things the hard way," Tylski said. "I never wanted to be told I couldn't do something. I always went out to prove people wrong. I've made some definite strides since, say, Stevens Point last year, but by no means am I satisfied or complacent. You keep trying to improve, and work the butt off. If you focus on things you do good, you get complacent, and satisfied. I don't want that."

Tylski made the roster, playing the first half of the season as a reserve, and when Brian DeMarco was injured, he became the starter. He sustained a series of neck burners—three in his first four games as a starter—that limited his time and effectiveness early, but the more he played, the more he held his own, and soon played so well that when DeMarco returned in early December, Tylski kept the job. "He was an unknown before he got in there when Brian got hurt," Dave Widell said. "We found out he was a pretty good player in his own right, so that makes everyone happy."

Peter Clark Mitchell was born October 9, 1971, in Royal Oak, Michigan, and played football, baseball, and basketball at Brother Rice High in Birmingham, Michigan. He signed with Boston College in 1990. Coughlin arrived at BC a year later, and Mitchell flourished in Coughlin's wide-open style.

Mitchell started four seasons at BC, finishing as the school's all-time receptions leader with 190 receptions for 2,388 yards and 20 touchdowns, and as a senior, he earned All–Big East and all-America honors with 55 receptions for 617 yards and seven touchdowns. Mitchell's size hurt him in the eyes of NFL scouts, and he was drafted in the fourth round that year by the Miami Dolphins.

Coughlin, meanwhile, had left BC before Mitchell's senior season. He liked Mitchell, and days before the 1996 season, dealt disgruntled receiver Mike Williams to Miami, and got Mitchell in return.

Mitchell, despite his size, flourished again under his college coach. He caught 41 passes in 1995 as a rookie for 527 yards and two touchdowns, and in 1996, emerged as one of Brunell's favorite targets. When the Jaguars needed a clutch catch or a big first down, often it was Mitchell who was the target.

"In critical situations, we go to Pete," Brunell said.

"That's the most important part of my game—to be consistent and dependable," Mitchell said. "I surprised people last year, but this year I wasn't expecting anything but to surpass that."

Thomas Edward McManus was born July 30, 1970, in Buffalo Grove, Illinois, and played football and threw the shot and discus at Wheeling High School in Wheeling, Illinois. If any Jaguars player was surprised to have been not only playing, but starting in the NFL on the final weekend of 1996, it was McManus.

McManus signed with Boston College in 1988, and after redshirting a year, became one of the most productive linebackers in school history. He started three seasons, and led BC in tackles as a junior and a senior, earning All–Big East honors both seasons. He was a prototype college linebacker—tough, hard-nosed—but he was also the kind of player who scouts questioned.

McManus could play, but his speed was a question and his size (6-foot-2, 240 pounds) was a concern, too. He went undrafted, and signed with the Saints as a free agent in 1993. The Saints released him in the first cut. Many players bounce from team to team after being released. McManus never even got a chance to do that.

He spent 1994 out of football, tending bar in a Chicago sports bar. There, he watched NFL games on Sundays, feeling he could play with the players he saw on television.

"It would drive me nuts," he said. "I'm thinking, 'Man, I should be out there somewhere.' Then, you realize how much of the NFL is timing."

His timing improved. When Coughlin got the Jaguars job, he offered McManus a chance. McManus went to camp with the Jaguars, but did so with a cautious optimism—if he didn't make the team that year, he figured, it was time to give up football and join the real world. "If it's not there this year, I'm done," he said.

He made it, and stuck.

He played with the Jaguars in 1995 as a backup, starting two games and playing extensively in short-yardage situations. In 1996, he again made the team as a backup to Bryan Schwartz, and when Schwartz was injured against New England in Week 4, McManus became the starter.

The Jaguars barely missed Schwartz. McManus took advantage of his opportunity, becoming one of the team's leading tacklers. Although not as big or physical as Schwartz, he made up for it with intelligence and solid tackling. McManus had made it at last, and he had made it by filling a specific role. The Jaguars needed a smart player, one who could stop the run, and McManus was that, but he bristled at times with his label of run-only player.

"I really hate being labeled, but I am," McManus said. "I'm labeled as a run stuffer, and that's the bottom line, but I don't feel like I have limitations on the field. I feel like when I'm out there, I'm flying around. I feel like I can cover the pass. I feel I can blitz. I feel I can stuff the run, but I will do what I'm asked to do.

"Since I was in college, it followed me, followed me, followed me. When I didn't make it my first year, it was my speed and my 40 time and blah, blah, blah."

Fair enough. By the time the Jaguars played the Falcons for a playoff spot, the bartender who had made his dream come true had earned the right to call himself what he wanted.

The 22nd day of December 1996 dawned cold and bright. Seventeen years had passed since the city of Jacksonville first began dreaming of the NFL, and by the end of the afternoon, their team—in only its second year— could do what was unthinkable only a month and a half before. The Jaguars could make the playoffs.

The day was about more than that, though. It was a day, too, for the city to at last embrace its team, its players, and even its coach. Jaguars fans, from the start, loved having a team. They supported it, too. The idea of a team, however, was different from the team itself, and Jaguars fans found the organization difficult to love. There were reasons for this, reasons ingrained in the consciousness of the collective Jacksonville football mind.

Jacksonville was a college football town. The people were passionate about football, but that passion came from years of watching Florida State and Florida. The NFL, at first, couldn't inspire such passion.

FSU and Florida, while fostering the passion for football, put the Jaguars in a difficult situation. They were winning programs, and if the Seminoles or Gators lost even one game during a season, it meant a disappointing season—11–1 and 12–1 were the norm for the schools. That made the NFL, where 11–5 could mean an extremely good season, a difficult idea for Jaguars fans to understand.

The first season was a learning process. Fans didn't like 4–12, but they understood expansion teams were supposed to lose. With Carolina's success early in the second year, that patience grew thin, and at times, it seemed there were as many critics in the stands as fans.

Making the Jaguars harder to embrace was Coughlin. Jacksonville was a town used to high-profile, media-friendly coaches—FSU coach Bobby Bowden and Florida's Steve Spurrier.

Their images made them easy to embrace.

Bowden was the riverboat gambler, a down-home friendly guy who never met a camera he didn't love. He was easy to love, and hard for even his enemies to hate. Spurrier was less camera-friendly, and less difficult for his enemies to hate, but he had godlike status among Gators fans in Jacksonville, and Gators fans made up much of the Jaguars' fan base. They were personalities, and by comparison, Coughlin paled at first.

Coughlin, unlike the college coaches, shunned attention. He refused to make television commercials, rarely ventured into the community, and kept team-related appearances to a minimum.

Most coaches—college and professional—use their weekly radio and television shows as vehicles to promote their personalities and increase popularity. Most coaches even conduct these shows at bars or restaurants, giving the fans a chance to meet them. Coughlin taped his TV show from a studio in the Jaguars' facility. His radio show was live, but broadcast from the stadium, and instead of staying for the entire hour of the show, Coughlin typically rushed out after a half hour. Coughlin viewed the shows as burdens that got in the way of preparation.

Out of sight, in Coughlin's case, meant being out of the public's heart. Jaguars fans wanted to support their team, but in the first season and a half, it seemed a distant relationship.

Coughlin didn't care. No matter how popular he was, Coughlin knew, he would be fired for losing. And even the most distant coach will stay forever if he wins. Everybody loves a winner, and if Coughlin was to be loved, he wanted it to be for winning—not because he spent time on a radio show, or shaking hands with the fans.

Still, in the first year, attendance was strong. The Jaguars' games were sold out for the first three seasons as a result of the NFL Now! drive, but in the second year, with the losses, crowds decreased slightly. Only 64,628 showed up for the November 11 game at JMS against the Ravens, and in the rainy December 1 victory over Cincinnati, 57,408 attended. Attendance in each game declined until the Game 15 victory over the Seahawks, and even for that game, 66,314 of a possible 73,000 attended.

On December 22, the days of dwindling crowds ended—71,449 showed up to see the Jaguars, the hottest team in the AFC, play the Atlanta Falcons. Fans, as Coughlin figured, did love a winner.

The town was as excited as the team. "We won't have to be watching the scoreboard," John Jurkovic said. "That's a nice situation to be in."

The Falcons, on paper, were the weakest opponent of the final half of the season. They were 3–12, and their coach, June Jones, would be fired afterward. They lost their quarterback, Jeff George, midway through the season, when he was suspended, then released. Defensive end Chuck Smith was suspended for the Jaguars game for "comments detrimental to the team."

The Jaguars, meanwhile, had won four consecutive games—double their previous best streak—and even oddsmakers had discovered what was fast becoming the league's most improbable story. The Jaguars were nine-point favorites, the most in team history. "We're very aware of what's going on, but we can't look past the Falcons," Jimmy Smith said. "If we do, we'll be sitting at home."

"There's all kinds of hype and talk about what can happen," Davey said, "but if we lose this weekend, nothing will happen. We'll all go home for Christmas."

Christmas was three days away, but the only present the fans wanted was a playoff berth. Early against the Falcons, it seemed an easy gift.

The fans had playoff fever, and the Jaguars started strong. They forced a Falcons punt in three plays. Driving from their 23, Brunell quickly moved the Jaguars. On the first play of the drive, he completed a 14-yard pass to Smith, and then two plays later, he scrambled left and passed 13 yards to Willie Jackson. First down at the Falcons' 44. Two plays later, a 17-yard pass to McCardell moved the Jaguars to the 28.

Means, who had been running better each week, ran six times for 22 yards on this drive. On the four plays after McCardell's receptions, Means's runs moved the Jaguars to the 11. On second-and-six, Brunell took a snap in the shotgun formation, and finding no one open, he scrambled left 11 yards. Touchdown. Jaguars 7, Falcons 0.

The teams traded punts until five plays into the second quarter, when Falcons kicker Morten Andersen converted a 46-yard field goal to make it 7–3, Jaguars.

The Falcons were struggling offensively, managing four first downs on the first five drives. Falcons quarterback Bobby Hebert was ineffective, and had just 56 yards passing at halftime. The Jaguars, meanwhile, were moving, but stalling in the red zone.

On the possession after Andersen's field goal, the Jaguars drove from their 25. With Brunell again completing short- to mid-range passes, they drove to the Falcons' 31, and from there, Means burst a 17-yard gain to the 14. On the next play, Brunell passed to Derek Brown to the Falcons' 5, but two runs by Means gained nothing. Hollis's 23-yard field goal made it 10–3.

The Jaguars again forced a punt in three plays, and again, Brunell drove the Jaguars. Starting at their 14, on second and 8 from the 27, Brunell passed 17 yards to Smith to the 44. On the next play, Means ran out of the shotgun formation to the Falcons' 42. Brunell then scrambled for 16 yards, and three plays later, on third-and-five, he passed 13 yards to Pete Mitchell to the Falcons' 8. Again, the drive stalled, and Hollis's 26-yard field goal made it 13–3, Jaguars, at halftime.

Meanwhile, Buffalo was pulling away from Kansas City. There would be no tie. A victory, and the Jaguars were in the playoffs. The crowd sensed it, and started celebrating.

The Jaguars began the second half as if the celebration might continue unabated. For a third consecutive series, Brunell and Means moved easily through the Falcons' defense. Starting from the 20, Means carried six times for 25 yards, and Brunell's quick passes hurt the Falcons. He passed 29 yards to Smith on the third play of the series to give the Jaguars a first down at the Falcons' 43. Six plays later, his 11-yard pass to Smith gave the

Jaguars first-and-goal at the 9. Yet again, the Jaguars stalled in the red zone. Hollis's field goal from 22 yards made it 16–3, Jaguars, with 8:11 remaining.

Not much worked for the Falcons, but on the next series, they used the plays that did work—quick handoffs and screens. A swing pass from Hebert to Richard Huntley gained 14 yards, a run up the middle by Craig Heyward gained 11, and on the next play, Hebert scrambled 15 yards. Three plays. Three first downs.

From the Jaguars' 32, the Falcons moved to third-and-goal from the 4. Hebert passed over the middle to Eric Metcalf. Touchdown with 2:34 remaining in the third quarter. Jaguars 16, Falcons 10.

The Jaguars' problems in the red zone had returned for the finale. They had driven inside the Falcons' 5 three times, but scored just three field goals. Touchdowns on those drives would have meant celebrating throughout the fourth quarter. Now, they had to worry.

On the first drive of the fourth quarter, the Jaguars got some insurance. Means was bruising the Falcons' middle. He ran four times for 15 yards, and went over the 100-yard mark for the first time with the Jaguars, but when the Jaguars reached the Falcons' 23, the drive stalled.

Hollis's field goal sailed toward the left upright. It hit it, but bounced inside for a 19–10 lead.

"There have been a few of those when I've hit the upright," Hollis said. "The majority of the time I missed them. Somebody was watching from above and guided it through."

The rest of the Jaguars' luck was dwindling. On the next drive, the Falcons moved 77 yards on 12 plays, a drive capped by a 2-yard touchdown run by Heyward to make it 19–17 with 5:39 remaining.

The Falcons, a run-and-shoot, pass-oriented team,

had surprised the Jaguars. After passing unsuccessfully in the first half, the Falcons changed to a two-tight-end, run-oriented offense featuring Heyward and Jamal Anderson. The strategy worked. The Falcons finished with 146 yards rushing, and throughout the second half hurt the Jaguars with strong inside running against defenses geared to stop the four-wide-receiver run-and-shoot.

With the Falcons' offense working, the Jaguars needed a time-consuming drive to clinch the victory. Instead, they punted after three downs, and the Falcons had possession at their 30 with 3:57 remaining.

Agonized, the 71,449 watched as the Falcons again moved easily through the Jaguars' defense. The Falcons had three second-half drives. One was for 72 yards; and one for 77. The third tore the heart out of the Jaguars' playoff hopes as the Falcons drove deep into Jaguars territory.

The Falcons had hurt the Jaguars all day on a play called the slip screen, when a receiver breaks toward the quarterback, takes a screen pass, and cuts quickly upfield. On second-and-seven from the Jaguars' 48 with just over two minutes remaining, Hebert threw a slip screen to the left to Tyrone Brown.

Brown caught it, broke free, and appeared headed for a touchdown, but Tony Brackens—who had rushed on the play—came from 20 yards away, and tackled Brown at the Jaguars' 25.

Still, the hopes were fading. The Falcons now were within range for a 42-yard field goal, and the Falcons had on their sideline one of the most accurate kickers in NFL history, Andersen. The final two minutes moved slowly, with the Falcons moving into better field-goal range. On third-and-five from the Jaguars' 20 with 1:36 remaining came the killer. The Jaguars needed a stop to get the ball back with enough time to score. Instead, Anderson ran 7 yards for a first down. The Jaguars called time-outs, hoping for a miracle. As Heyward ran for a yard, the Jaguars were out of time-outs, and the clock ticked to 11 seconds.

The crowd, meanwhile, was losing hope, too. At the beginning of the drive, it had been loud, cheering for a decisive stop, but as the drive went on, particularly after Brown's reception, the crowd grew quiet. The playoffs were increasingly unlikely. Finally, with eight seconds remaining, Hebert lost a yard moving the ball to the center of the field. The Falcons called time-out on third-and-10 from the Jaguars' 13.

"I thought the game was over," Beasley said. "It was point-blank. I thought we were done."

Andersen came on and lined up for the kick, and the fans again began to cheer. "Sweet Home Alabama," a local favorite by Jacksonville-based band Lynyrd Skynyrd, played, and the fans danced and cheered, hoping for a miracle, but mostly, celebrating a season better than they could have hoped.

On the sidelines, Coughlin stood, watching.

Some players chose not to watch. Others prayed.

Lageman, who usually didn't play special teams but had waited too long for this, forced his way onto the field for the play. During the time-out, as fans danced, Jaxon DeVille—the Jaguars' mascot—stood in the end zone, furiously shaking the goal post at which Andersen was set to kick. As the time-out ended, he was told to stop by the back judge, but it was still slightly shaking even as Andersen attempted the kick.

Which didn't matter. The kick wasn't that close.

The snap was true, and the hold was good, but as Andersen approached, his plant foot slipped in the soft turf. He appeared balanced as he kicked, but after the kick sailed away, he slipped to the ground.

The kick sailed far left.

No good.

"A heckuva present," Coughlin called it.

Coughlin, as the kick went up, jumped in the air, then couldn't see if it had gone through. After a second, he heard the crowd cheering, and leapt again. "My six-inch vertical," he called it.

Three seconds remained. Time for Brunell to take a knee.

Players rolled on the field, hugging. Andersen kneeled in disbelief. Lageman walked from the field, hands held high. The Jaguars, improbably, were in the playoffs.

"From 30 yards out, that's a kick I make in my sleep," Andersen said.

"Who would have thought that guy in that situation would have missed that?" Davey said. "He's done that a thousand times in his career and won those games. This time, he missed, and gave us a real nice Christmas present."

"That's automatic," Smith said. "You just knew he was going to make it. But I guess you have to believe in destiny when something like that happens."

The gun sounded. Bucky Brooks and Aaron Beasley leapt into the crowd. Other Jaguars players did, too. The crowd embraced its team. As they cheered and celebrated and sang and wondered how the NFL's best kicker—maybe ever—had missed a chip shot, stadium officials worked to set up a podium at midfield. Players and fans gathered around, and much of the crowd of 71,449 was still there when Weaver and Coughlin climbed up to speak. They spoke to the crowd, told it the victory was for Jacksonville, and each thanked the fans for supporting the team—in good times, and bad.

In the locker room afterward, Coughlin delivered his message to the team. "We've got an opportunity now to do something about this playoff thing," he told his team.

"And we're gonna . . . We're not going to be just happy to be in here.

"We're in this thing to win."

The players cheered and high-fived, and Coughlin left the dressing room, still stunned that Andersen had missed. This simply didn't happen, but it had. Something else that simply didn't happen had happened, too, and you noticed it when you looked at Coughlin as he walked to his postgame press conference.

Coughlin was wet.

Late in the game, team trainers had mixed Gatorade to be poured on the head coach in case of victory. Never in the two-year history of the Jaguars had the team participated in this old and overused tradition. Never had there been a victory big enough to merit breaking that barrier with Coughlin. As the clock ticked toward zero, with Atlanta driving for the apparent game-winning field goal, the Gatorade was all but forgotten.

When Andersen missed, Jurkovic and Davey grabbed the container, ran to their coach and doused him— seconds after his six-inch celebratory vertical.

"It was teal, too," Jurkovic said, laughing.

"It was cold, but the circumstances were fine," Coughlin said.

He didn't mind a bit.

16
THE END OF
ONE ERA . . .

*"All we're going to do is seize the moment.
We just hope teams keep saying this is an
expansion team, keep hoping they don't
give us the respect they deserve."*

—LEON SEARCY
December 28, 1996

The impossible had happened. The Jaguars, 4–7 in mid-November, had won their final five games of the season to make the playoffs. That meant the Jaguars would be working Christmas. That meant the Jaguars were suddenly ahead of their three-year plan. That meant instant excitement in Jacksonville.

What it didn't mean was instant respect.

The Jaguars were the fifth seed in the playoffs, and would travel to Buffalo for the first round of the AFC playoffs. Two more-opposite teams were hard to imagine. The Jaguars never had made the playoffs; the Bills had made it six times in seven seasons during the 1990s.

When the Bills beat Kansas City on the final Sunday

of the regular season, their players were asked to comment on their first-round playoff opponent.

"The only thing I know about 'em is they have a left-handed quarterback," Bills defensive end Phil Hansen said as the Bills celebrated their sixth playoff appearance of the 1990s.

Television crews in Buffalo scrambled through the Bills' locker room that day at the same time the Jaguars celebrated and cheered raucously in Jacksonville. When the Jaguars watched their television news that night, they saw a sound bite from Bills running back Thurman Thomas, one of the greatest players of his era and a spokesman of sorts for his veteran teammates.

"Jacksonville who?" the camera showed Thomas saying, laughing.

No one asked, "Buffalo who?" If you didn't know the Bills on the final week of 1996, you hadn't been following the NFL—not that season, and not in the 1990s.

Jim Kelly.

Bruce Smith.

Thurman Thomas.

Andre Reed.

The Bills' stars were some of the biggest of their era. Together, they had led the Bills to four Super Bowls from 1990 to 1993. That they lost all four often overshadowed the fact that they played in four consecutive Super Bowls, something no NFL team had ever done. Ever.

So no one asked, "Buffalo who?" But they did tell Bills jokes. They joked about the Bills being losers, and chokers, and fans once prayed the Bills never would make the Super Bowl again.

Those, however, were uneducated jokesters, for any team with that much success always was a dangerous team, particularly in the playoffs. The Bills, contrary to the jokes, were one of the NFL's all-time success stories, and if any team was the AFC's team of the 1990s, it was the Bills.

Yes, they were older. Kelly, Thomas, Reed, and Smith all were over 30, and their careers were closer to their ends than their primes, but as they prepared for the December 28 AFC wild-card playoff game at Rich Stadium in Orchard Park, New York, they were far from a broken-down old team.

Nearly as impressive as the Super Bowl run was the Bills' ability in the mid-1990s not to slip to the bottom of the division immediately afterward, as was the trend of many teams after a peak winning era. The Bills had shuffled personnel, staying among the AFC's better teams by reloading throughout the lineup—and undergoing a change in philosophy along the way.

The Bills' Super Bowl teams were known for their high-powered, no-huddle, K-Gun offenses—Kelly, Thomas, and Reed were among the biggest stars of the early 1990s. The mid-1990s Bills were a defensive-oriented team, with Smith the team's dominant player, and the league's dominant defensive end.

The change in philosophy meant the Bills team that would play the Jaguars in the wild-card game was a far different team than the ones that had made the Super Bowl. Kelly, Thomas, and Reed were still the cogs on offense, but all were aging. Kelly, once a daring down-the-field quarterback, had struggled at times in 1996, having lost some of the velocity of his passes. One particularly memorable scene had Kelly questioning whether he should play anymore after a midseason loss to the Dolphins.

Thomas, too, was no longer the player he had been two or three years before. He rushed for 1,000 yards for an NFL-record eighth consecutive season, but whereas in the early 1990s he was perhaps the best combination receiver/runner ever, he now was less of a breakaway threat.

Still, the Bills firmly resisted any talk of a last stand. "We're not a team that's creaking along," Kelly said. "We're a team that has a lot of young players who are playing great roles."

However, Kelly did speak with a tough nostalgia during the week of the Jaguars game. "It's something to do what we've done," he said. "The thing is, we've been asked that for the last three years, 'Is this your last time?' After our second Super Bowl, they were saying that. After our third Super Bowl, they were saying that. After the fourth Super Bowl, they were saying that. We continue to keep plugging away."

They had rebuilt so well that before the season many picked them to win the AFC.

The reason they were picked was they had rebuilt while maintaining their core of the 1990s Super Bowl teams. At the same time, the Bills did what many considered one of the most masterful jobs of retooling in the last two decades. Instead of crumbling, they retooled around their core, adding Bryce Paup, Quinn Early, and Ted Washington as free agents and drafting Reuben Brown and Thomas Smith.

So, despite heavy losses such as Cornelius Bennett, Darryl Talley, James Lofton, and Will Wolford, they stayed strong—at least strong enough to make the play-offs.

"There's no sense whatsoever of last chance," Bills coach Marv Levy said. "There's a sense of this is a chance—that's all. There's no sense of nostalgia or anything other than a sense of concentration on the task at hand."

Whatever the Bills were sensing, the signs were different, which was only logical.

Age did at last seem to be catching up.

Before the season, people thought they were going to be back. They started strongly, struggled, Kelly almost quit, but the Bills had gotten there, and they were an experienced, veteran team—a dangerous team to face in the early round of the playoffs. Making the Bills most dangerous was Bruce Smith.

Smith was a great player who seemed to get better with age. He had dominated that season, and many considered him the best defensive end ever. The player who would have to stop him: Tony Boselli.

Don Anthony Boselli Jr. was born April 17, 1972, in Modesto, California, and played basketball and football at Fairview High School in Boulder, Colorado. He was a quarterback in junior high school, and his feet were quick enough to start at power forward on the Fairview basketball team, but he always wanted to be a lineman.

A defensive lineman, that was.

Early in his career at Fairview, his father, Don Boselli, told his coach, Sam Pagano, this.

"He's an offensive lineman," Pagano replied.

"Defensive linemen make all the money," Don Boselli told Pagano, a family friend.

"He'll make a million as an offensive lineman," Pagano said.

And then some. Boselli played offensive tackle, then signed with the University of Southern California, where he was a freshman all-American in 1991 and a Walter Camp all-American the following year. In 1993, he was a consensus preseason all-American, but dislocated his right kneecap against Arizona midway through the season. He missed five games, and played the season finale against UCLA. He considered declaring for the NFL draft during the season, but his stock had fallen because of his injury, and he returned for his senior year, when he was a consensus all-American.

"Tony is the greatest college football lineman I've ever coached," said his coach at Southern Cal, John Robinson, who had also coached NFL linemen such as Anthony Munoz, Marvin Powell, Bruce Matthews, Keith Van Horne, and Don Mosebar in college. "He is absolutely a dominating player on this level, and I expect he'll be that way in the NFL."

So did the Jaguars. They selected him No. 2 overall in 1995. He was their first draft selection.

"He is a cornerstone," Tom Coughlin said.

Coughlin knew he couldn't waste his first draft selection, and he particularly couldn't waste a selection as high as No. 2. An NFL team could go years without the opportunity to draft a premiere top-five player, and mishandling such picks can doom a franchise. Which was why Coughlin loved Boselli.

Boselli was reared on hard work. Don Boselli owned two McDonald's in the Boulder area, and Tony grew to know them well. "When he was seven, he would pick weeds, sweep the lot . . . that kind of thing," Don said. "As he got older, he would cook burgers and wait on customers. That's the one thing I always wanted for my kids. They were going to work."

Little Tony had incentive, too. He was growing fast, and a growing kid needed food. Don's rule was no work, no food. So Tony worked—and ate. Quarter Pounders. Big Macs. Anything.

"Every hour little Tony would come to the front door and ask, 'Can I have something to eat?' " Don Boselli said. "I'd say, 'Get back to work. Concentrate on your job.' "

Later, after his freshman year at USC, he worked at

the Abbey of St. Walburga in Boulder, where he helped the Benedictine nuns tend their 150-acre farm. The work ethic translated into football. Boselli was a huge fan of the game, and wanted to be known as the best. "To be better than the next guy you have to work," Boselli said. "You have to stay a cut above. Talent, no matter what you're doing, will take you so far. That's what separates the great ones."

What separated Boselli once he made the NFL was an unusual athleticism and balance for his size. Boselli was prototypical in size for an offensive tackle at 6-foot-7, 325 pounds, but to look at him, he didn't seem like an offensive lineman. "He's a very, very large human being," Coughlin said, "but he moves with the grace of someone smaller. Here's a man 50 pounds heavier than any premiere NFL pass rusher, but he has the athleticism, maneuverability, and speed to compete with them."

From the start, Boselli usually did more than compete. With rare exceptions, he dominated.

He sustained a knee injury early in his first training camp that forced him to miss the first three games of his rookie season. He returned in Week 4 of that season against the Green Bay Packers, and showed why he was rated so highly, holding veteran end Sean Jones to no sacks and one tackle. He allowed just one sack in 13 games, and was named to the All-Rookie team.

By the start of his second year, he was a mainstay, and was not only known in NFL circles as a future star, he was a celebrity of rare status for an offensive tackle. The night he was drafted, Boselli told reporters, "I'm an offensive lineman. I'm not comfortable in the spotlight. I'll probably never be interviewed again." But Boselli's career was not to be one of anonymity. His jerseys were among the most popular in Jacksonville. He made regular radio appearances, and had a weekly television

show—making him one of the Jaguar's most recogniz-
able faces along with Brunell, one of his closest friends
of the team. Adding to the mystique was the glamour of
being married to a former Miss California, the former
Angie Aylor.

He improved on the field in the second year, too. In
the first year, Boselli was a dominant pass blocker, using
his natural footwork and instincts to excel in that area.
By the second year, he improved his weakness—run
blocking—enough to be considered strong in that area.
He recovered from a preseason ankle injury, started the
opener, and again allowed just one sack for the season.
He was an alternate for the Pro Bowl, but most NFL observers believed it only a matter of time before he was a
perennial choice.

What was usually needed for a lineman to attain such
status was publicity—either a season so dominant that
his peers couldn't help but vote for him, or a benchmark
nationally televised game against a marquee opponent.

A playoff game was just such a game.

Bruce Smith was just such an opponent.

Smith was not only the NFL's dominant player at his
position that season, most agreed he was the NFL's dominant defensive player. Boselli, however, never had been
one to worry about an opponent's ability. It was often
said of Boselli that he had the potential to be one of the
NFL's all-time greats. Boselli never said that publicly, but
he believed it, and when he played a great player he expected not only to match the player, but overmatch him.
Smith was no different.

"I'm excited. That's why you play this game," Boselli
said. "To play one of the best. I'm going to do what I do,
and what I do I do pretty good."

Smith had 13½ sacks for the season, and as a future
Hall of Famer, was hardly intimidated by a second-year

player—even one looking at the game as a way to establish a reputation. "Unfortunately, it's like that every week," Smith said. "Everybody wants to measure themselves against me. Therefore, I can't have an off week. I have to be prepared each and every week."

Smith had one advantage over Boselli, an advantage shared by his team—a wealth of playoff experience. That was something the Jaguars couldn't manufacture or fake. You had to earn playoff experience, and the Bills had done just that. The game, then, set up with clear contrasts between each team:

—Veterans versus youth.
—The upstart Jaguars versus the ageless Bills.
—The wide-eyed kids versus the old, wise men.

It was a story line as old as competitive sports—the veterans hanging on for one last bit of glory, trying to hold off the up-and-comers who could taste it for the first time.

The Jaguars had 24 players who had been with playoff teams with 19 playing in playoff games. Only 13 of those players had started a playoff game. The Bills, who finished 10–6, had eight players who had played in four Super Bowls. Smith, for example, had played in 17 postseason games; Boselli, none.

"There's no question about the Bills being a veteran football team," Coughlin said. "That's a plus, being able to call upon their experience to put them in a frame of mind that goes with the playoffs. But we have some guys that have been in the playoffs. There's no question that when you talk about teams, though, they are a veteran team."

The Jaguars' playoff-tested veterans included Leon Searcy, Clyde Simmons, John Jurkovic, Dave Widell,

Dana Hall, and Robert Massey—players brought in not only for their ability, but for just this situation. They were about production, Coughlin knew, but they also knew how to prepare for big games, which made them valuable.

An NFL player hears stories about the playoffs, and those are the kinds of stories players listen to; the NFL is about money, but there is a pride in winning come playoff time. Rookies and younger players on the Jaguars wanted to know how to win in the playoffs, and the Jaguars' veterans made it a point to tell them.

The game changes, the younger players were told. Massey recounted what veterans told him when he was a second-year player with the Saints preparing for a playoff game. "They told me to take my hardest hit of the regular season and multiply it by 10 times," Massey said. "That's how the level of the intensity goes up. I took a hell of a hit during the season, so I knew I was going to have to pick it up."

The veterans also stressed to the rookies that being in the playoffs was not something to be taken for granted. A player could play for years without making it, and once they were in, they had to take advantage of the situation.

"We've been riding the coattails of our veterans," Ben Coleman said. "We've relied on them to get us ready. That's all we can do until we get the experience."

"We've learned a lot from our veterans," Pete Mitchell said. "There won't be that awe. We just have to go play them."

The Jaguars, though, were also developing a feeling that they did belong. They had won five straight games, the defense was credible, and the offense had finished No. 2 in the NFL. This was a team with producers and playmakers, players such as Boselli, Brunell, Smith, and McCardell. In recent weeks, Searcy and Means had helped give the Jaguars the running game they envisioned when they acquired the players in the off-season. Means, since taking over as a starter, was showing why he had made the 1994 Pro Bowl. His rushing total had increased weekly with his confidence, and his 110-yard game against the Falcons was his first 100-yard day with the Jaguars.

Not that the Bills were impressed. The Jaguars, since hearing the comments of Thomas and Hansen the previous Sunday, had suspected the Bills weren't taking them seriously. Upon arrival in Buffalo Friday, they quickly discovered those suspicions were correct.

The Jaguars learned firsthand that the Bills' disrespect was more than a media creation. On his television show the Friday night before the game, Kelly talked at length about the big edge the Bills had because the Jaguars had not seen the Bills' K-Gun no-huddle offense. The Jaguars had played against a similar scheme twice in two victories over the Ravens, whose coach, Ted Marchibroda, helped develop the scheme as Buffalo's offensive coordinator in the early 1990s. Most players saw the show. In case some hadn't, coaches talked about it at the team meeting that night.

"There was an attitude from Buffalo since we got off the plane—not only from the Bills, but from hotel employees," John Jurkovic said. "And when you went out to dinner, the fans. People were saying we were lucky to be in the playoffs. We got tired of that condescending attitude."

The morning of the game, the Jaguars awoke to read Bills linebacker Sam Rogers saying in the *Buffalo News* that the Jaguars would be "shell-shocked" by the crowd, and indeed, the venue appeared likely to be a factor. The Bills hadn't lost at Rich Stadium in nine playoff games there, a streak dating to 1988. During their Super Bowl run, it had been the rowdy and raucous atmosphere that often catapulted the Bills to the top of the AFC, but like the Bills, the atmosphere was different now.

Sellout crowds were the norm at Rich Stadium—the second-biggest stadium in the NFL—during the Super Bowl run. Now, however, with the Bills struggling into the playoffs and playing a 9–7 second-year team, interest had waned, and only 70,213 attended, meaning the game was blacked out locally.

Sellout or not, the Bills were confident.

"The Jaguars are talking a lot of noise," Thomas said before the game. "They act like they've been in the league 10 or 12 years. Just as quick as they got in is as quick as they're going to get their ass out."

For much of a quarter, he was right. The Jaguars got a break with the weather—it was mild, in the mid-40s—but early on, the Bills dominated, and seemed likely to win in a blowout.

The Jaguars, on their first series, looked exactly like the Bills had expected—young and panicky. Taking possession at their 9 after an illegal block on the kickoff, Brunell threw incomplete, then Means ran for no gain. On third-and-10, Bills defensive end Jim Jeffcoat pressured Brunell, who threw incomplete, and was called for intentional grounding. That made it fourth-and-18 at the Jaguars' 1. Bryan Barker punted 42 yards and the Bills took over at the Jaguars' 43.

The Jaguars' defense was as shaky as the offense. Kelly threw 15 yards to Quinn Early on the first play, and five plays later, Thomas caught a pass from Kelly alone in the flat and scored on a 7-yard touchdown with just 3:30 elapsed. Bills 7, Jaguars 0.

The Jaguars lost 3 yards on their next possession, gained 7 on their next, and were reeling when the Bills took over at their 13 with 6:51 remaining in the first quarter still leading 7–0. After an 11-yard completion to Early, Kelly dropped and tried what was a staple of the K-Gun—an inside screen.

On the play, Kelly dropped as if to pass downfield with the offensive linemen blocking for a second, then released the defensive linemen to pursue Kelly. As the defenders approached, Kelly flipped the ball to Thomas, who in theory would be free because the linemen had vacated the area.

On this play, Kelly again flipped to Thomas, but Clyde Simmons read the play, and stepped in front for the interception. He shed several tacklers, and scored on a 20-yard return. Jaguars 7, Bills 7.

"I knew he was trying to get me upfield," Simmons said. "I could feel the tackle throwing me. I saw Jim sliding toward me, and Thurman did that little shovel. I just held the tackle until he [Kelly] pitched the ball. I stepped in front and made a little run."

Some Jaguars players jokingly said later they wished Simmons would have approached the run part differently. Over the final 15 yards, he held the ball out with one hand, leaving it vulnerable to defenders. "I hadn't seen anyone hold the ball like that since [Walter] Payton," Jurkovic said, laughing. "We're just happy he didn't fumble."

Still, the Jaguars' defense wasn't yet stopping the Bills, who drove 68 yards on their ensuing possession, needing 10 plays and only four minutes. Again, Thomas capped the drive—this time with a 2-yard touchdown run with 2:26 remaining in the first quarter. Bills 14, Jaguars 7.

The Jaguars, for the most part, were struggling, doing little defensively and nothing offensively. On defense the exception was Simmons. On offense, it was Boselli.

Boselli, despite the offense's struggles in the first few series, realized he could handle Smith—both run blocking and in pass protection. On the possession after Thomas's touchdown run, Smith—trying to get an edge—jumped offsides. On the next play, Boselli drove Smith 4 yards off the ball. Boselli stayed with Smith, then moved him to the side, and Means ran through a gaping hole on the left side of the line.

Sixty-two yards later, the Jaguars had first-and-goal at the 5.

The drive stalled, but Hollis's 27-yard field goal made it 14–10 with 10 seconds remaining in the quarter, and the Jaguars somehow were in a game that already could have been lost. The Bills had dominated. Aside from Means's run, the Jaguars had no yards in the first quarter. The Bills had 117 yards and two long touchdown drives, but led by just four points. "We were in the game, and we knew we hadn't played well," Ben Coleman said. "We knew once we got it cranked upon we could win the thing."

Early in the second quarter, the Jaguars began to do just that. On the first drive of the second quarter, the Bills drove from their 20 to the Jaguars' 16, where they faced a fourth-and-one. Kelly tried to sneak into the middle, but Lageman stuffed him at the line for no gain. The Jaguars took possession, and on third-and-14 from the Jaguars' 23, the Bills blitzed. Brunell read it, and threw a quick pass to Mitchell over the middle. Mitchell broke two tackles, rambling 47 yards to Bills' 30. On the next play, Means ran into the middle. There, he was hit by Smith, but he bounced off and ran around the right end. By now, he was outside the defense, and after he got a block from McCardell, he ran to the end zone.

Jaguars 17, Bills 14.

"Bruce missed me and didn't wrap up, and he bounced me to the outside," Means said. "Keenan made a great block on the safety and after that it was a straight shot, and I tried to dive into the end zone."

Steve Christie's 33-yard field goal tied it at 17–17 with 1:56 remaining in the half, and at halftime, the game no longer looked or felt like a domination. The Jaguars, with their big plays, had matched the steady production of the K-Gun. The Bills had 14 first downs to the Jaguars' six, but the Bills' total yardage advantage was now just 222–200. "We're as cool as alley cats," McCardell said. "We stayed composed, and knew that we were going to come back."

One goal on the road in the playoffs is to stay in the game in the second half. The Jaguars were doing that, and they realized now they were reaching another pre-game goal—stopping Thomas. In the 1990s, it was often Thomas who keyed the Bills' playoff victories in Rich Stadium. Stop the run, and run well yourself—that was a credo many teams used in the playoffs, and few did it as well as the Bills. Today, the Jaguars were doing it to the Bills.

At halftime, Means had 104 yards on 10 carries; Thomas had carried nine times for 31 yards.

The third quarter was even. Christie made a 47-yard field goal, and Hollis made a 24-yarder. It ended tied 20–20.

On the second play of the fourth quarter, the Bills blitzed linebacker David White. Brunell tried to pass over White, who leapt and tipped the pass. The ball hung in the right flat in front of McCardell, whose momentum carried him away from the pass. Bills cornerback Thomas Smith intercepted, and ran untouched 38 yards for the go-ahead touchdown. Bills 27, Jaguars 20.

The interception couldn't have come at a worse time. The Jaguars had fought back from their early jitters, and seemed to have gained control of the game. The defense hadn't allowed a touchdown since Thomas's run with 2:26 remaining in the first quarter, and the offense was moving consistently. Then, the interception—the sort of play the Bills had made often in Rich Stadium in the playoffs in the 1990s, the sort of play that wins and loses playoff games.

Lageman and a few other defenders called the offense together over the sideline.

You've been moving all day, the defensive players said. The interception was a mistake. Let it go.

On the next series, Brunell did seem to forget the interception. The day, until now, had belonged to Means. No more. Now, it was Brunell's time. On the second play, he passed 20 yards to McCardell to the Bills' 40. Three plays later, the Jaguars faced fourth-and-one at the Buffalo 31. Means ran 2 yards. First down.

On the next play, Brunell again passed to McCardell—this time for 19 yards to the Bills' 10. Three plays later, he threw a wide-receiver screen to Jimmy Smith. In New Orleans, Smith had fumbled on a similar play. This time, he dodged several defenders and dove into the end zone with 8:40 remaining. Jaguars 27, Bills 27.

The game was turning into a classic. The crowd had begun to sense it, and even at 10,000 less than capacity, the noise was deafening. The atmosphere was a playoff atmosphere. There was urgency in the air.

This was Kelly time.

Often in his 12 NFL seasons, Kelly—a gritty, tough competitor—had led the Bills from behind late in games. This was a situation in which playoff experience beat inexperience, and the Bills began to drive.

After a false start by Reed, Kelly passed on first-and-15 for 25 yards to Early. First down at the Bills' 47. On first down, he passed incomplete, and on second down, Thomas ran 3 yards to the 50.

On third-and-seven, Kelly lined up in the shotgun, Lageman pressured from the left, and as Kelly ran from the pocket, Lageman reached and poked the ball from Kelly. It bounced, Kelly picked it up, and ran around the right side. Kelly stumbled to the Jaguars' 45, and as his knee touched the turf, Chris Hudson hit him hard on the head and shoulder, knocking the ball free. Aaron Beasley recovered at the 42. Although Kelly was down on the play, officials ruled it a fumble, and the Jaguars had a first down. As the Jaguars celebrated, Bills teammates and trainers helped Kelly from the field.

Brunell passed 14 yards to Smith for a first down at the Bills' 44, and three plays later, they faced third-and-seven from the 41. White again blitzed and pressured Brunell. This time, instead of passing over White, Brunell broke free to the right, throwing to McCardell in the middle of the field near the Bills' 37. McCardell, still needing 3 yards for the first down, ran away from the first down to evade a tackler, then broke free for an 11-yard gain and a first down at the Bills' 30. The Bills then held, and with 3:07 remaining, Hollis's 45-yard field goal off the right upright was good.

Jaguars 30, Bills 27.

"There may be a little luck in those situations," Hollis said. "You've got to think about what got us here in the first place."

The Bills had time, but the Jaguars knew with three minutes remaining—and second-year player Todd Collins replacing Kelly—it wouldn't be enough time. "When you bring a young quarterback in and he hasn't played all game, and he hasn't seen the pass rush, he gets back there, and he doesn't really have a chance," Dana Hall said. "Jim Kelly was standing back there and finding open receivers. They had the same routes without Jim in there, but Collins wasn't going to stick around. He was going to get out of there and make something happen. Once Jim went out, it made it real tough on them. That was a tough situation for him to come in. We had our ears back."

Just before the next drive, Kelly—still appearing stunned and dazed—rode a golf cart around Rich Stadium and down the tunnel to the locker room. No one knew it then, but these were to be his last moments in the NFL. A month later, Kelly announced his retirement. On Collins's first drive, Simmons sacked him on the first play, and he threw two incomplete passes. The Bills punted, and didn't regain possession until 42 seconds remained. Collins completed one pass for 7 yards to Thomas, but after spiking the ball to stop the clock, Collins was sacked by Brackens. The hit forced a fumble that Eddie Robinson recovered at the Bills' 18 with 11 seconds remaining.

"Now they know who were are, damn it," Kevin Hardy yelled as the Jaguars celebrated.

The unknown Jaguars left the field rejoicing. They deserved it, having dominated the second half with 209 total yards to Buffalo's 86. Means finished with 175 yards on 31 carries. Thomas had 50 yards on 14 carries. The Bills had 92 yards on 29 carries. "I told you if we stopped the run and put it all on the quarterback's shoulders, we'd have a chance," Lageman said.

Brunell, with two interceptions, walked by a reporter afterward, smiling. "Who says we don't win if I throw interceptions, huh?"

"They were looking ahead," Searcy said. "They didn't respect us."

"We listened to them all last week say, 'Jacksonwho?'" Boselli said.

The Jaguars had answered that question. Boselli had answered his own. If anybody said, "Boselli who?" before the Bills game, they weren't saying it anymore. Boselli dominated Smith. Next to Smith's name on the statistics was this:

—Three tackles.
—Zero sacks.

"He did a tremendous job," Kevin Gilbride said. "Who else would you want blocking Bruce Smith?"

Smith, for his part, declined to give Boselli much credit. Although ABC replays again and again showed Boselli handling Smith one-on-one in both passing and running situations, Smith said afterward, "It wasn't like he was one-on-one all day. They were sliding to protect him, and they kept a tight end in sometimes. They had a very good blocking scheme."

Boselli, for the most part, *was* that scheme.

"The way I approached it was it was just another game," Boselli said later. "I had to do my thing. He's a great player, sure, but people can block him, so I just went out and played my best. I wasn't worried about the circumstances. If I played well, we had a chance to win, but other players had to play well. If I didn't play well, it would be a long day, but to me, it was just another day."

Afterward, Jaguars players were incredulous at the degree to which the Bills had overlooked them. Kelly's comments regarding the K-Gun in particular seemed silly. "Doesn't he watch film?" Hall said. "That upset us. I took it personally, and so did some of the other guys. They thought they would come out, jump on us early, and we would quit. They didn't know we'd be around for four quarters."

The theme in the postgame was broader than just one playoff game. The Bills, it seemed, faced the end of an era. People were already suspecting Kelly might retire, and center Kent Hull was rumored to be retiring in a few days. Thomas had shown his age in the game, as had Reed. Of the players who had helped the Bills to four Super Bowls, only Smith still appeared to be playing at a peak level.

The Jaguars, meanwhile, were a young team, and suddenly, were a playoff-tough team on a six-game winning streak. As his team celebrated what many considered one of the biggest playoff upsets in recent memory, Coughlin was asked if, perhaps, it was the end of an era. He saw it differently.

"It's the beginning of one, maybe, for us," he said. And maybe it was.

17
AN UPSET FOR THE AGES

"There's not a person in America who picked us. The only ones who picked us were the guys in this locker room. I knew we would do it. I just didn't know how."

—TOM COUGHLIN
January 4, 1997

"They played perfect."

—JOHN ELWAY
January 4, 1997

The roads leading to Jacksonville International Airport were lined with cars, on the night of December 28, 1996. Fans stood outside their cars, waving pennants, yelling.

Earlier in the day, the town that once knew only college football shut down for a day to watch its professional team. More than 5,000 fans had flown to Buffalo for the game, and most Jacksonville sports bars were so crowded before the game that people had to leave or step outside. At the JCPenney at the Avenues Mall, fans stopped in the customer service department to watch the game.

After the 30–27 victory, they made their way to the airport just north of town to greet their heroes.

"We had watched the game, and we just couldn't stand it—we had to come out here [to the airport]," Gyn Crane told a reporter from the *Florida Times-Union*.

Some fans left their homes that afternoon early enough to park in the airport parking lot, early enough to make it inside the airport for the chartered flight that would be arriving from Buffalo at 8:15.

By 8 P.M., 5,000 people crowded into the airport's Concourse C, chanting, "J-A-G-U-A-R-S. J-A-G-U-A-R-S, J-A-G-U-A-R-S."

Kids sat on the shoulders of parents. Others climbed on tables, planters—anywhere to get a better view. The airport was overcrowded. It was bedlam.

"It was more than we could handle," said Charles Hardrick, operations manager for the Jacksonville Port Authority, which ran the airport.

And no one talked about firing the coach.

The Jaguars' victory over the Bills meant they would be playing the following week, but they didn't yet know the opponent. The Steelers and the Colts played an AFC wild-card game the following day. If the Colts won, the Jaguars would travel to New England the next weekend. If the Steelers won, the Jaguars traveled to Denver. The Steelers beat the Colts, 42–14, so for the third time in two seasons, the Jaguars would travel to Denver to play the Broncos.

This time, the winner would play in the AFC Championship Game.

Despite the victory in Buffalo, the Jaguars didn't feel as if they had gained the respect of many. The week opened with the Broncos 13½-point favorites over the

Jaguars, and the line quickly jumped to 14. On paper, the line didn't seem too ridiculous. The Jaguars, in the eyes of many, had fluked into the playoffs on an unlikely missed field goal, then beaten an aging team, the Bills, that had played poorly late in the season.

The Jaguars were a nice little story. Little more.

The opponent was much more—the AFC's top seed, with a quarterback, John Elway, having perhaps the best season of a Hall of Fame career.

The AFC hadn't won a Super Bowl since the 1983 season, but with the Dallas Cowboys and the San Francisco 49ers not looking as strong as in years past, the theory around the NFL was an AFC team could break that streak. If any team was capable, that theory went, it was the Broncos.

They had finished the season 13–3, and clinched the AFC's best record with three games remaining. No AFC team in the 1990s had clinched home field as early as the Broncos did in 1996. That seemed to make the Broncos an overwhelming favorite at least to make their fifth Super Bowl, their fourth since Elway joined the team in 1983.

"We have two facets on offense—a running game and a passing game—that are very good," Broncos tight end Shannon Sharpe said as the Jaguars game approached. "And we have a defense that is very solid. That's what you need, but more, you need a Hall of Fame quarterback. In order to win the Super Bowl, you must run the football, and you must have a Hall of Fame quarterback. I can't think of a team that won the Super Bowl without a Hall of Fame quarterback.

"This year, we have all the facets."

The Broncos indeed seemed invincible, but if the Jaguars were familiar with any team outside their division, it was Denver. They had played Denver in their two pre-seasons, and once in their first season, but they weren't all pleasant memories. In a regular-season game at Mile High Stadium in the Jaguars' first season, Elway shredded the Jaguars in a 31–23 victory, a game not as close as the score indicated. In the 1996 preseason, the Jaguars again traveled to Mile High. That was the site of Coughlin's preseason halftime Gatorade tantrum, but perhaps more significantly, when Elway played in that game, he was practically perfect, and all but unstoppable.

The Broncos had moved at will against the Jaguars. They led 17–0 at the end of the first quarter with Elway leaving after two series. The Jaguars rallied to win, but that was preseason. Elway had played five quarters against the Jaguars in his career, and thrown five touchdown passes. As the AFC Divisional Playoff approached, there was genuine concern over whether the Jaguars' defense could stop Elway. Or even come close.

Elway had been dominant all season. Mike Shanahan had taken over as Broncos head coach before the previous season, and Elway had adapted spectacularly to Shanahan's West Coast offense. The Jaguars had seen an example of that in their meeting the previous regular season, when Elway threw for 286 yards and four touchdowns. This season, Elway was receiving consideration for league MVP, and many in Denver thought this was the best Elway had ever been. "He's playing as well as I've seen him play," Sharpe said, "and for John, that's pretty good."

As with any great, aging athlete who has never won a championship in his sport, public sentiment was with Elway in his quest to win the Super Bowl. The Broncos had made it in 1986, 1987, and 1989, but lost all three.

"I'd like to win one—no question about it," Elway said, "but I feel good about the situation we're in right now. I don't look at it like it's Elway's last stand."

To stop Denver and Elway, the Jaguars figured they had to stop what allowed Elway to be so effective, and that was an improved running game. Terrell Davis, the Broncos' second-year running back, was the NFL's second-leading rusher in 1996 with 1,538 yards and 13 touchdowns and an average of 4.5 yards per carry. Stopping Davis meant putting Elway in obvious passing situations, which made it easier to rush him.

"You have to get Elway in a situation where you can pin your ears back," Jeff Lageman said. "When you talk about Buffalo, I didn't think Jim Kelly could win a football game all by himself. John Elway can."

"John's a fast man and very quick," Clyde Simmons said. "We just have to find a way to get it done. You don't know how to do it. We just have to do it. You have to contain him from exploding on you."

The Super Bowl talk, Broncos players said, added pressure to their situation. They had thought of the play-offs for five weeks, and hadn't played a meaningful game in that span.

"If we lose this game, our whole season is for naught," Davis said.

After the Buffalo victory, the Jaguars were in the opposite situation. Whether they won or lost in Denver, the season now was a success. Not that the Jaguars thought that way.

"I don't want to go in there and if it doesn't work out, we say, 'We shouldn't have been there,'" Massey said. "That's bullshit. I feel there's pressure on us, too. We're not in this to be a hell of a story for the year. We deserve the right to go to the Super Bowl, just like any other team. What have they done that we haven't?"

Should the Jaguars have been there? Recent results indicated yes. In the NFL, teams that win in the playoffs typically are different from teams that win only in the regular season. The difference usually is a strong defense and a powerful running game, because playoff football often is cold-weather football. In the first 12 games of the season, the Jaguars were essentially a run-and-shoot team, with the offense not moving unless Mark Brunell was effective. In the last four games of the season—and in Buffalo, too—the offense underwent a transformation. The Jaguars still depended on the pass, but no longer did they depend upon it solely.

Natrone Means, a bruising, physical runner, had taken over for James Stewart, and the result was a team that—for the first time in its history—could run as well as it could pass. Means, in essence, made the Jaguars a playoff team.

Natrone Jermain Means was born April 26, 1972, in Harrisburg, North Carolina, and was a Parade all-American at Central Cabarrus High School in Concord, North Carolina. Means rushed for 2,023 yards and 33 touchdowns in his senior season in high school. He signed with the University of North Carolina, where he played three seasons before being drafted in the second round of the 1993 NFL draft by the San Diego Chargers.

Means played in 16 games as a rookie, and became a Pro Bowl player in 1994. He gained 1,350 yards on 343 carries and scored 12 touchdowns in 1994.

His career in San Diego thereafter was a story of falling out of favor and falling fast.

The Chargers went to the Super Bowl in 1994 largely because of Means, but in the 1995 off-season, his relationship with the team, and particularly General Manager Bobby Beathard, deteriorated. Although under contract, Means held out, and the situation quickly turned ugly between Beathard and Means's agent, Tank Black.

Means eventually reported. He led the AFC in rushing after nine games, but then injured his groin, and played only two more games—a playoff game and regular-season game—finishing with 730 yards.

The Chargers, meanwhile, never recaptured the magic that took them to the Super Bowl. They started 4–7, and barely made the playoffs, losing to the Indianapolis Colts, 35–20, in the first round. Means, though effective when he played, bore much of the blame from the Chargers' front office.

Beathard, from the time Means held out, questioned Means's work ethic in conversations with San Diego media, implying the groin injury was a result of Means reporting to camp late and out of shape. Beathard also privately questioned Means's off-the-field activities. Means, Beathard told people, stayed out too late, and drank too often. It was a disappointing turn of events for Means, who felt miscast in the role of lazy, uncaring malcontent.

Means called Beathard's actions "a character assassination," particularly the reports he had a drinking problem, something Means said he heard in the final weeks at San Diego.

"I never got into any trouble," Means said. "I never got a DUI. I never got into trouble with the law. It was almost as if I was a scapegoat. It was always like, 'Natrone was out late last night, out again late this night.'

"I wasn't the only one going out. Nine times out of 10, I was going out with guys on the team. If I had a problem, then everybody on the whole damn team had a problem. They almost tried to single me out. It was like all their problems were my fault. It was like they were going to make people believe I was this evil person."

Those closest to Means found this new Chargers-perpetuated bad-boy image ironic. Means was a self-proclaimed "mama's boy." He and his mother, Gwendo- lyn Means, spoke often on the phone during the season, and whenever Means could during the season, he flew home to Harrisburg to be with his family. That off-sea- son, Means was planning to build a home less than 10 miles from where he grew up in Harrisburg. He was a homebody, and a family guy. The image of drinker and malcontent didn't fit. At times, his mother said later, he was near tears.

"The pressure was getting to him," Gwen recalled. "He said, 'I don't understand it. My stats are better than last year, but no matter what I do, they want more, more, more.'"

Finally, in February of 1996, the Chargers waived him, citing salary-cap reasons. Suddenly, the Jaguars had an opportunity to acquire a player two years removed from the Pro Bowl. Not only that, he fit their profile. He was young, 23, and with no major injuries in his past. All that remained was for the Jaguars to determine how much of what was coming out of San Diego was true.

The Jaguars conducted an intensive background check on Means before claiming him, and talked to him. "He never gave me an idea it was real problem," Coughlin said of his drinking.

"We were all convinced Natrone would fit into this system," Weaver said.

Still, the Jaguars did have one major concern— Means's weight, which was always a concern in San Diego. He played between 240 and 250 pounds—heavy for a featured running back—but when the Jaguars claimed him, he weighed 275 pounds. A few days after he was claimed by the Jaguars, Means was concerned enough about his image that he released a statement, as- suring fans in Jacksonville he was serious about football, and would not be a problem. That day, a reporter asked him about his weight.

"It ain't that bad, bro," he said, smiling.

It was that bad, but not for long. Means, Jaguars coaches said later, responded well to the program. He was put on a strict diet by the team nutritionist, and was an everyday participant in the workouts. By the second minicamp in June, he weighed 242 pounds, and he called it good weight. When training camp opened, he was at 232.

Success came slower on the field. He struggled in the preseason, and was beaten out by James Stewart, a second-year player many figured would back up Means. A workhorse, Means never could get in a groove sharing time, yet with Stewart playing well, Jaguars coaches were reluctant to give Means the 20 to 25 carries a game he felt he needed to be effective. So, by the time he tore ligaments in his thumb in the final preseason game—against Denver—he already was No. 2 behind Stewart.

He stayed at No. 2 even after he returned in Week 3. The ensuing two months were frustrating. "I was about to pull my hair out," Means said. "It was different for me, but I had to deal with it."

How he dealt with it impressed Coughlin—enough, even to sign him to a contract extension while he was a backup. During that time, Means approached the staff and told them he would do anything to play, even playing special teams in several games. "I have the utmost respect for that young man, and the way that he conducted himself," Coughlin said. "He was never a negative on our football team."

Means had flashes of his old self. In New Orleans he broke a 35-yard run, and in an October loss to the Bengals, his 11-yard pass reception from Brunell gave the Jaguars a late lead. Mostly, though, he struggled in a limited role, rarely carrying more than four or five times a game, and those carries were often ineffective, 1- or 2-yard gains in the middle.

Then, in Game 12 against Baltimore, Stewart injured his toe. Means filled in, breaking off several tough 7- and 8-yard runs in overtime. Means finished that game with 39 yards on 10 carries. "I told him, 'With the way you run, I don't know why you ever run right to left,' " Coughlin said.

The inference was clear: Coughlin, who loved a power running game from his days with the Giants, loved Means's straight-ahead, intelligent power style. Means became the starter the next week, and even when Stewart returned late in the season, kept the job. His yardage total increased weekly, and in the season finale against the Falcons, he had his first 100-yard game in more than a season. Against the Bills, he had a career-high 175 yards, and by the time the Jaguars traveled to Denver, he had returned to Pro Bowl form, with the following total in his most recent six games: 39, 56, 67, 92, 110, and 175.

"I never thought things would work out like this," Means said.

Who could have? Not Beathard, who still backed his decision even with Means reemerging as a premiere back.

"He did what a lot of guys don't do, and he'd disagree with me on this," Beathard said, "but he woke up. Our worries were that something outside of football would screw him up."

San Diego's loss was Jacksonville's gain, and the result was a team with one more weapon as it prepared for the latest, biggest game of what was becoming a remarkable season.

* * *

On Friday, January 3, 1997, 5,000 fans stood outside Jacksonville Municipal Stadium. The night before, the Florida Gators had beaten Florida State for college football's national championship. Once, a Florida-FSU game would have so overcome the city—particularly a Florida victory in the game—that it would have been the main topic of conversation not just for days, but weeks and months. Today, though, Florida-FSU wasn't the topic.

"Florida wins the national championship, and half the calls to the show were Jaguars calls," said local radio talk-show host David Lamm, a Jacksonville sports personality since the late 1970s. "I never thought we'd see that."

The 5,000 fans were at JMS to send off what had become *the* story, the Jaguars—*their* Jaguars. Fans cheered. Fans clapped. Fans screamed. Several players addressed the crowd. "Everybody gives us about as much chance at winning as a one-legged man at an ass-kicking contest," John Jurkovic told the crowd.

Few gave them that much hope.

The Jaguars were used to their chances being discounted. Not surprisingly, many in Denver took a similar view of the Jaguars. A victory in Buffalo and a six-game winning streak mattered little to people who had watched the Broncos win 13 games that year. "The Jaguars?" one Broncos fan said that week, echoing the feelings of many. "No way the Broncos lose to the Jaguars."

The Denver media agreed—particularly *Denver Post* columnist Woody Paige.

When the Jaguars awoke in the team hotel Saturday, many awoke to Paige's column, in which he referred to the Jaguars as "Jagwads" and a USFL team. Paige wondered why the NFL couldn't have sent a "real opponent" to Denver for the Broncos' biggest game of the season, and also wrote:

—"Jacksonville—is that a semipro team or a theme park?"

—"Wasn't Jackson State available?"

—"Instead of The Drive and The Fumble," he wrote, referring to past legendary Broncos playoff victories, "Jacksonville will be known as the blowout."

—"This is where you get off Jagwads. Broncos 31, Jaguars 10."

—"Can we get a legitimate NFL team in here next Sunday?"

Typically, Coughlin maintained an indifferent stance to such stories. This time, he was furious, and players felt the same. The story brought out all the old inadequacies the team had felt during the first year and a half. It was what the coaches and players knew everyone thought, but no one had written it in quite so sarcastic a way. Nerves were touched, and it hurt reading it when the team had accomplished so much. For anyone who might have missed it, Coughlin had copies taped to the locker-room walls before the game.

"You bet I read it and you bet it upset me," Coughlin said. "It was uncalled for. I don't mind being called an expansion team, but for someone to abuse our name after what we've put into this program . . . that bothers me a lot."

That morning, Coughlin had a worse concern. Tony Boselli, who dominated Bruce Smith the week before and was needed to block Broncos defensive end Alfred Williams, was stricken with the flu. The previous night, Boselli was too sick to eat dinner, and when he wasn't vomiting, he spent much of the evening in bed.

Boselli, like his road roommate and close friend, Mark Brunell, was deeply religious. He prayed daily, and was a regular at the team's Bible study groups. The night before the game, Boselli was feverish and fell asleep around 9:30. Shortly thereafter, 10 teammates, including Brunell, came to the room to pray for him.

He fell asleep immediately.

"I woke up the next morning, read my Bible, and prayed," Boselli said. "I pray to myself the whole time before a game. I was still throwing up a couple of hours before the game—I thought there was no way with the way I felt I would go out and play."

Game time was 2 P.M. mountain time. "Two o'clock came—the throwing up stopped, the headaches went away," Boselli said. "I hadn't eaten all day, but I had energy. It was amazing. Two o'clock came, and I felt fine."

Many Jaguars players believed Boselli's newfound health a sign, and used it as inspiration. What they saw moments before the game could only be described as motivation.

As they warmed up, a few players looked into the right corner of the open end zone in Mile High Stadium. "We looked up, and there was the scaffolding for [NBC analysts] Ahmad [Rashad], [Mike] Ditka, Joe Gibbs, and the boys to come in the next week to host the studio show," John Jurkovic said. "We walked out onto the field, and everybody goes, 'What's that?' We were all made aware of it. We said, 'Hey, if that's the way they want it, then that's the way they get it.'

"I knew it would give us a little edge."

Even with NBC providing motivation, the game started as the Bills game had a week before—with 75,678 fans watching as the Jaguars nearly were blown out of the stadium in the first quarter.

The Broncos, as in preseason, moved at will early. Elway had time, Davis had holes, and on the Broncos' first series, Davis blew through a huge hole on a sweep left, breaking a 47-yard run to the Jaguars' 2. The Jaguars' defense made a stand, but on fourth-and-goal from the 1, Vaughn Hebron scored on a dive, and the Broncos led 6–0.

Clyde Simmons blocked the extra point, but when the Jaguars failed to gain a first down for the third consecutive series to start the game, the Broncos were in a position to take a commanding lead.

And they did. Starting at the Broncos' 36, Elway worked quickly, moving the Broncos to the Jaguars' 18 on a drive keyed by passes of 16 yards to Anthony Miller and 13 yards to Ed McCaffrey. On second-and-nine, Elway passed to Shannon Sharpe, who was alone in the end zone. Sharpe then dropped Elway's two-point conversion pass.

Broncos 12, Jaguars 0.

The quarter ended that way, and a trend had been established. The first quarter, clearly, was not the Jaguars' playoff quarter. As in Buffalo the previous week, the Jaguars were dominated. This time, the Broncos had outgained them 146–28. The difference was that in Buffalo the defense made a big play to keep the Jaguars in the game. Against the Broncos, there was no big play—only a desperate clawing to stay in the game.

The first quarter was worse than the score in one way. On the first play, center Dave Widell injured his knee, and was lost for the game. Widell, a nine-year veteran, was a leader of the young team, and the Broncos game was in a very real way a homecoming for him. He spent five seasons in Denver, and was a member of the 1991 Broncos who advanced to the AFC Championship Game. Popular in the Denver market, Widell had a radio show there late in his career, and he did in Jacksonville, too. Soon after signing, Widell became a leader on what was then a young line featuring two rookie tackles, Brian DeMarco and Tony Boselli. Although he was often criticized throughout the first two seasons, his teammates valued his veteran leadership, and when he was injured early in the year, all talked of his value upon his return. Now, he was out again, which left the Jaguars only Michael Cheever, a rookie from Georgia Tech.

After the miserable first quarter, the Jaguars rallied. The offense, stifled in the first quarter, began to find itself. Brunell gained confidence, and the line cleared holes for Means. On third-and-six at the Jaguars' 25, the first play of the second quarter, Brunell passed 11 yards to Jimmy Smith for the Jaguars' first first down of the game. That led to a 46-yard field goal by Mike Hollis.

That made it 12–3, but the Broncos still had momentum. The Jaguars forced a punt, and on third-and-10 from their 20, Brunell passed to Willie Jackson, but Tory James intercepted at the Jaguars' 30. The Broncos had a first down at the . . .

Wait.

Penalty.

Officials ruled that James had interfered with Jackson, and although James and Broncos coaches protested, the penalty not only negated the interception, it gave the Jaguars a first down. Three plays later, on third-and-six from the Jaguars' 29, Brunell passed to Means for a 29-yard gain. Three plays after that, the Jaguars again converted on third down when Brunell passed 19 yards to Willie Jackson on third-and-three from the Broncos' 35. Means ran 8 yards on the next play, and on the play after that ran 8 yards again. This time, it was enough for a touchdown with 2:58 remaining in the half. Hollis added the point after. Broncos 12, Jaguars 10.

The Jaguars forced a punt, and took possession with 58 seconds remaining on their 11. Means, on the first play, ran 21 yards, and on the ensuing play, Brunell threw deep to the right side of the field to Jimmy Smith for a 44-yard gain to the Broncos' 24.

The Broncos were reeling now. Momentum had changed. Twenty-four seconds remained. Only 15 minutes before, the Broncos had led 12–0, and the Jaguars had seemed like the Jagwads. Now, with 14 seconds remaining in the half and with the Jaguars out of timeouts, Hollis kicked a 42-yard field goal.

Jaguars 13, Broncos 12.

"They seemed to pick up momentum when they scored right before halftime," Broncos rookie linebacker John Mobley said.

As in Buffalo the week before, the Jaguars did have momentum at the half, and they had it for the same reason. They were shutting down the run, and running well themselves. Means had 79 yards on 10 carries and a touchdown. Davis had 71 yards on eight carries, but only 24 on seven carries besides the 47-yarder to set up the Broncos' touchdown.

Boselli, by now, was feeling 100 percent, with one exception. He had taken fluids intravenously before the game. He felt fine, he said later, except, "I had to pee about 50 times on the sidelines." Teammates surrounded him several times throughout the game, enabling him to do so.

The Jaguars' momentum carried into the third quarter. The Jaguars didn't make a first down on their first three series of the game, but they scored on the next three, and on their first series of the third quarter, they drove 75 yards on seven plays, with Brunell passing 31 yards to McCardell for a touchdown. Hollis added the extra point with 8:41 remaining in the third quarter.

Jaguars 20, Broncos 12.

The Broncos' offense was faltering as the Jaguars' offense gained momentum. The Broncos had scored on their second and third possessions of the first quarter, but were stopped on two second-quarter series, and on their first series of the third quarter, the Jaguars stopped the Broncos after one first down, setting up the series that ended with McCardell's touchdown. Now, having allowed 20 consecutive points to the Jaguars, the Broncos trailed by eight with 8:51 remaining in the third quarter. They managed two first downs, but the Jaguars' defense stiffened, and again forced a punt.

The Jaguars took possession at their 8, and again were driving when the third quarter ended. With 10:51 remaining in the fourth quarter, Hollis ended a 17-play, 88-yard drive with a 22-yard field goal.

Jaguars 23, Broncos 12.

The Jaguars led by 11 points with less than a quarter remaining, and even the most fervent Jaguars follower might have had trouble if someone, right then, had asked the following question: When was the last time the Jaguars led by 11 or more points?

Answer: Carolina—13 games and more than three months before. The statistic revealed the nature of the Jaguars' late-season run. This was a team that had lived on the edge over the last half of the season. They were winning, but they hadn't been dominant—not until the playoffs anyway. And were they dominant in the playoffs?

Take away the first quarter, very much so. Against the Bills and Broncos, the Jaguars trailed by a cumulative 26–10 at the end of the first quarters. The Jaguars had outscored the two teams 43–13 after the first quarter.

Denver outgained the Jaguars 133–28 in the first quarter and the Bills outgained them 117–62. The Jaguars outgained the Bills 347–199 in the final three quarters, and since the debacle in the first quarter against Denver, the Jaguars were outgaining the Broncos 349–77.

The Jaguars had scored on five consecutive possessions. The Broncos hadn't scored in five possessions.

The Jaguars had outscored the Broncos 23–0 over
that span.

Now, the question—was it enough? The reason the
answer was unclear was Elway.

Throughout his career, Elway had compiled a legendary list of fourth-quarter comebacks, often in scenarios
such as this one—his team having been dominated much
of the game. In the 1986 AFC Championship Game
against Cleveland, he drove the Broncos 98 yards for a
game-tying touchdown with 39 seconds remaining, and
the Broncos won in overtime. In a playoff game following
the 1991 season, he led an 87-yard drive—against starting from the Broncos' 2—that ended with a 28-yard field
goal with 20 seconds remaining, giving the Broncos a
26–24 victory over Houston.

Now, the stage was set for another Elway comeback.

On the drive after Hollis's field goal, Elway drove the
Broncos quickly from the Broncos' 43. Five plays, 57
yards, ending with a 2-yard run by Terrell Davis. Jaguars
23, Broncos 20—7:37 remaining. Plenty of time for
Elway.

The Broncos, though, hadn't stopped the Jaguars
since the first quarter. Now, with the game on the line,
Denver's defense again wilted. Rather, Brunell—who
couldn't lead a clutch late drive in the first half of the
season—strung together a series of plays for the ages.

—On second-and-nine from the Jaguars' 27, he
scrambled left. Twelve yards. First down.

—On second-and-five from the 44, Means ran over left
tackle for a 6-yard gain. First down.

—On second-and-10 from the 50, Brunell again
scrambled. He dodged defenders, and finally, ran over

safety Tim Hauck. Twenty-nine yards. First down at the Broncos' 21.

—On third-and-five from the Broncos' 16, Brunell called a pass in the huddle. He told Jimmy Smith to run a fade if the defender tried to play him close at the line of scrimmage. On a fade, Smith was to take one step forward, then run to the corner of the end zone. The defender indeed tried to jam Smith.

Brunell read it. So did Smith. Brunell threw a lob into the corner of the end zone. Smith dove behind the defender, catching it with 3:39 remaining. Jaguars 30, Broncos 20.

Elway needed more than a miracle now. He drove the Broncos 80 yards in eight plays, and with 1:50 remaining, he passed 15 yards to Ed McCaffrey for a touchdown. Jaguars 30, Broncos 27.

The theme from *Rocky III*, "Eye of the Tiger," played in Mile High. On the sideline, Aaron Beasley stood on the bench, shaking his head at the crowd. "It's done!" Beasley shouted. "You ain't getting back into it. It's done. Rocky ain't getting back up no more."

And he didn't. Broncos kicker Jason Elam tried to dribble an onside kick. The idea was to surprise the Jaguars, and get the team going toward one side of the field or the other. Elam would then fall on the ball. Elam dribbled, but Le'Shai Maston stayed in the middle of the field and recovered. Brunell kneeled four times. Time expired.

"Without question, this is the toughest loss I've ever faced," Shanahan said. "You work the whole year for this opportunity, to play on our home backyard, and we had a lot of success this year. But when somebody comes in and takes the game away from us—it hurts a lot."

Elway walked from the field, stunned.

"You'll get another chance," a fan yelled.

Elway looked into the stands, and forced a smile.

"They played perfect," Elway said later.

And for three quarters, they had.

"It was neat," said Boselli, who grew up in Boulder, which is just outside Denver. "Everyone [on the Broncos] was like, 'All right, let's get this game out of the way so we can go into the championship game.' It was special for me knowing what it did to that city. They thought for sure they were going to the Super Bowl that year, and it was just a walk in the park. They thought they'd just step over us and keep on going."

The Jaguars scored on six consecutive possessions, and in the final three quarters, the only time the Jaguars didn't score was when Brunell kneeled to end the game. The Broncos were stagnant until too late, scoring twice when the Jaguars were in prevent, kill-the-clock defense.

"People weren't expecting this," Jurkovic said, laughing. "That one-legged man must've been an agile motherfucker today."

Indeed he was. Brunell completed 18 of 29 passes for 245 yards and two touchdowns with no interceptions. Elway completed 25 of 38 passes for 226 yards and two touchdowns, also with no interceptions.

Means, for a second consecutive week, helped the Jaguars control the clock, rushing 21 times for 140 yards. The Jaguars had outrushed a second consecutive playoff opponent. Davis rushed 14 timers for 91 yards and a touchdown.

After the first quarter, the Jaguars dominated:

—Rushing yards: Jaguars 184, Broncos 46.
—Total yards: Jaguars 415, Broncos 208.
—First downs: Jaguars 21, Broncos 14.

The Jaguars had dominated games that way before. That was in October, and the result each time was a loss.

This time, the result was a trip to the AFC Championship Game. The result was also a Jaguars locker room ready to have the last laugh at a certain local columnist.

"Tell Woody that the golden rule is that you cannot write a check that your body can't cash, defensive line coach John Pease said.

"Woody wants a real team in here next week?" offensive line coach Mike Maser said. "He's going to get a real team. Nobody."

Whatever that meant, the Jaguars had proved a point. The Broncos had been favored by 14 points. Some called it the biggest upset in the playoffs since the Jets, 18-point underdogs, beat the Colts in Super Bowl III.

"We overcame the odds," Jurkovic said. "We don't care how the glass slipper fits. The bottom line is the Jaguars are still playing football. That's all that matters."

The Jagwads? A USFL team?

"On paper, it said a second-year expansion team was playing a four-time Super Bowl participant with the Buffalo Bills, and the team with the best record in football," Dana Hall said. "I think the odds were a million to one that we could win both of these, but the game is played on the field.

"Not in the paper. Not in Vegas. In between the white lines. Period."

Meanwhile, Jacksonville was preparing the biggest non-game crowd in the stadium since Irsay's helicopter ride. The city again packed its sports bars and crowded around living-room television sets. This time, when their team won, the Jaguars, the town, and the airport were ready. The previous week, the airport had been unprepared for the inundation of people, but this week, the fans had their celebration orders: Be at JMS at 11 P.M.

Fans began arriving at 7:30 P.M. When the team plane

flew over JMS, players were stunned. Over 40,000 people filled JMS.

"It was an amazing sight," Boselli said.

By the time the team arrived at 1:30 A.M., 45,000 people were in JMS.

"I've played in Green Bay," Brunell told the crowd when the team arrived. "They say the Packers have great fans. These are the best fans in the NFL."

And the crowd cheered and cheered and cheered.

18

"WE JUST COULDN'T TAKE IT"

"To think where we are today is beyond imagination."

—WAYNE WEAVER
January 9, 1997

ours after the 1 A.M. celebration, Coughlin was working. This was Sunday. Players had the day off. Most watched the AFC Divisional Playoff game in Foxboro, Massachusetts, between the Steelers and the Patriots.

The Jaguars would visit the winner in the AFC Championship Game the following Sunday.

Coughlin watched between watching film of the victory in Denver. What he saw on TV was as impressive as what he saw on his team's films. The Patriots, coached by his former boss, Bill Parcells, took a 14–0 lead after the first quarter, and led 21–0 at halftime. By now, it was obvious the championship game would be Teacher versus Pupil II. The Patriots won 28–3.

"I'm going to put a little message on his voice mail

when I get back to the office," Coughlin said at a midafternoon meeting with the media shortly after the Patriots' victory. "I'll tell him I don't know if we should show up there with that outstanding performance I saw today."

False modesty never did play well on Coughlin. Whether he was coaching against Parcells or not, he shared a feeling with every player on his team—that the team that lost a Week 4 overtime game to New England, 28–25, was a very different team than the one that would travel to Foxboro the next weekend. The changes were obvious, but one stood out most of all.

The team that lost in September had won five games—ever.

The team playing in January was a victory away from the Super Bowl.

On Monday, January 6, 1997, Jaguars players arrived at work to a new scene. The schedule was the same, the meetings were the same, and so were the workouts, but the atmosphere was as different as one could imagine. The Jaguars, previously the least covered team in the NFL, were no longer just a little story. They were more, even, than a big story. They were *the* story.

ABC *World News Tonight* ran a story on the team and the late-night celebration Sunday.

CNN. ESPN. NBC. The *Boston Herald*. The *Boston Globe*. The *New York Post*.

All were in the Jaguars' locker room Monday.

"The calls are coming in faster than we can answer the phone," Communications Director Dan Edwards said.

The Jaguars were a national story not just because they were in the AFC Championship Game, but because of the manner in which they had made it. A 4–7 start. A five-game winning streak to finish the season. Two unlikely, classic playoff victories. The second-year status. Coughlin's maniacal image.

All were easy story lines for media descending upon the once sleepy little town. As the week continued, the story seemed to get bigger. *Sports Illustrated* arrived. So did the BBC. Even *Hard Copy.*

If *Hard Copy* wanted a story that week, all they needed to do was turn their attention north to Green Bay. There, Andre Rison—seven games removed from his Jaguars career—was talking about his former team. The Packers claimed Rison two days after his release from the Jaguars, and both teams improved drastically thereafter. The Packers, a preseason Super Bowl favorite who struggled in October and early November, won six consecutive games after Rison's arrival. That included a 35–14 victory over the 49ers in the NFC Divisional Playoff game the week before. The Jaguars had won seven consecutive games. Ironically, Rison received credit for both streaks.

Few on the Jaguars now doubted the team was better without Rison, but some insisted Rison's presence still was helping the team. Rison, many pointed out, had brought a confidence to the team, and when he left, that confidence stayed. "I taught them how to win," Rison proclaimed that week, and indeed, many around the Jaguars doubted they would have learned to win as quickly had it not been for Rison.

"He taught all of us something about being competitors," Jimmy Smith said. "I can't tell you how much I learned from him."

If the Jaguars' feelings about Rison were mixed, they learned the week of the AFC Championship Game that Rison's were less so. Rison, who had been comparatively quiet about his former team since his release, told a reporter in Green Bay that while he liked many of his Jaguars teammates, he was bitter toward others.

"Fuck Brunell," he said. "I have no love for Brunell." Rison also called Brunell a "wanna-be."

"Me and the players are close except for Jimmy Smith. He had some things to say when I left. I didn't know he felt like that. There's backstabbers everywhere . . .

"I haven't heard Kevin Gilbride's name up for no coaching jobs. . . .

"They can all kiss my ass."

Reaction was swift. Brunell recalled Rison's days in Jacksonville when the receiver constantly praised him, comparing him to Steve Young. "I used to be the best in the league," Brunell said, laughing.

Smith, who when Rison was released said Rison had been given every chance to stay in Jacksonville, shrugged when told of Rison's comments.

"Why did he call me a backstabber?" Smith said. "I only said the truth. The truth is, they tried to keep him here. They gave him a chance to be here. He just didn't perform. We were surprised he got away with a lot of things he got away with, but he's Andre Rison. If he thinks I'm a backstabber, that's fine.

"I'm not mad at him. I just said the truth."

Said Tony Boselli, "I don't think there was a for–Andre Rison or an against–Andre Rison group. I liked Andre a lot. I don't think it was a black/white thing. I got along with him great. I was sorry to see him leave. He was a good guy on the team. I was sorry he said what he said when he left. That leaves a bitter taste in your mouth."

The Rison issue was a diversion, but the Jaguars didn't stay diverted long. They had a championship game to play against a team with a somewhat similar story to their own.

The Patriots, when 1996 began, weren't expected to make the AFC Championship Game, either. Parcells had taken the job four years before, and in 1994—his second season—guided the team to an unlikely playoff appearance, where they lost to Cleveland in the first round. That Patriots team won their final seven games to finish 10–6, and did so because of Drew Bledsoe, then a second-year quarterback who threw for 4,555 yards and 25 touchdowns.

The Patriots slipped in 1995, finishing 6–10, and when the Patriots began 1996 0–2, many had doubts about the team, Parcells, and especially Bledsoe, who had regressed since 1994.

After the slow start, the Patriots improved quickly, winning 11 of their last 14 games before routing the Steelers in the playoffs. Bledsoe, inconsistent early in the season, improved, completing 373 of 623 passes for 4,086 yards and 27 touchdowns with 15 interceptions. And unlike 1994, the Patriots were balanced. Curtis Martin, a second-year running back, rushed for 1,152 yards on 316 carries with 14 touchdowns. The defense, suspect early in the year, improved late in the season, and allowed more than 12 points only once in six games leading to the championship game.

Overshadowing the success, however, was an ongoing feud between Parcells and his boss, Patriots owner Robert Kraft. Parcells had been the coach a year when Kraft bought the team in 1994, and the two quarreled constantly. During the 1996 draft, Parcells wanted to draft a defensive player in the first round, but Kraft's personnel people wanted to take Ohio State wide receiver Terry Glenn. Kraft sided with the personnel people, the Patriots took Glenn, and although Glenn excelled, the incident strained an already fragile relationship.

By the week of the championship game, Parcells was rumored to already have agreed to take the New York Jets head coaching job, a rumor that later proved true. That was the story in New England that week—would Parcells stay or would he go?—but the most amazing story of the week was the team that would be visiting Foxboro.

What the national media wanted to know was how.

How could a second-year team be a victory away from the Super Bowl? How could a team in disarray two months before win seven consecutive games? How could a team that would have missed the playoffs but for a missed *30-yard* field goal, win two playoff games?

The first question had lost some of its novelty. There was a dual aspect to the Jaguars' success story. The Panthers were in the NFC Championship Game. As unlikely as that was, the Jaguars' appearance was even more so. The Panthers had won their division and gone 12–4. The idea of the Panthers being in the title game was strange to many NFL fans, but at least they had had a few months to adjust to it. Two expansion teams?

Well, excuse the public if that seemed a bit odd—especially when one had seemed destined for a top-10 draft selection at midseason.

A 9–7 team making the AFC Championship Game was surprising, but it had been done before. As recently as 1995, the Colts made the AFC title game with the same record, but the Colts had been consistent all season. The Jaguars were three games under .500 in mid-November at 4–7, and trailed the Ravens 25–10 in the fourth quarter.

"To think where we are today is beyond imagination," owner Wayne Weaver said.

The reasons were many. Rison was gone. That had helped team unity, and helped reduce Brunell's interceptions. Also, as Tony Boselli later said, "It got a better receiver on the field. Jimmy Smith, at this point in his career, is a better player than Andre Rison." A young team was maturing. Brunell was a more mature, better player than in September and October. The offensive line, which struggled in the first half of the season and allowed an AFC-high 50 sacks in the regular season, had improved, too. Boselli was a base all season, but Searcy improved drastically in the second half, and Coleman and Tylski had played well in the playoffs. Dave Widell had played well against Buffalo, and when he was injured against Denver, Michael Cheever made the future look bright by excelling in his stead.

Defensively, too, the team was improving, and playing well enough to win. It gave up 14 points against Buffalo in the first quarter, but only allowed two field goals in the final two quarters (the touchdown came on an interception return). After the 12-point first quarter, the Broncos didn't score until the Jaguars had an 11-point lead.

Those were the technical reasons, the obvious reasons.

The reason behind the reasons, players said, was Coughlin.

Coughlin's change, most players agreed, was at the heart of the turnaround. Since the bye, the Jaguars had half days on Mondays, and that week, Coughlin began having the team practice without pads twice a week. That meant only one day of practice with full pads.

"The way he approached practice and things like that—it made a huge difference," Kevin Hardy said. "After the bye, we pulled back on the contact in practice. We still went hard one day a week, but it was no longer two, three days a week. That keeps guys a lot fresher. Like Brunell—he wasn't practicing as much and his play picked up dramatically.

"It's a long year, and you need that kind of break."

Players recalled the day Coughlin first gave them Monday off as a benchmark. "Guys were elated when he said, 'Get your lifts and conditioning in, and go home,' "

Jurkovic said. "We had all Monday and Tuesday to relax, which was a good feeling.

"The mind is a crazy thing. Anytime the mind tells you things are going good, your psyche is a little up. Your biorhythms are up. You come back Wednesday and you're ready to attack."

Another factor contributing to the late-season surge, Jurkovic believed, was the struggles of September and October. Nothing made winning feel good like having been through the losing.

"The time we had spent together and the trials and tribulations we were going through seemed to make us tighter and have a little more cohesiveness," Jurkovic said. "We started to do what we had to do to win games in the fourth quarter. When it came time for crunch time, we did what we had to do to win. That's exactly what we weren't doing early in the season."

Boselli thought the turnaround was just a matter of a young team learning to win.

"I thought we were going to have a good team, but we struggled early, but even when we struggled, you could see that if we just stopped making mistakes we could be a good team," Boselli said. "Earlier in the year when we won a game, it was like, 'Wow, we won.' With Houston [Game 14], winning was becoming like, 'OK, we won. Now, let's go on to the next thing.' We got used to winning, which was good. That's when I said, if this team gets rolling . . .

"After the Pittsburgh game, when Andre got cut, if we wouldn't have won that Baltimore game, things might have gotten ugly. It was a situation we were 4–7, and still had an outside hope. Clyde [Simmons] said, 'If we win the rest of them, we can get in the playoffs. That's our chance.' If we had lost that game, we would have been

4–8, and struggling to get done with the season. That was a big game for us, to get us going.

"My theory is when you're winning, everything's better. When you're winning, all of a sudden, everyone's like, 'Hey, practice is better. Things are easier.' When you're losing, it seems a lot longer. The last five weeks, practice got a little lighter. That gave us a chance to get our legs back. Besides that, he [Coughlin] joked around a little bit, but I think he wants to do that. I think he wanted to have fun with this team."

Coughlin, by the AFC Championship Game, was indeed having fun. It was his sort of fun—winning, and doing it his way. How much he had changed—and the genesis of that change—remained a point of issue to Coughlin. Yes, he had changed, he said, but not as much as people wanted to think. And not for the reasons many thought.

The reality was he changed, and although he insisted he planned it, that was only partly true. Yes, he planned the change in schedule. Coughlin, at heart, is a psychologist. In Year One, he never saw a need to relax practices. That team wasn't going to win, no matter how they felt physically. Better, Coughlin figured, to treat that whole season like an extended training camp, and to see how the players would respond, to see who were "Coughlin" players.

"The first year, I knew a certain portion of that locker room wasn't there for the same reason I was there," he said. "If you're going to do something, do it to the best of your ability. That's the whole deal for me. Don't involve the rest of us with this pettiness. That's not what I'm doing here. When I make the commitment, I make the commitment."

By the second season, particularly after the dedicated practices during the bye week, Coughlin knew he had players in the locker room there for the same reason he was. Coughlin relaxed immediately thereafter.

Another change, however, he couldn't plan, and that was the manner in which he related to his players. He approached the team over doughnuts in mid-October, and at first, players rejected him. His plan was to reach out, but the interaction he couldn't have planned. What happened was a team responding to a coach and a coach responding to a team. It happened, and it changed the course of the Jaguars' remarkable 1996 season.

After the season, Coughlin explained:

"There's always an adjustment," he said several months after the championship game. "The adjustment comes from people getting to know one another. Then the knowledge of what the level of expectation is, the give and play of the human element—that's what really happens. When the players find out what the standards are, and they find out that you are a human being, that's a big step, and we reached that this year. That was satisfying.

"We got this idea that maybe each side has to do a little better job adjusting to the other. We had some work to do there, and that work got done.

"It's a combination of a lot of things. Any season is. Every year is a new year, and every team is a new team. You're always calling upon the experiences you had somewhere in the past, and that will help you. You had a player who was like that, and you recall some positive opportunities that you had with that player—or a situation, or a circumstance, the way you dealt with training camp, or a bye week, or something like that. . . .

"Everything is cumulative, but I don't think you ever stop learning. You're always trying."

The first year, Coughlin explained, had been about establishing trust. "A big word, in any profession, is trust," he said. "It's a huge word. One of my faults is you've got to show me you can handle it, and then I'll show you. The big thing there is I don't want people to ever abuse anything. People need to know the level of expectations. Then, within the concept of organization and structure, people—intelligent people—begin to realize what their responsibilities are. Within those responsibilities, they make contributions.

"It's better to understand those things with some degree of sacrifice than it is to think that there's going to be an easy orientation, then have to firm it up. That just doesn't make any sense to me."

How much did he change? Not as much as people wanted to believe, Coughlin said.

Winning, he believed, brought a perception of change.

"I don't know that there was a lot of compromise," he said. "The relationship with the players got better before the winning. I also really believe that while you're losing these games in the fourth quarter, if you have good players, good people, good athletes, these experiences are cumulative, and at some time, you get better.

"At some time, Mark Brunell will be comfortable with the two-minute drill, and will succeed. At some time while it doesn't look like our clock management is any good and it doesn't look like we get things done fast, at some point that improves with time. Eventually, that happened, too."

The injuries in Cincinnati, he said, had more to do with the change than anything.

"The truth of the matter was Andre speaking out had nothing to do with it," Coughlin said. "What it had to do with was when those two kids were on the field. Without a doubt, after the injuries in Cincinnati, I took a step back, and tried to analyze the role and position that I had taken in terms of relentlessly driving these players. It wasn't all physical. It was probably more mental. I have a burning desire to correct when I see something wrong, when I don't like something. Sometimes, it's not very tactfully done. The nice thing was, when we did start winning some football games, I could get across to my players the key issues, under different kinds of circumstances. I didn't have to have a one o'clock meeting on Monday to go in with my list. I could do it some different ways. I could slip down to the weight room on a Monday morning. I could go in and have a doughnut with a couple of guys on Saturday mornings. I could walk up to somebody on the way to practice and say something about it. That was the good part about it—with the winning, I could find a way to give them something back. It allowed them to have an extra day without the pressure of football, but you know what? I was going to do that at that point in the season anyway."

All part of the plan, Coughlin insisted—down to the doughnuts.

"The Saturday morning drop-by—that was something I had planned to do. What I was doing at that point in time was taking myself and putting myself into the players' territory, and making them realize I was there as an individual. I wasn't wearing my stripes. I was there. I was busting balls. I was eating doughnuts, and taking shots as they all came by."

Showing players that side, Coughlin said after the season, was not something that came naturally.

"I do show that side," he said, "but I try not to wear a lot of things on my sleeve. I don't stop to think about me. I always think ahead. I'm not satisfied with today, and I try not to think about dwelling on yesterday. I'm always trying to be out front. I try to think about consistency. I don't think people need to be stroked all the time. I think that's phony. I think true character comes in different ways. I'm not going to say, 'Everybody gather round.

Here's how I'm going to show you how I care for you.'
I'm never going to do that. I don't believe in that."

On Saturday, January 11, 1997, the day before the AFC
Championship Game, residents of Providence, Rhode Island—site of the Jaguars' team hotel—awoke to find their
city blanketed in snow. This was new to the Jaguars, who
had avoided cold weather in their first 34 games as a
franchise.

That morning, the Jaguars went to Brown University
for a walk-through. Afterward, they played in the snow,
throwing snowballs at one another. The team traveled
back to the Biltmore in Providence around noon. Players
had the afternoon off. A few lingered in the lobby, doing
interviews with NBC, who would televise the game the
next day, and *Sports Illustrated*. Coughlin did, too, and he
was reflective. Game time was nearing, and yes, he said,
there were ramifications of this game beyond simply a
conference championship.

He would be coaching against one of his only friends
in coaching, Parcells, for the right to go to the biggest
game in their profession. The two talked often during the
season, but except for the Sunday message on Parcells's
voice mail, they hadn't spoken this week. Parcells versus
Coughlin had been the topic all week, but as happened
in September, Coughlin discounted any relevance their
relationship had on the game. Now, though, the day before the game, Coughlin admitted there were feelings involved in coaching against Parcells.

"I think there are probably some emotions that go
along with the first time that aren't there the second
time," Coughlin said. "I had some emotions that I don't
have right now."

The emotions were there the first time, but now, the
winner went to the Super Bowl.

The Jaguars, in two seasons, never had played a game in below-freezing temperatures. That changed in Foxboro. As they took the field in front of 60,190 at Foxboro Stadium, it was clear and bright, but also 27 degrees, with a zero wind chill.

On their first possession, the Jaguars failed to move. On fourth down, Rich Griffith snapped high and wide right. Punter Bryan Barker leapt to catch the snap, and seeing the rush closing, attempted to run. Patriots special-team specialist Larry Whigham tackled Barker at the Jaguars' 4.

The Jaguars had been getting breaks throughout the playoffs. Now, the first break of the championship game had gone against them. Two plays later, with 12:34 remaining in the first quarter, Martin scored on a 1-yard run. Patriots 7, Jaguars 0. "We felt it would be a little helter-skelter," Parcells said. "We hoped we could have the edge on special teams, and we did do that with the early turnover, and that helped."

As in Buffalo and Denver, the Jaguars regained their composure. The offense still struggled, but made no more mistakes. Late in the quarter, the Patriots put together their first drive, moving from their 33 to the Jaguars' 19—a drive keyed by a 23-yard pass from Bledsoe to Shawn Jefferson on third-and-seven from the Patriots' 36. Martin and Dave Meggett ran for 22 yards on three plays to move the Patriots to the Jaguars' 19. There, Bledsoe tried to pass to Coates. Tom McManus tipped it, and Aaron Beasley intercepted at the Jaguars' 8. He returned it 15 yards, and the threat was thwarted.

On their previous series, the Jaguars had produced their first two downs of the game. Now, the Jaguars built on that momentum. On first down from the Jaguars' 23, Brunell passed 22 yards to Jimmy Smith, and when the first quarter ended two plays later, the Jaguars had a first down on the Patriots' 45.

With the weather hurting the chance to throw deep, Brunell worked underneath. He threw three times to Pete Mitchell on the first six plays of the quarter for 24 yards, and his final completion to Mitchell—an 8-yarder—gave the Jaguars a first down at the Patriots' 21. The drive stalled, and on third-and-four, Patriots end Chris Slade forced Brunell to throw incomplete. Hollis's 32-yard field goal made it 7–3.

The Jaguars were back in it, and on the new series, they held the Patriots. The Jaguars had momentum, but on the ensuing punt, Chris Hudson fumbled and Mike Bartrum recovered at the Jaguars' 20.

The Patriots failed to make a first down, driving 7 yards on three plays. Adam Vinatieri lined up to kick a 29-yard field goal, but before the Patriots could snap, the lights at Foxboro Stadium dimmed suddenly, leaving the stadium in half darkness. The outage delayed the game 11 minutes, after which Vinatieri made the field goal.

Patriots 10, Jaguars 3.

Throughout the first quarter and a half, the Jaguars' defense kept them in the game. The first Patriots touchdown came on a 4-yard drive, and the field goal also came after an error by the special teams. With less than two minutes remaining, the Patriots took possession on their 29. On second-and-11 from the Jaguars' 41, Bledsoe—ineffective until now—found Shawn Jefferson behind the Jaguars' defense for a 38-yard gain to the Jaguars' 3. Again, the Jaguars held, and Vinatieri's 20-yard field goal on the final play of the half gave the Patriots a 10-point lead, 13–3.

"In the first half we gave them 10 points, and in a good game like this, you just can't do that," Brunell said.

The Jaguars were in their toughest halftime situation

of the postseason. Against the Bills and Broncos, they struggled in the first quarter, then recovered, and led at halftime. Now, the Jaguars trailed by 10—their largest halftime deficit since Game 11 against Pittsburgh, their last loss.

Still, the Jaguars steadied in the second half. They stopped the Patriots on three plays to start the half, then took possession at their 36 after a punt. Starting from their 36 with 13:25 remaining in the third quarter, Brunell passed 13 yards to McCardell on third-and-10 to move the Jaguars' 49. A 7-yard pass to Mitchell and a 4-yard run by Means gave the Jaguars another first down, and when Means ran 9 yards on second-and-10, the Jaguars had momentum.

Third-and-one at the Patriots' 31.

Means, nursing an ankle he injured in the first half, left for one play.

The Jaguars tried Stewart over Searcy at right tackle. No gain.

On fourth-and-one from the 31, in the cold conditions and on the shoddy Foxboro Stadium turf, a field goal was all but impossible. A punt was worthless. Coughlin decided to go for the first down.

The run with Stewart hadn't worked, but conventional wisdom in the NFL said if you can't gain a first down on fourth-and-short you don't deserve to win. Brunell tried a sneak. Again, no gain.

On the next series, the Jaguars got a break. Finally. With just under eight minutes remaining in the third quarter, on third-and-eight from the Patriots' 33, Bledsoe dropped to pass, but was pressured. He ran for 4 yards, and Hardy hit him, forcing a fumble. Eddie Robinson recovered at the Patriots' 37.

The Jaguars briefly recaptured the momentum-building run blocking that had won two playoff games. Means ran 9 yards over Boselli on first down, then around Searcy on the right for 4 yards. First down at the Patriots' 24. On third-and-13, Brunell scrambled around right end and leapt over defensive back Scooter McGruder for a first down. Suddenly, this felt like Buffalo. Or Denver. The drive stalled, however, and Hollis made it 13–6 with a 28-yard field goal with 2:47 remaining in the quarter.

And then it stayed that way.

And stayed that way.

Neither team scored in the early part of the fourth quarter, trading punts. Then, from the Patriots' 44, Bledsoe pieced together a short drive to the Jaguars' 29. Despite the conditions, Parcells opted for a field goal attempt from 46 yards that would have meant a 10-point lead. Wide left.

Eight minutes, 42 seconds remained. Jaguars ball at their own 37. At last, they drove, and they did it quickly. This looked again like the team that won twice. There was hope.

—First-and-10, Jaguars' 37: Brunell 15-yard pass to McCardell.

—First-and-10, Patriots' 48: Stewart 2-yard run over left tackle.

—Second-and-eight, Patriots' 46. Brunell 13-yard pass to Mitchell. Next play: Brunell 8-yard pass to Stewart.

—First-and-10, Patriots' 25. Brunell 9-yard pass to McCardell, then a 6-yard run by Stewart over Tylski.

—First-and-10, Patriots' 16. Stewart 6-yard run, and a 4-yarder by Means.

First down Jaguars at the 6. Means then ran over Boselli for a yard and the Jaguars faced second-and-five. Less than four minutes remained now, and overtime looked like a real possibility. Again, the Jaguars had fought back, and Team Miracle looked poised for another.

On second-and-goal from the 5, Brunell dropped and scanned the end zone. The play was a four-receiver slant in the end zone—with Smith crossing from the left, and Derek Brown, Pete Mitchell, and Keenan McCardell all crossing from various spots on the right. Brown broke open and Brunell threw a hard pass. Patriots safety Willie Clay stepped in front.

Interception. Touchback.

"Just me not seeing the back-side safety," Brunell said. "That's been a great play for us. We run it a lot, and with a lot of success. It was a poor read on my part. That was the turnover that really hurt us, obviously.

"To have a scoring opportunity like that after a long drive and turn the ball over and come away with nothing in a game like this is tough to overcome. That is what's going to be bother me for a little while."

After the interception, the defense—which allowed a field goal and 234 yards total offense in the game—again held. The defense forced a punt in three plays, and the Jaguars took possession at their 42.

Two minutes, 36 seconds remained.

Time for another miracle.

On first down, Stewart—who rushed impressively, seven times for 40 yards, replacing Means—ran a draw over Ben Coleman. A hole opened, but after a 5-yard gain, he was hit by Slade. "I came through the hole, and there was a lineman standing there," Stewart said. "I was trying to make a move on him. As I was making a move, I extended my arm out. Another guy came from behind and hit it out."

The ball flipped into the air, and Patriots cornerback Otis Smith caught it, returning it 47 yards for a touchdown.

"I saw Corwin [Brown] react to the running back," Smith said. "I jumped up to support the play, and take away the outside. The ball just bounced up to me. I saw Brunell there, and just cut it back inside and saw all that running room."

Patriots' 20, Jaguars 6—2:24 remained. Neither team scored again.

"I think that's one of those things that will stick with me forever," Stewart said. "You're tying to make something happen, and it just turns around on you."

Afterward, the Jaguars were stunned. Any satisfaction from the season faded with the realization of how close they had come. "We pissed one down our pants," Jurkovic said.

"With two minutes, three minutes, to go, we felt for sure we would go into overtime," Davey said. "And then duke it out in overtime to go to the Super Bowl. We just blew the chance.

"The thing that stings is that you don't get this far very often. It's tough to get where we are. We had a great chance, and we didn't play up to our potential. We blew a great opportunity. There were no guarantees we'll get back to this point. It's an opportunity we hope we get many more times, but we wasted one today."

Said Boselli, "That was upsetting. They didn't play very good. We drove the ball, but just couldn't get it into the end zone. Our defense played awesome. They played good defense also, but we turned the ball over. We gave them the game. Going into the first two games, we had to play well and we did. Going into the third game, we knew if we just played our game, the way we're capable . . .

"We played horrible, and still had a chance to win."

And that was what was killing Coughlin. The team he built in his image attained a height few imagined possible at the start of the season—even two months ago. The team won seven consecutive games, evolved into a national story, and—whether he cared to admit it or not—justified how he built Jacksonville's NFL franchise.

Lunatic? Maniac? Taskmaster? Too tough and too strict for the NFL?

Maybe, but somehow, he had turned a ragtag group into a team that came one turnover away from having a chance to play in the Super Bowl. And it was that—that one turnover, knowing that without an interception or with one break the Jaguars could have won—that was killing Coughlin inside. He spoke to the media, then walked through the locker room in Foxboro, talking to a few players. Finally, he showered, and by the time he was ready, most of the team had boarded the bus that would take them to the plane.

Months before, Vinnie Clark had stood in this spot, teary eyed and telling his agent to get him released. Now, that day seemed like years ago. Coughlin, bags in hand, walked toward his wife, Judy. She hugged him for a final time this season.

"We gave the other guy 17 points," Coughlin said as he walked. "How do you overcome that?"

Consistency, in the end, had hurt. The irony was obvious. The team that had played mistake-free football over the last two months to turn their season around reverted to their September and October form at the worst possible time.

"It's the worst feeling in the world, because it was there," Coughlin said. "It was there all day, and we just couldn't take it."

Then the coach walked up the long hill into the Foxboro night, where the buses were waiting to take him—and his team, *his team*—home at last.

19
EPILOGUE

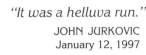

"It was a helluva run."
JOHN JURKOVIC
January 12, 1997

On the day after the championship loss, the Jaguars players cleaned out their lockers. The players were going home, but the coaches were going back to work. First, Tom Coughlin had to go the dentist.

Three weeks before, he had lost a filling, but he had coached through the pain.

"No time," he said.

Now, there was time—but not much. One of the ironies of the NFL schedule is the coaches of successful teams have scant time off as reward. On the Tuesday following the Patriots game, Jaguars coaches went to Mobile, Alabama, for the Senior Bowl, where many of the nation's best college players gathered.

That day, Kevin Gilbride interviewed for the vacant San Diego Chargers head coaching job. That Friday, Gilbride interviewed for the St. Louis Rams job. Apparently, some around the league thought Gilbride was more than a "run-and-shoot" guy, after all. That Saturday, Gilbride turned down the Rams, and accepted the Chargers job. A successful coach in the NFL often was measured by his "family tree," coaches who had worked for him and gone on to hold head jobs. Coughlin now had a branch.

"It's something we've been preparing for," Coughlin said. "We thought there was a chance Kevin might be leaving."

The next week was Super Bowl week. Then, the Jaguars had the pleasure of watching three former teammates, Andre Rison, Bruce Wilkerson, and Desmond Howard, win the Super Bowl with the Green Bay Packers. Rison scored the game's first points, catching a 54-yard touchdown from Brett Favre, in a 35–21 victory over the Patriots.

"I guess all those wrong routes I was running don't matter anymore," Rison said afterward.

Howard, whom the Jaguars did not try to re-sign the previous off-season, returned a kickoff 99 yards for a touchdown and was the game's Most Valuable Player.

"The cream always rises to the top," Howard said.

A week later came another residue of the team's success. Under league rules, the coaching staffs from the losing team in the AFC and NFC Championship Games coach their conference in the Pro Bowl. Coughlin, who would rather have been scouting and preparing for free agency, wasn't crazy about the task, but the game *was* in Honolulu, Hawaii, and hey, a league rule is a league rule.

Coughlin and the coaches didn't go alone. Broncos tackle Gary Zimmerman opted not to play, so Boselli went as first alternate. Dan Marino and John Elway also skipped the game, making room for Brunell. With McCardell having been voted to the team, that made three Jaguars players. Brunell did more than make the trip. He enhanced his image as the league's rising star, completing 12 of 22 passes for 236 yards and a touchdown with no interceptions in a 26–23 come-from-behind overtime victory.

Brunell's 80-yard pass to Tim Brown of the Raiders tied the game late in regulation at 23–23. He then led a scoring drive that ended with Cary Blanchard's 37-yard field goal. Brunell was named the game's Most Valuable Player.

Two days after the Pro Bowl, on February 5, Coughlin hired former Patriots quarterback coach Chris Palmer to replace Gilbride, who later hired Jaguars assistant Nick Nicolau to be Chargers tight-ends coach. That left one vacancy on the Jaguars staff. Coughlin filled it with his best friend in coaching, former Patriots offensive line coach Fred Hoaglin.

The staff in place, Coughlin turned to free agency, which had a decidedly different tone than in years past. The Jaguars pursued Gilbert Brown, a defensive tackle from the Packers and the run stuffer the Jaguars needed. They offered Brown $3 million a year to start, and went even higher after several days of negotiating. The sides agreed to a deal, and Brown was scheduled to fly to Jacksonville to sign the contract on Wednesday, February 18.

On February 17, Brown re-signed with Green Bay for a three-year deal that averaged $2.75 million per season—at least $250,000 a year less than the Jaguars were offering. "It just had ahold of me, and I couldn't go nowhere else," Brown said. "I love it here in Green Bay."

"It's tough because it was us or them," Michael Huyghue said. "We fought like crazy."

With Brown returning to Green Bay, the Jaguars made signing their unrestricted free agents—Ben Coleman, Derek Brown, and Dave Thomas—the priority.

They signed all three, and signed only one free agent from another team, cornerback Deon Figures.

A few weeks later, another prominent player became available, but the Jaguars didn't try to sign him. This time. The Packers released Rison, citing salary-cap reasons. Rison, Packers coach Mike Holmgren said, was going to be the Packers' third receiver, and Rison deserved to start. That's what Holmgren said publicly. Packers sources said Holmgren was irritated by Rison's behavior.

More than that, Holmgren worried not only about Rison's influence in the locker room, but that he was no longer capable of playing up to his $2 million salary. A familiar refrain.

As of April 15, Rison had not signed elsewhere.

On March 26, 1997, the NFL released its 1997 schedule. The Jaguars, particularly owner Wayne Weaver, scanned it eagerly. The Jaguars had had two prime-time television appearances in two seasons, but an AFC Championship Game appearance, most figured, would increase that total. They figured wrong.

The Jaguars would have one prime-time, national TV appearance—September 22, against Pittsburgh.

The other three teams that played in the championship games—the Packers, Patriots, and Panthers—all would have five prime-time appearances.

"To say I was not happy is an understatement," Weaver said.

The Jaguars were unhappy, but in retrospect, not surprised. The 1996 season was unexpected and unbelievable, but it was clear the NFL and the television networks perceived it as a fluke.

"It's a slap in the face, that Carolina has five and we have one," Tony Boselli said, "but that's fine. That's how we were treated all last year. We'll come in this year, and we'll fight."

"It sure is tough, but we'll be OK," Natrone Means said. "I'm disappointed we're not on TV more, but we proved a point to a lot of people last year, and we'll just have to do it again."

As Means spoke, the pieces were in place to do just that. All key players from 1996 were under contract. There was the matter of Mark Brunell, whose contract expired after the season, but Brunell and the Jaguars each had expressed serious interest in getting the matter resolved. Elsewhere, all seemed well. Means was signed for another season, McCardell for three, Smith for two, and Boselli and Searcy for five years each.

"The way the season ended, I think, left a hunger for everyone," Boselli said. "We felt like we could have gone to the Super Bowl, and I think everyone wants to work hard to get back. The season was a great story—especially for a second-year franchise that got no respect coming in. We started off 4–7 and no one even cared about us, no one even recognized us. We're one of the worst teams in the NFL in everyone else's eyes. To go from there, and get on this hot streak and to be one play basically away from the Super Bowl—one play in the end zone.

"It was pretty amazing. It was fun."